TRANSACTIONS

of the

American Philosophical Society

Held at Philadelphia for Promoting Useful Knowledge

VOLUME 77, Part 6, 1987

Literature and Political Change: Budapest, 1908–1918

MARIO D. FENYO

Fayetteville State University

THE AMERICAN PHILOSOPHICAL SOCIETY

Independence Square, Philadelphia

1987

Copyright © 1987 by The American Philosophical Society

Library of Congress Catalog
Card Number 86-72880
International Standard Book Number 0-87169-776-9
US ISSN 0065-9746

CONTENTS

		Page
I.	In Lieu of an Introduction	1
II.	The Historical Context	15
III.	The Literary Context	28
IV.	The Financial Context	40
V.	The Political Attitudes of the Nyugat Writers	53
VI.	Numbers and Literature	76
VII.	The Nyugat and the Intellectuals	87
VIII.	The Nyugat and the Working Class	107
IX.	The Nyugat versus the Establishment	120
X.	The Mirror or the Hammer	135
Bibliography		147
Index		153

LIST OF ILLUSTRATIONS
(Between Chapters V and VI.)

Fig. 1. Margit (Margaret) Kaffka, poet and novelist.
Fig. 2. Ernö (Ernest) Osvát, founder and editor of the *Nyugat*.
Fig. 3. View of Budapest and the Danube with the Parliament building in the center.
Fig. 4. A scene from the revolution of October 1918, the "Chrysanthemum Revolution."
Fig. 5. Endre Ady and Mihàly Babits, the two most outstanding poets of Hungary and of the Nyugat.
Fig. 6. Bèla Bartók, Hungarian composer.
Fig. 7. View of Budapest, Kàlvin (Calvin) Square, with the National Museum in the background.
Fig. 8. Budapest, the Andrássy on Andrássy Street, 1911.
Fig. 9. Miksa (Max) Fenyö, an editor and founder of Nyugat.
Fig. 10. Portrait of Frigyes (Frederick) Kariuthy.
Fig. 11. The cover of *Nyugat* Vol. 1911, No. 8 with an illustration by "E. Falus."
Fig. 12. Pál (Paul) Igustus, the first editor-in-chief of *Nyugat*.
Fig. 13. Inside the Café Central at the turn of the century.
Fig. 14. The cover of *Nyugat,* July, 1911.

To Mother

"If it totters, it deserves to be knocked over."
—my father's favorite Nietzsche aphorism.

I. IN LIEU OF AN INTRODUCTION

VIENNA, PRAGUE, OR BUDAPEST?

Vienna, Prague, and Budapest were not only the cultural centers of the Austro-Hungarian Empire; by the end of the nineteenth century these three cities had grown into the cultural centers of Europe, on a par with Paris or London, even if their residents, and other Europeans, were seldom aware of it. The Empire itself was far from the greatest of the great powers of nineteenth-century Europe, even at the time of Metternich, "the coachman of Europe," even more after the disastrous defeat at Sadowa, the beginning of the end. The Habsburg Empire, variously known, in its last stages, the final fifty years, as the Austro-Hungarian Empire, the Dual Monarchy, or simply the Monarchy, did assume a central cultural significance out of proportion to its political, military, or economic importance, in part because of its analogy to Europe at large. Like Europe, the Monarchy comprised many nations living together in a relatively small space, often at odds with one another. The decline of the Monarchy, its multinationality, its anachronisms, its troubles and ailments already manifest at the time of its creation in 1867, were parallel to or foreshadowed the decline of Europe. No wonder the Europe-wide conflagration now known as World War I started as an even more localized conflict involving the Monarchy, and ended in its dissolution. Austria-Hungary was the very core of Europe, and not simply geographically.

Historians of ideas have gradually come to realize the significance of Vienna. Books have appeared on the world of Freud, of Wittgenstein, of Hofmannsthal, on the "Austrian Mind," and on the Austrian mind as the prototype of the "European imagination." Kakania—the land of the KK, the Kaiserliche und Königliche (Imperial and Royal)—boasts of a culture which is, "or appears to be at first sight, our own twentieth-century culture in its infancy."[1] While Peter Gay argues that "Vienna is an invention of cultural historians in search of quick explanations," he concedes, in the same breath, that the "salons" of the city fostered new poems, new compositions, new ideas.[2] The Prague of Franz Kafka, of the Čapek brothers, and of Jaroslav Hašek, has also received its share of attention. But Budapest? The "Queen of the Danube"? It remained, to contemporary Western trav-

---

[1] Allan Janik and Stephen Toulmin, *Wittgenstein's Vienna* (New York: Simon and Schuster, 1973), 13.
[2] *Freud, Jews, and other Germans* (New York: Oxford, 1978), 34.

elers, a provincial city filled with exoticism, the capital of a backward, Eastern, and semi-feudal district. The border between Austria and Hungary was the frontier of Western civilization, nay of civilization itself (whereas Hungarians tended and still tend to refer to their country as the "easternmost outpost" of civilization). And if, according to some more careful observers, Hungary nevertheless fell within the pale of Western civilization, it was because the border between Austria and Hungary ceased to have much political importance as soon as Hungary became a domain of the Habsburgs; whereas Budapest, the "Queen of the Danube," borrowed its lustre from Vienna, presumably the king.

To be sure, those travelers who saw in Budapest a provincial town were not altogether mistaken. In a sense, the "culture" of Budapest was but a distinguished subsidiary of that of Vienna or Berlin. The intellectual fermentation taking place in Budapest was noticed even less than the fermentation in Prague or Vienna, by contemporaries no more than by present-day historians. Arthur Schnitzler or Freud, Richard Strauss or Hugo von Hofmannsthal, Arnold Schönberg, Rainer Maria Rilke, to pick names at random, did become international celebrities shortly after their works appeared or were performed in Vienna; and if others, like Wittgenstein, Kafka, or Hašek, remained obscure for a while, maybe they preferred it that way.

But Budapest? Who would have known, in 1910, that the Café Bristol (the Budapest equivalent of the Café Griensteidl) at the foot of the Elisabeth Bridge, one of the five hundred cafés that flourished in Budapest at the turn of the century,[3] was the refuge of a dozen or so young men whose world of ideas was to have an impact comparable to that of any pleiad, who were to make major contributions to the natural and social sciences of our century, albeit in different languages, usually far from their native land. In 1910 Sándor Ferenczi was thirty-seven years old, Oszkár Jászi thirty-five, Ernö Dohnányi thirty-three, Jenö (Eugene) Varga thirty-one, Béla Bartók twenty-nine, Zoltán Kodály twenty-eight, Béla Balázs thirty-six, György (Georg) Lukács twenty-five, Károly (Karl) Polányi twenty-four and his brother Mihály (Michael) nineteen, Arnold Hauser also twenty-four, Frigyes Antal twenty-three, Vilmos Szilasi twenty-one, Géza Roheim nineteen, Károly (Karl) Mannheim seventeen, László Moholy-Nagy fifteen, Károly Kerényi thirteen, and Charles Tolnai a mere eleven. Ferenczi and Roheim made significant contributions to psychoanalysis and psychoanthropology, the former having been, for a number of years, Freud's closest associate. Bartók and Kodály, whose achievements—it is true—were eventually fully recognized in their own country, can be counted among the most distinguished composers of the century, and were largely responsible for the initiation of the scientific study of folk music (not to mention Kodály's contributions to music education). Szilasi became a noted existentialist philosopher at Heidelberg and in Switzerland. Karl Mannheim achieved fame

---

[3] "There were more cafés in Budapest than in Vienna. . . . In Vienna you could spend a few hours in a café. In Budapest you could live there," writes Ernst Roth, in *A Tale of Three Cities* (New York: Charles Scribner's Sons, 1971), p. 90.

as a pioneer in the sociology of knowledge in Germany and the United Kingdom. Charles Tolnai taught art history at the Sorbonne, Princeton, and Harvard. Karl Polányi was a man of many achievements, but is perhaps best known for his elaboration of economic anthropology; whereas his younger brother became a noted "thinker," in addition to his accomplishments in physics, chemistry, and the social sciences. Hauser and Antal were pioneers, perhaps *the* pioneers, in the sociology of art. Balázs is known, in the West, as the first to have undertaken the sociological study, or at least the serious study of the cinema. Jászi, having played a prominent political role in Hungary for two decades, became a noted historian and political scientist in exile. Moholy-Nagy was to become an all-around artist and architect, first with the review *Ma* in Vienna, later with Bauhaus, and finally in Chicago. Jenö Varga, better known as Eugene Varga, became one of the most prominent economists in the Soviet Union. As for Lukács, he is often reckoned as the most significant Marxist philosopher of the twentieth century.

I have mentioned only the less significant part of their aspirations. They were in search of some deeper synthesis, rejecting the contemporary trend towards the division of labor, and towards the cellular division of disciplines and "specialties." Many of them had attended the Lutheran "Gymnázium," where they met with stimulating teachers, and where their religious affiliation or ethnic background was not an issue. Later many of them were to meet at the Bristol, in the Sunday Circle, or elsewhere, not just to play cards (although card-playing was not beneath their concerns), but to present their ideas, receive those of others, understand and stimulate one another. The intellectual world of Budapest, or Vienna, was not dispersed like that of the United States; for here, on the one hand, we have the creative minds of New York City, a country in itself and, on the other, the bright lights scattered around the United States. But even in New York the creative minds remain scattered, isolated. There are no cafés, no Circles; the "Irish bars" are an inadequate substitute, and those who do meet at occasional parties are the "jet-set" intellectuals, whom I do not have in mind. Even colleagues working at the same university hardly communicate with one another if they happen to belong to different "departments." It should come as no surprise that in lesser cities such as Vienna, Prague, or Budapest at the turn of the century where, because of tradition and a perennial inadequacy of living quarters, people spend much time in cafés, intellectual intercourse was so much more intense.

My list of celebrities, to be sure, was somewhat one-sided; I included thinkers who had made a name for themselves outside of Hungary. Even so I had omitted the "tinkerers," the scientists of the caliber of Leo Szilárd (1898), György Hevesy (1885), György Békésy (1899), Eugen Wigner (1902), János (John von) Neumann (1903), Todor Kármán (1881), or Albert Szent-Györgyi (1893), who seldom moved in the same circles.[4] Nor have I men-

---

[4] Nor have I mentioned musicians of the caliber of David Popper, József Szigeti, Eugene Ormandy, and Jenö Hubay.

tioned the names of writers or poets, who did move in the same circles, but most of whom did not acquire any sort of reputation abroad, because of lack of translations and the "isolation" of their language—an isolation Hungarians never cease to bemoan.

Of course, it was not simply coincidence that a certain group of intellectuals gathered in Budapest at a particular time. Nor is it sufficient to argue that all the creative activity that ensued was simply fermentation due to a certain lack of barriers between the sciences, or between the sciences and the arts. It is not enough to refer to the cafés, to intellectual cross-fertilization. Specialization, over-specialization, the "division of labor," are recent phenomena; the cross-fertilization characteristic of Vienna, Prague, or Budapest was not a new development, it was characteristic of cultural centers in general, until recently.

There is, however, another dimension to this process of cross-fertilization more peculiar to the time and to the places, to the intercourse among Budapest, Prague and Vienna. In Prague, for instance, Jaroslav Hašek published a number of satires and short stories excoriating the program of assimilation inflicted on the Slovaks by the Hungarian authorities; yet other works of his dealt romantically with traditional Magyar themes, such as Gypsies and *betyárs* (Hašek understood Magyar tolerably well). Nor was this choice fortuitous: Hašek consciously endeavored to create a Central European literature.

"Böhmen and Mähren" was an integral part of the Monarchy, culturally and otherwise. The majority of the Jewish-born big industrialists and, by the same token, Maecenas of the arts, came to Hungary not from Galicia, as the so-called "little Jews" had done, but from Bohemia, Moravia, or Pozsony (Bratislava), that is from the West, from the area of present-day Czechoslovakia, back in the eighteenth century. Presumably, the Jews who immigrated from the West were educationally or culturally better prepared to assume the role of the big bourgeoisie within the Monarchy. But the Jews who migrated from Bohemia or Moravia did not invariably become capitalists. Sigmund Freud also hailed from Moravia. Victor Adler, a German-speaking Jew from Prague, was to become the leader of the Austrian Social Democrats.

The visit of Karl Kraus to Budapest, in 1913, may also serve to illustrate the phenomenon of intellectual intercourse among the three great capitals of the Monarchy. The Hungarian poet Endre Ady was bold enough to encourage his public to attend the lecture given by Kraus in preference to the one by Thomas Mann, scheduled for the same day. The choice of programs may be an indication that Budapest was not simply a provincial capital. Ady's taste in the matter was not necessarily the result of inadequate information: for Kraus was as brilliant a social critic and satirist as Mann was to become a novelist.

Of course, Hungary's economic and political weight within the Monarchy was greater than its immediate intellectual influence; nevertheless, such influence was not negligible. One might mention, in this context, the Hungarian background of Theodor Herzl, the originator of political Zionism, who published *Der Judenstaat* in Vienna in 1896.[5] The operetta music of Franz Lehár and Imre Kálmán, Hungarians both, was setting the tone in Vienna (to the considerable chagrin of the intelligent Karl Kraus, who preferred Offenbach). But it would be equally pertinent to mention that Gustav Mahler had been director of the opera at Budapest before he was appointed music director of the Vienna Opera: the anti-Semitism of Hungarian society had compelled him to renounce his post in Budapest!

It is hardly necessary to argue that Budapest was subject to Austrian influence. If several famous Austrians were actually born in Hungary, the reverse is true of some Hungarian celebrities. Karl Polányi, for one, was born in Vienna, and was influenced, during his studies, by the ideas of Ernst Mach and of Wilhelm Ostwald. Typically, Hungarian scholars and artists traveled (at the beginning of the century it was still something of a journey) to Vienna, and many learned German well. Austrian authors were read in Budapest, either in Hungarian translation or in the original. My father, Miksa Fenyö, wrote an enthusiastic review of Robert Musil's *Young Törless*, long before Musil became appreciated or even known outside of Austria. Austrian fashions, styles, and currents had an impact on life in Budapest. The Hungarian version of the style internationally known as *art nouveau* can be traced directly to the *Sezession* movement in Vienna in 1893 (which, to be sure, had French and British antecedents). In Budapest Sezession as a decorative style was discussed by Ignotus in 1899; as an architectural trend, its influence can be detected already in 1896, the year of the Hungarian "millennium," when the Museum of Applied Arts designed by Ödön Lechner was completed.

But was it always a matter of "cultural diffusion" rather than parallel development? The Monarchy had evolved certain liberal political institutions which favored a certain type of cultural development.[6] One manifestation of the kind of liberalism I have in mind was the ennobling of a number of ethnic Jews in the period of the Dual Monarchy; the ennoblement does not explain the emergence of talent, but it does imply a degree of acceptance which was a prerequisite for achievement.[7] It may be argued, however, that the social obstacles placed in the way of assimilation also encouraged achievement. At the basis of liberalization, of partial assimilation, of partial integration we find certain fundamental socioeconomic changes: the Hungarian economy was changing from predominantly agricultural to partly industrial; Hungarian society was being transformed from one that had most of the characteristics of a feudal society to one that could be described as semi-feudal, semi-capitalist.

---

[5] See Andrew Handler, *Dori; the Life and Times of Theodor Herzl in Budapest* (U. of Alabama Press, 1983).
[6] To be sure, this liberalism had its limits. Lajos Biró's play "Yellow Lily" was banned from the Vienna stage in January 1912 because it portrayed officers of the K.u.K. (Imperial-Royal) army. The problem did not arise when performed in Budapest, in its original version. *Népszava*, 2 January 1912.
[7] William O. McCagg, *Jewish Nobles and Geniuses in Modern Hungary* (Boulder: East European Quarterly, 1972), 163.

The exchange of activity among Vienna, Berlin, Prague, and Budapest was not so much the result of the predominance of one center over the others. It had its roots in the evolution of a central European urban culture that was by and large promoted by Jews. Pre-Marxist Hungarian historians have stressed (and often deplored) the importance of the simultaneous advance of the Jewish element in business and industry, in the professions, in journalism, in art, in literature. The nuclear physicist Leo Szilárd ascribed the emergence of talent in Hungary to a feeling of economic security.[8] He might have added, the economic security of the Jewish city-dweller. To mention but one statistic: while the number of lawyers in Hungary increased by 7.2 percent between 1890 and 1900, the number of Jews among them increased by 68.6 percent.[9] And Oszkár Jászi stated in the twenties that judging from the people involved in the press, in the arts, in literature, it would seem that 90 percent of the country was Jewish, rather than a negligible percentage of the population.[10] Indeed, four-fifths of the names I had listed on the previous pages pertain to persons whose background was Jewish. Progressive (Jászi) and conservative (Szekfü) observers are agreed on these facts; they disagree in their estimate of the "peril" involved to the Hungarian nation as a whole.

If similar lists of names were compiled for Prague or Vienna, the results would be almost as striking. In Prague, too, the Jewish minority produced some outstanding individuals a few of whom, like Max Brod, remained conscious of their Jewishness. But the differences were also significant: in Prague the Jewish and German minorities were both quite small. In Prague the Jewish minority amounted to twenty-five thousand persons out of a total population of four hundred and fifty thousand, or a little more than 5 percent.[11] In Vienna the Jews represented some 10 percent of the population, while in Budapest they were not at all negligible; they amounted to over 20 percent. Furthermore, in Prague, partly as a result of the political status of Bohemia, many of the Jews, particularly those intellectually prominent, did not assimilate to the Czechs but, on the contrary, tended to become German nationalists.

Lest we be inclined to consider these data as evidence of some kind of triumph for East European Jewry or, worse yet, as the basis for an ethno-religious interpretation of history, it should be noted: with a handful of exceptions, these prominent individuals had either explicitly rejected Judaism as a religion, or disregarded it altogether in their thinking and activity, that is, insofar as they were allowed to disregard it. The explanation of the prominence and achievement of these groups of individuals in Prague, Vienna, or Budapest is to be sought not in their *ethnos*, but in their *ethos*.

Furthermore, the interdisciplinary cross-fertilization and fermentation

---

[8] McCagg, op. cit., 47.
[9] Gyula Szekfü, *Három nemzedék és ami utána következik* [Three generations, and the aftermath], (Budapest: Magyar Királyi Egyetem, 1934), 333.
[10] *Magyar kálvária, magyar feltámadás* [Hungarian calvary, Hungarian resurrection], 121.
[11] Max Brod, *Der Prager Kreis* (Stuttgart: W. Kohlhammer, 1966), 65.

discussed above did not result from the free interaction among classes and strata but, on the contrary, pertained to a specific and relatively homogeneous stratum. The Wittgensteins, the Lukács, the Jászis, the Hatvanys, the Polányis, the Hofmannsthals, could have met roughly at the same social level, even if there had been no intellectual accomplishments to their credit. They were Jews or part-Jews from an upper-middle class; yet they were not so upper class, not so far removed from the ghetto, that they could not interact with the "little Jews," with other persons of Jewish descent.

Intellectual cross-fertilization and ethnic factors were but symptoms rather than a convincing final explanation of the intellectual ferment at the beginning of the century. The Jewish element was far from being invariably the preponderant one; the three most prominent leaders of the literary revolution in Hungary, the three whose works were to acquire a specific political function (even if two of the three were not politically *engagés*)—that is, Endre Ady, Mihály Babits, and Zsigmond Móricz—did not have any Jewish ancestors whatever. During one of his drinking bouts, Ady, otherwise known as a pro-Semite, exclaimed, with true indignation, that he was tired of being financed by Jews! Indeed, being Jewish was not a prerequisite for talent or genius. The ethnic factor was not a cause, but a symptom: the assimilation of Jews, rapid as it was, incomplete as it remained, had something to do with the fermentation I am speaking about.

The intellectual fermentation, moreover, was not unique to the Austro-Hungarian Monarchy. It could be felt in other lands and cultures, particularly on the periphery of Europe. I mean periphery in the economic as well as in the geographical sense. Consider the Russian Empire in the second half of the nineteenth century. Consider the flurry of literary activity in Ireland immediately prior to the establishment of the Free State (as well as immediately after). Better yet, consider Spain of the "Generation of '98" where a political crisis and a military rout were reflected in a cultural and philosophical renaissance. Yet there were few Jewish intellectuals in Ireland, practically none in Spain.

What may be the explanation of this flurry of intellectual activity at opposite ends of Europe? On the one hand, we are dealing with a socioeconomic process of modernization roughly similar and approximately simultaneous in Ireland, Spain, the Russian Empire, and the Austro-Hungarian Monarchy (to stick to our preceding examples). On the other hand, we are dealing with an approaching crisis, a European crisis of world significance: the outbreak of the Great War. To use the language of Lukács: "The great crisis which led Europe to the First World War manifested itself in practically every literature in the world, more or less consciously, through various underground wires."[12]

Not always consciously. In the "Heidelberg Aesthetics" Lukács argued that the esthetic effect of a given opus is due precisely to the fact that it

---

[12] György Lukács, *Magyar irodalom--magyar kultura* [Hungarian literature-Hungarian culture], Selected Works, Vol. 3 (Budapest: Gondolat, 1970), 606.

says more, or something different from what the artist meant to put in it. It says more than its own period, than its contemporaries were able to discover in it. Hence the role of "misunderstanding" in the interpretation of the work of art. Perhaps it is only with two world wars behind us that we understand, or misunderstand, prewar literature to the fullest. The great poets of the beginning of the century met with incomprehension, even by those who actually understood them! The fact that the coming of the world cataclysm may have been mirrored in their work could not prevent or even attenuate that cataclysm. To paraphrase Mikos Kazantzakis, the task of the writer is to act as a kind of seismograph, registering and predicting the tremors before anyone else, keeping "his people" on the alert.[13] Yet the earthquake will take place.

It is only incidentally, however, that this study may provide an intellectual portrait of Budapest at the beginning of the century. My basic purpose is quite different.

My basic purpose is to undertake a case study of the political function of literature. The world-renowned thinkers mentioned above are peripheral to my main concern; the heroes of this book are relatively unknown to Western readers, even to those more especially interested in literary criticism or comparative literature. As I have mentioned, part of my undertaking is to introduce these writers, hoping to awaken a more general interest, hoping that eventually they will be accorded the rank they deserve in the literary heritage of the world. The *porte-parole* of these writers was the review *Nyugat* (the title has been rendered in English as "West" or "Occident") which, rather than a literary journal, was a metaphor, a symbol objectifying abomination for some, cultural progress and even revolution for others.

The most important names around the review *Nyugat* in 1908–1918, that is the first generation of Nyugat writers, comprises, according to the consensus of critics: Endre Ady, Zoltán Ambrus, Mihály Babits, Béla Balázs, Artur Elek, Milán Füst, Oszkár Gellért, Lajos Hatvany, Ignotus, Gyula Juhász, Géza Lackó, Géza Lengyel, Anna Lesznai, Menyhért Lengyel, Margit Kaffka, Frigyes Karinthy, Lajos Kassák, Dezsö Kosztolányi, Gyula Krudy, Aladár Kuncz, Zsigmond Móricz, Lajos Nagy, Aladár Schöpflin, Dezsö Szabó, Ernö Szép, Gyula Szini, Dezsö Szomory, Jozsi-Jenö Tersánszky, Árpád Tóth, and Wanda Tóth.[14] This list does not include György Lukács, Béla Bartók, Ferenc Molnár or the minor writers, but it does include some who are not usually or not primarily associated with the *Nyugat*: for instance, Zoltán Ambrus, Lajos Kassák, or Gyula Krudy.

To be sure, most of these names are not likely to ring a bell for the English-speaking reader. Their repeated mention, however, may serve to

---

[13] Peter Bien, "Nikos Kazantzakis (1885–1957)," in George Panichas, ed., *The Politics of Twentieth Century Novelists* (New York: Hawthorn Books, 1971), 41.

[14] Based on an incomplete listing by Dezsö Keresztury, in "A Hatvan éves Nyugat" [The Nyugat was born sixty years ago], *Irodalomtörténet*, I (1969): 61–75. Strangely enough, the list includes neither Ignotus, the editor-in-chief and a distinguished writer, nor Ambrus who, in addition to being a fine writer, eventually became an editor of the review. His omission of Artur Elek, Anna Lesznai, Menyhért Lengyel, Gyula Szini, Aladár Kuncz, or Wanda Toth can be explained, *à la rigueur,* as a matter of esthetic judgment.

bring these worthwhile writers, if not their writings, into the mainstream of international consciousness.

Among all these distinguished writers a special role must be conceded to Ady. A monograph similar in theme and scope to this one might have been written with Ady as the protagonist: the political function of Ady. As Oszkár Jászi stated in 1914:

> Just as Petőfi symbolizes the entire range of sentiments and objectives of the generation of 1848's revolutionary Magyarism, more clearly than Kossuth or any other political leader, so the future historian will study Ady if he is seeking to understand the great spiritual crisis of twentieth-century Hungary.[15]

Ady was first a poet, though he also wrote short stories, a journalist by occupation, a polemicist by temperament. His prose, his polemics are eminently quotable. It may be a truism to state that it was in his political writings that he expressed most clearly his political views. But his poetry, as I shall attempt to demonstrate, was no less effective as a political weapon; Jean-Paul Sartre was wrong in claiming that poetry, unlike prose, could have no political function, that "poetry can have nothing to do with the criteria of commitment,"[16] that the poet, like the painter or the composer, cannot become *engagé*.[17] Sartre's contention may be valid within the French context, and may apply to the United Kingdom, or to the United States. But in Latin America or in Eastern Europe, poetry is not merely a literary genre, it is not a game with (or without) rhymes, it is not simply a manifestation of "culture." "In Russia," wrote Yevgeni Yevtushenko, "the poet is more than a poet. Only those are born poets in whom a proud civic spirit dwells, for whom there is no comfort. The poet is the image of his own age and the phantom herald of the future."[18] Ady was that kind of a poet, the image of his age, the herald of the future.

I think it behooves the author to reveal all the subjective and objective motivations which led him to undertake a study, to write a book. I will confess, therefore, that filial piety has played a part in this endeavor: one of the protagonists of this study, one of the organizers of the Nyugat movement, happened to be my father. I would be tempted to claim that this book has autobiographical elements in it, were it not for the fact that its story ends many years before I was born.

It is certainly not my intention to present a distorted image of the times, of the movement; some historians, myself included, have developed a sense, a technique of objectivity that becomes second nature to them, a basic

---

[15] Quoted by Lee Congdon, "Endre Ady's Summons to National Regeneration in Hungary, 1900–1919," *Slavic Review*, 33, No. 2 (June 1974): 305.
[16] *Politics and Literature* (London: Caldar and Boyars, 1973), 106.
[17] *What is Literature?* (New York: Harper and Row, 1965, [1st ed. 1949]), 5 ff.
[18] Quoted by Edward Shils, "The Intellectuals and the Powers: Some Perspectives for Comparative Analysis," in Philip Rieff, ed., *On Intellectuals* (Garden City, N.Y.: Doubleday, 1970), 95. Yevtushenko is, of course, reiterating a conviction held by committed poets everywhere, from Shelley to Pablo Neruda. The Argentinian Gabriel Celaya writes: "La poesia no es un fin en si. La poesia es un instrumento para transformar el mundo." *Poesia urgente* (Buenos Aires: Losada, 1972), 7.

element of their personality. Among Koreans, the well-bred person does not praise his relatives, for that would be too much like self-praise; and if you should praise the wife, husband, or father of a Korean to his face he will feel honor-bound to protest: "But my father is a good-for-nothing!" I am not Korean; but I see their virtue as universally commendable.

Other subjective factors have played a role in my choice of topic. For instance, the fact that since I have begun the practice of my profession, the teaching and research of history, I have had little opportunity to read belles-lettres; it seemed as if my interest in novels and poetry had been but a teenage fancy. It was with design, therefore, that I selected a theme which would allow and even oblige me to read and reread great literary works.

This study, nevertheless, has nothing to do with literary criticism in any sense of the term; nor is it literary history in the narrow sense. The quotations scattered through the book are not intended to give a taste of Hungarian literature, to be "tid-bits" of literary value; in any case, these quotations are usually from the lesser works rather than the masterpieces. The quotations are meant to support an argument.

The objective purpose of this study is twofold.

First, it is an attempt to formulate a methodology, a theory of the political function of literature. I was stimulated in particular by Lucien Goldmann's remark calling for more empirical study,

notamment sur la nature de la lecture et de la participation au spectacle . . . et aussi sur les relations entre les créateurs et le groupe relativement étroit d'individus qui, dans les sociétés contemporaines, participent à la prise de décisions dans les domaines économique, social et politique.[19]

Second, it is a case study. On the one hand, we are confronted by a body of literature that constitutes a whole, a unit, even though it would be awkward to classify these literary works under a single literary style, trend, or current. These works came about as a process that can best be described as a literary revolution. The authors of the new multivolume history of Hungary are even more precise and categorical: the appearance of the *Nyugat* in 1908, and of the two anthologies of poetry titled *Holnap*, signified the beginnings of an artistic revolution.[20] The journal *Nyugat* was not simply a symptom of this process but was, by and large, identical with it. "A full critical assessment of the *Nyugat*," argued the anonymous critic of the *Times Literary Supplement*, "would mean narrating the whole story of modern Hungarian literature."[21]

Ten years after the beginnings of the *Nyugat*, in 1918 and 1919, Hungary experienced two revolutions, the first of which can be characterized, for the sake of simplification, as a bourgeois revolution, and the second as a proletarian revolution. While both these revolutions failed (at least in the

---

[19] *Pour une sociologie du roman* (Paris: Gallimard, 1964), 371–72.
[20] *Magyarország története* [The History of Hungary], chapter 12, 703.
[21] Issue of 25 September 1969, 1109. See also *Ignotus válogatott írásai* [Selected Writings of Ignotus], ed. Aladár Komlos (Budapest: Szépirodalmi Kiadó, 1969), 704.

short run), they can be termed the most nearly successful violent upheavals in any country in Europe in the aftermath of World War I save, of course, the Great October Socialist Revolution.[22] My question then is: was there some connection between the two processes, between the literary and political revolutions? Can one formulate some general laws regarding the political function of literature?

I do not claim that literature in general, or modern Hungarian literature in particular, must be ranked alongside economic, social, or technological factors in accounting for changes in the course of history. In no sense is this study a discussion of the causes of the revolutions of 1918–19, but merely of one factor, which may have hastened the coming of those revolutions; and *a priori* it is not impossible that it may have hindered their coming. Nor have I selected the Nyugat movement because I am convinced that it was the most important intellectual or cultural factor. Not for a moment would I deny that the journal *Huszadik század*, rallying as it did bourgeois radicals, socialists, and the most progressive exponents of the social sciences, played an equally important role in raising the level of consciousness of certain groups and classes. The explicitly socialist literature published in the organs of the socialist press, intellectual currents coming from abroad or, for that matter, the organized workers' movement itself, should be accorded as extensive a treatment, or a more extensive treatment, in any historical survey of the period. J. Barrington Moore's sobering analysis of the role of the poet, of the writer, of the intellectual in general, is surely close to the truth:

The discontented intellectual with his sane searchings has attracted attention wholly out of proportion to his political importance, partly because these searchings leave behind them written records and also because those who write history are themselves intellectuals.[23]

Nevertheless, I have opted to write about the Nyugat movement, for reasons I have mentioned, and for further reasons I shall mention below.

The problem of definitions. To avoid misunderstandings I mean literature in the sense of belles-lettres. Yet we must deal with writers as well as their works. What about writers engaged in journalism—the rule rather than the exception in Hungary at the beginning of the century? And not only in Hungary. The poet and the sociologist, the poet and the politician were compatible aspects of the same personality in England, as Raymond Williams explains: Wordsworth wrote political pamphlets; Blake was a friend of Tom Paine and was tried for sedition; Coleridge wrote political journalism and social philosophy; Shelley, in addition to all this, distributed pamphlets in the streets; Southey was a constant political commentator, and Byron spoke in the frame-riots and died as a volunteer in a war of liberation. These activities of theirs "were neither marginal, nor incidental, but were

---

[22] Of course, one might argue that the establishment of new states in Eastern Europe, or the triumph of Fascism in Italy and Germany are even more momentous consequences of World War I.

[23] *Social Origins of Dictatorship and Democracy* (Boston, 1966), 480.

essentially related to a large part of the experience from which the poetry itself was made."[24] Yet the role of the poet in Hungary, and perhaps in Eastern Europe as a whole, is even more political, as the facts will show. In any case, the "New Critics" notwithstanding, it would serve no purpose to dissociate the literary work from its author, and it would make no sense to separate the author-as-poet from the author-as-journalist.

Furthermore, this study is concerned with a movement rather than with literary works, or with a review. Here I must add a word of explanation. It is by no means generally admitted that there was such a thing as the Nyugat movement. But that is mainly because the journal and the literature around it have never been the subject of an analytical, synthesizing study; what we have instead is thousands of monographs, books, and articles dealing with individual authors—an atomized view of historical and literary reality. A lifetime would be needed to read all the material published in connection with the hundredth anniversary of the birth of Ady, in 1977. No Hungarian scholar would venture to undertake an analytical study of the review: for it would result in ten volumes, or else remain a small collection of superficial generalizations already familiar to the Hungarian public. The Nyugat writers themselves, wrote Aladár Schöpflin, did not consider their work as "merely a series of poems, short stories, and books, but rather as a movement which will guide Hungarian literature onto untrodden paths."[25] And Aladár Komlos: "The Nyugat was more than a review; it was an entire movement, practically an entire period . . ."[26]

If my undertaking will seem too ambitious to literary historians, so will it seem to sociologists. Even the study of the reception of a single novel, that of *Madame Bovary*, was a task that required five years, and was never completed; that approach might necessitate "ten dissertations" for a single author, argued Robert Escarpit, during a discussion of the methodology of the sociology of literature.[27]

This kind of project is rather different from a doctoral dissertation.[28] Ideally, it should not be the work of an individual. Rather, it should be a matter of painstaking interdisciplinary research, touching on intellectual history, the sociology of literature, the psychology of the reading public, and mass communications. To cite a list of disciplines suggested by sociologists from the German Democratic Republic: there should be collaboration among estheticians, historians of art, linguists, historians, psychol-

---

[24] *Culture and Society, 1780–1950* (Garden City, N.Y.: Doubleday, 1960), 34–35. "Wordsworth is really the first . . . to annex new authority for the poet, to meddle with social affairs . . ." wrote the anti-meddler, T. S. Eliot, in *The Use of Poetry and the Use of Criticism* (London: Faber and Faber, 1964), 87.

[25] *A magyar irodalom története a XX. században* [The History of Hungarian literature in the 20th century] (Budapest: Grill, 1937), 121.

[26] *Vereckétől Dévényig* [From Verecke to Dévény] (Budapest: Szépirodalmi, 1972), 280.

[27] ". . . j'ai fait faire une thèse sur la réception de l'oeuvre de Flaubert, mais nous avons été obligés de nous en tenir á *Madame Bovary*, et cela nous a pris cinq ans . . ." *Littérature et société* (Bruxelles: Institut de Sociologie, 1967), 84.

[28] Ibid., 92.

ogists, sociologists, physiologists, and other natural scientists, information and communication specialists, specialists in semiotics and cybernetics, in order to arrive at an adequate analysis of the reception of literature.[29] Hence this kind of research should be carried out in interdisciplinary collaboration.

Thus the critic need not be too severe if the present study falls short of even limited expectations; it is bound to be incomplete, lopsided. It does not purport to be the definitive, the authoritative work. Quite to the contrary: it broaches the subject. I hope it will prove sufficient stimulation to prompt others to collaborate, to investigate similar topics, either within the same period, or pertaining to other times and places. I hope I myself may become part of such endeavors.

A few more words of warning. As will become clear in the course of reading, the archival materials pertaining to the *Nyugat* have perished, by and large. I have found no letters received, no subscriptions lists, few accounts, no official data on circulation. Hence this undertaking would have to remain incomplete even if greater resources of talent, scholarship, and interdisciplinary knowledge had been mustered. The editorial offices of the journal were never impressive: the Bristol Café, and a series of addresses, including a room adjoining the apartment of the editor Ernö Osvát. The staff consisted of a part-time secretary. The materials pertaining to "my period" were already depleted during the Republic of Councils. In the period 1922–24 the journal was unable to file tax returns because the company had no regular office, and the books had disappeared "during the period of Communism. . . . It was only after intensive search that some of these could be located."[30]

What became of the books that were located at that time I do not know. By 1935 they had again disappeared, for in a dissertation submitted that year Lujza Farkas complained that it was no longer possible to determine who had been the first readers of the *Nyugat*, "the business books having been misplaced."[31]

According to Professor István Király's communication, whatever material remained in the early forties must have perished when the editorial office in the last years of the journal, the Baumgarten building in Sas street, was hit by a firebomb during an air raid in 1944; and this piece of information was confirmed to me by the former librarians of the Baumgarten foundation.[32]

The archival sources that remain are scattered among several institutions;

---

[29] Manfred Naumann, Karlheinz Barck, Dieter Kliche, Rosemarie Lenzer, *Gesellschaft, Literatur, Lesen* (Berlin: Aufbau, 1975), 10. The Swede Karl Erik Rosengren observes that most of what has been written so far in sociology of literature, and catalogued by librarians as such, has been "the unique excursions of sensitive individuals" rather than sustained and collaborative scientific effort. *Sociological Aspects of Literary Systems* (Stockholm: Natur och Kultur, 1968), 17.
[30] Attorney Sándor Török to the Royal Court of Justice, circa May 1925, Cégbiroság Archives, Cg 628.
[31] *A Nyugat és a századeleji irodalomforduló* [The *Nyugat* and the literary revolution at the turn of the century], (Budapest: Gyarmati, 1935), 42–43.
[32] Communications of Endre Illés and B. Juhász Erzsébet to author.

and their provenance is not the editorial office of the *Nyugat*. These sources include the judiciary materials in the Budapest municipal archives, the archives of the business courts (Cégbiroság) where there are two files pertaining to the *Nyugat*, the archives of certain publishing houses, accessioned by the State Archives, and other materials in the State Archives.

Some of the lacunae are difficult to explain. For instance, the materials from the press office of the Prime Minister contain data regarding the number of copies of certain journals sent through the mails (that is, to subscribers). The *Nyugat* should figure among these journals as of 22 October 1916, when it officially opted to become a "political" review, in addition to being "literary, social, scientific, and economic."[33] Yet there is no mention of the *Nyugat*, either before that date or thereafter. These deficiencies, however, should cause no great surprise to anyone who has conducted research in recent Hungarian history; it is not the lacuna that are surprising, but rather that certain records did survive, what with two world wars, invasions, occupations, sieges, fires, and floods and the fact that the art nouveau structure of the State Archives happens to stand at the most exposed corner of the "Castle" district of Buda!

Already a state-owned company, in the spring of 1949 the Nyugat publishing house was absorbed by the Révai National Publishing Company, the historically significant records of which were eventually transferred to the State Archives.[34] But once again my search through the fonds of the Révai company proved to be in vain.

A few more words of warning. I have deliberately neglected the theater, but not because the theater had little significance. On the contrary, in their columns headed "literature" the daily papers were actually commenting on the theater for the most part, and the space devoted to drama reviews was at least three times the space devoted to other genres. Moreover, a number of Nyugat writers were involved in the theater as well, or even primarily, e.g. Menyhért Lengyel, Dezsö Szomory, not to mention their contemporary, Ferenc Molnár. Nor would I deny that drama can become an effective weapon for the transformation of the world: "The Enlightenment mastered the theater," we are told, "and it was precisely on untutored minds that it had the greatest effect."[35] I have neglected the theater simply because the amount of data available is overwhelming, and research has not yet begun! There are no analyses of theater audiences for the period 1908 to 1918.

For the sake of clarity, the term Nyugat will be italicized whenever it refers specifically to the review; regular type will be used whenever I have primarily the movement in mind.

---

[33] Reports of 21 October 1916, and 16 February 1918, Mayor's Office, I 7875/907.
[34] Miniszterelnökség to Budapesti Törvényszék, 22 April 1949, Cégbiroság Archives, 16001.
[35] *Gesellschaft, Literatur, und Lesen*, 190. Lunacharski claims that the theater becomes particularly rich during and immediately preceding a revolution. He quotes Kautsky who wrote that drama and revolution are related since both are catastrophes which are prepared unnoticed, but inevitably, and explode all of a sudden. A. V. Lunacharski, *Müvészet és forradalom* [Art and Revolution] (Bucharest: Kriterion, 1975), 44–47.

II. THE HISTORICAL CONTEXT

The following summary is not intended as an introduction to the history of the period. I compiled it *a posteriori*, after writing the subsequent chapters. The information contained herein has not been selected with a view to presenting objectively the most significant developments, although that may well be the case, but rather to render the main body of my argumentation comprehensible, to place the Nyugat within its political, social, and economic contexts.

More comprehensive or better rounded descriptions of Hungary at the beginning of the century may be found in a number of adequate and better than adequate treatments of the subject in English and other Western languages. These treatments reflect a consensus on at least some basic trends or processes. For instance, by and large they are agreed that Hungary at the beginning of the century was a semi-feudal country, that is a feudal country in which industrialization, industrial capitalism, or modernization were under way.

Political power was still largely in the hands of the aristocracy and of the gentry. The term "gentry," although transcribed from the English some time in the 1880s, was ascribed a modified meaning to designate the middle ranks of the Hungarian nobility. Paradoxically enough, this stratum was to form the bulk of the middle-class, including the middle and upper ranks of officials—hence its status and role were rather different from what they had been in England. The structure of Hungarian society also differed markedly from that of Western European countries, where a middle-class had evolved economically as well as politically over a long period rather than as a result of the downward social mobility of déclassé nobility. The structure of Hungarian society resembled more nearly that of other East European countries, notably Poland.[1]

The big bourgeoisie, on the other hand, had not yet (and never will have) acquired a political importance commensurate with its economic or even social position; rather, it was the owners of landed estates who proved more aggressive and effective in consolidating their power at this time.[2] The numbers and power of great landowners reminded a contemporary French observer of the ancien régime of France in the decades preceding the Revolution.[3] The aristocracy did not simply own land; it owned much

---

[1] *Magyarország története* [History of Hungary], 5: 22.
[2] Miklós Szabó, "A századforduloi konzervatizmus új vonásai" [The New Traits of Conservatism at the Turn of the Century], *Századok* 108 (1974): 29. Michael Löwy argues the Hungarian bourgeosie was not anti-federal. Op. cit., passim.
[3] René Gonnard, *La Hongrie au XXe siècle* (Paris: Armand Colin, 1908), 158, 178.

of the country. Of the fifteen prime ministers since the Compromise of 1867, nine had been aristocrats, four had been members of the lesser nobility, and only two were of non-noble background.[4] In the lower house of Parliament 58.4 percent of the members belonged either to the aristocracy or to the gentry (there is no need to discuss the upper house which, in any case, had been designed as a "brake" on transformation, entirely in the hands of the aristocracy, although its composition was somewhat more variegated than that of the British House of Lords). Every tenth adult magnate was a member of Parliament.[5] Furthermore, the aristocracy and the gentry dominated the civil service, particularly the administration of the provinces.[6] The regime's claim to political liberalism had little foundation in practice, and certainly did not imply democracy, or a distribution of power; political power remained largely in the hands of the aristocracy and of the gentry until 1918—indeed, except for the revolutions of 1918–19, until October 1944. Other classes either collaborated or simply did not partake of power.[7]

But we must be wary of oversimplification; in addition to magnates, the Hungarian Parliament was well supplied with lawyers and journalists. In 1917 almost one percent of the country's 6,743 lawyers were in parliament, whereas 10 to 15 percent of the members were journalists turned politicians.[8] At about the same period (between 1902 and 1906) the French Parliament included 74 deputies of "professions littéraires" out of a total of 587, and 189 lawyers. The "professions littéraires" included teachers, journalists, and men of letters.[9]

Although the data presented above may denote a static structure, few societies present a clearer picture of transformation and transfer of power from one class to another, both through revolutions, and by gradual process. The gentry's economic decline or even rout was not simply an interpretation imposed by historians of a subsequent generation. It was a phenomenon that could not escape the attention of even the mildly observant contemporary, and which became a major theme in contemporary literature. The gentry played cards, gambled away its land and fortune, drank to excess, sobbed to gypsy music, and entertained lavishly even after it could no longer afford to do so.[10]

On the other hand, the big bourgeoisie was rapidly developing its industries, and becoming increasingly dependent on foreign, even Austrian investment. Industrialization was redeeming Hungary from a peripheral

---

[4] Ernö Lakatos, *A magyar politikai vezetöréteg, 1848–1918* [The Hungarian Ruling Stratum] (Budapest: Pázmány Péter Egyetem, 1942), *passim*. Also, Gyula Szekfü, *Magyar történet* 5: 512–513.
[5] Lakatos, op. cit., 29–30.
[6] *Revolution in Perspective; Essays on the Hungarian Soviet Republic of 1919*, eds. Andrew Janos and William B. Slottman (Berkeley: Univ. of California Press, 1971), 7–8.
[7] Lakatos, op. cit., 35.
[8] Ibid., 84–87.
[9] Frédéric Bon, Michel-Antoine Burnier, *Les nouveaux intellectuels* (Paris: Cujas, 1966), 81.
[10] Szekfü, *Magyar Történet* 5: 517.

role around the Austrian center. True enough, while in Austria 22 percent of the population was engaged in industrial work at the turn of the century, in Hungary the proportion was only 13.4 percent. But ten years later, by 1910, 18.3 percent of the population was engaged in industrial and commercial activity (as opposed to 23 percent in Austria and Italy, 38 percent in Germany, and 46 percent in Great Britain); and it was estimated that about a fourth of the national income was derived from industry (as opposed to 62.4 percent from agriculture).[11] Between 1890 and 1910 industrial employees increased by 62 percent, as opposed to 42 percent in Germany, and only a 33 percent increase in Austria.[12] Hence the rate of industrialization was accelerating, and Hungary reached a stage Austria and Germany had reached considerably earlier. Although there were ups and downs in the rate of industrialization, development itself was continuous. While the GNP grew 2.5 percent per year on the average, industrial growth averaged 4 percent in the period between 1890 and 1914.[13] Of all European countries only Sweden seems to have experienced more rapid industrial growth in this period.[14]

Incidentally, literacy among industrial workers was 87.2 percent in 1910, far above the national average. Literacy of the inhabitants of Budapest was even higher, 89.3 percent, as opposed to 59 percent in the rest of the country (in 1900).[15]

One indirect consequence of modernization and the increase in the number of industrial workers was the rise in working class consciousness manifested in the spread of trade unionism and the growth of the Social Democratic Party, which culminated in 1907 with a membership of 152,332. To be sure, the Hungarian Social Democratic Party remained small compared to the Social Democratic parties of some Western countries; but party membership, like industry itself, was concentrated in the capital.[16] As the Minister of Interior saw it, the workers dominated the streets of Budapest.[17]

Both trade unionism and the Social Democratic Party experienced vicissitudes, even if we limit our examination to the brief period from 1908 to 1918. By 1906–07 membership in unions had risen to about one hundred

---

[11] *Magyarország története* 4: 108. Péter Hanák, "Skizzen uber die ungarische Gesellschaft am Anfang des 20. Jahrhunderts," *Acta Historica* 10 (1963): 6. Iván Berend and György Ránki, *Magyarország gyáripara az imperializmus elsö világháboru elötti idöszakában* [Hungarian industry before World War I] (Budapest: Szikra, 1955).
[12] *Magyarország története* 4: 108.
[13] Ibid., 4: 4–5.
[14] *Magyarország története* 4: 114–15.
[15] Ervin Szabó, "Községi nyilvános könyvtár Budapesten" [Community public library in Budapest], *Városi szemle* 3 (1910): 449.
[16] On the other hand, a large percentage of the Hungarian POW's in Russia joined the Bolsheviks and fought on their side in 1917–18 (circa 80–100,000). The Hungarian contingent outnumbered all other nationality groups save the Russian. Iván Völgyes, "Hungarian Prisoners of War in Russia, 1916–1919," *Cahiers du monde russe et soviétique* 14 (1973): 54–85.
[17] Jószef Kristoffy, *Magyarország kálváriája* [The Calvary of Hungary] (Budapest: Wodianer F. és fiai, 1927), 489.

and thirty thousand.[18] Thereafter membership in the Party and the unions dropped, only to rise again in 1912. After March 1913, membership began to decline once again as a consequence of the Party's decision to call off a general strike.[19] The Party leadership disappointed many workers by its timidity. The program and practice of the Party, modeled on that of Austria, had been timid all along. In 1899 a party leader, Dezső Bokányi (who also happened to be the Party's most effective speaker) declared that the Party expected to achieve its ends by peaceful means;[20] and, indeed, the Party was not directly responsible for the bloody street clashes in 1905 and 1912, or for the violent demonstrations, and even more violent repression, of the agricultural workers during several hot summers. As for the goals of the Party, it consistently stressed, as item number one on its agenda: general, secret, and equal suffrage, as did one of the basic resolutions of the First Socialist Congress of 1899. Thus the Social Democrats and the bourgeois liberals (officially the Bourgeois Radical Party) were in agreement as to what should constitute the major objective, and on how to achieve it.[21]

Although the workers may have ruled the streets, their political impact remained limited. A major economic intervention of the state was the artificial depression of the wage level, and the shifting of the cost of overhead onto the workers, in order to allow higher profits for the large enterprises, and in order to make Hungarian goods more competitive on the international (i.e. Austrian and Balkan) markets.[22] According to some authors, money wages increased substantially between 1901 and 1913 "under the threat of social rebellion," although the gains were partly canceled out by the rise in the cost of living.[23] More recently, it has been argued that though nominal wages increased by about 25 percent in that period, this increase was more than offset by a 35 percent increase in the cost of basic goods.[24] Even if we choose to agree with those who claim the standard of living was rising, we must recognize that with an annual income of around 300 crowns, the average worker had little or nothing to spare for the purchase of books.

Apart from their intrinsic significance, these data lead to certain conclusions more directly pertinent to the object of my investigation. They indicate that the revolutions of 1918–19, particularly the "proletarian dictatorship" of 1919, cannot be explained simply by the rise in consciousness and the

---

[18] Szekfü, *Magyar történet* 5: 558.
[19] Only to rise again during the war, as a result of strike activity, to 215,222 by the end of 1917.
[20] Tibor Süle, op. cit., 41.
[21] See Oszkár Jászi's definition of the goals of Socialism as interpreted by Tibor Süle, op. cit., 86.
[22] *Revolution in Perspective*, 22.
[23] *Revolution in Perspective*, 43–44.
[24] Hanák, "Skizzen . . . ," 35. According to Bruce F. Pauley, real income increased by 75 percent between 1903 and 1913. *The Habsburg Legacy, 1867–1939* (New York: Holt, Rinehart, and Winston, 1972), 24. Arthur J. May is more guarded in *The Habsburg Monarchy*, 246.

power of the working class. If we should extend our study to parallel phenomena in the states of Western Europe, class consciousness would seem even less adequate as the explanation for the revolutions in Hungary; for countries with Social Democratic (i.e. Communist) parties more effective than the one in Hungary remained largely unaffected by the revolutionary tide in the aftermath of World War I. If, nevertheless, a few Hungarian intellectuals were able to predict the coming of the revolution—and here I discount the element of deliberate incitement such predictions often contain—it was because they also took other factors into consideration, or were able to sense those factors instinctively. "Some beasts," wrote the poet Gyula Juhász, "can feel an earthquake coming, but there will be an earthquake, even if some beasts cannot feel it coming."[25]

One pertinent factor was the role played by the big bourgeoisie. The organization of industrialists, the GyOSz (the equivalent of the National Manufacturers Association in the United States), was established only in 1902, well after the landholders had felt it necessary to organize in order to safeguard their class interests. The GyOSz was intended to represent and harmonize the interests of the industrial capitalists. It did not directly challenge the landholders, for it was conscious of its inferiority; but any significant issue confronting the industrialists was also bound to affect the landholders, and more or less overt clashes did ensue.[26] For instance, while the landholders eventually became indifferent to the problem of mass emigration from Hungarian territory, perhaps because the price of land seemed to rise as a result (more money in the hands of certain elements of the peasantry?), the industrialists regarded emigration as "the greatest enemy and vampire" of capitalist development: witness the conference organized by the GyOSz on the subject in July 1907.[27]

I singled out the GyOSz as representative of the big bourgeoisie, for I have an ulterior motive. On one hand, the GyOSz was, as a matter of course, the natural enemy of the Social Democratic Party and its press organ, the *Népszava*. The paper frequently published attacks against the organization and its individual members. Yet if the Party was indeed concerned primarily with the introduction of universal suffrage, the conflict with the industrialists was avoidable; the latter had no objections against the granting of civil liberties, against the introduction of "Western" democracy. One of the Party leaders argued that the task of the Social Democrats consisted in convincing the bourgeoisie: "it must intervene against agrarianism in its own interest, and it must ally itself with the Social Demo-

---

[25] *A magyar irodalom története*, ed. Miklós Szabolcsi [The History of Hungarian Literature] (Budapest: Akadémia, 1965), 303.
[26] Miksa Fenyö, "Önélatrajz VIII" [Autobiography] (*Uj látóhatár*, Munich), 548. This statement is contradicted by Andrew Janos, who argues that politicians and the government gave preferential treatment to banking and industrial interests. *Revolution in Perspective*, 22. Indeed, the National Work Party, the party in power, enjoyed the support of important industrialists, and vice-versa. See Loránt Hegedüs, *Ady és Tisza* (Nyugat, n. d. ca. 1940), 48.
[27] Zoltán Horváth, *Jahrhundertwende*, 346.

crats in the struggle for the right to vote."[28] And the same Party leader, Kunfi, was to repeat, in December 1908, that the workers must use all their strength to force Hungary to embark on the road from a feudal to a capitalist state! Surely, the capitalists might have argued likewise! But it is not for me to rule on the validity of the thesis of "the need for a capitalist stage of development"; suffice it to say that the relationship between Social Democrats and Hungarian industrialists was at times ambiguous rather than antagonistic (as was the relationship between the big bourgeoisie and the radical bourgeois), and open conflict was avoided until the outbreak of revolution in October 1918.

Here we are not primarily interested in the relationship between the Hungarian bourgeoisie and the working class. I am particularly interested in the GyOSz, hence in the industrial bourgeoisie, because of the support it lent to the periodical *Nyugat*. I shall furnish evidence regarding the importance of this support in Chapter 4; my purpose here was to identify the organization within the framework of Hungarian class society and of economic life.

The Bourgeois Radicals constituted one of the links between the big bourgeoisie and the working class. The Bourgeois Radical Party received financial support from elements of the big bourgeoisie. At the same time, the bourgeois radicals collaborated with the Social Democrats on certain issues, particularly general suffrage. Oszkár Jászi, who was to establish and lead the Party, wrote in 1907: there, in the West, the order of the day is the transition from a bourgeois democracy to a workers' democracy; "here, in Hungary, we must first bring about bourgeois democracy."[29] Clearly, then, Jászi and Kunfi were in full agreement, at least on the basic issue.

But the most immediate issues of Hungarian history at the beginning of the century were not the class struggle which, in any case, could not be singled out as peculiar to Hungarian society; nor was it the revolution, the rise of the bourgeoisie, or the rise of the working class. These issues did not constitute a "problem," for there were no alternatives to choose from, it was not a matter of volition, of decisions adopted or rejected. The most immediate issues may not have been so readily apparent to contemporaries. The officials of the regime certainly failed to concede to these issues the importance they deserved.

In 1910 the Socialist Zsigmond Kunfi wrote: "The fear and horror inspired by the minorities has become a determining factor of political struggles as if all the nationalities living in Hungary had already awakened from the

---

[28] Quoted in *Magyar történet* 11: 26. In the State Archives I have found a lengthy petition from the landowners' organization (OMGE) requesting government intervention against peasant strikes, union activities, and "international socialism." 29 March 1906, ME 536 (1907) and 2802 (1908). The GyOSz did not support such initiatives.
[29] André Karátson, *Le symbolisme en Hongrie*, 54.

slumber of national unconsciousness."³⁰ Indeed, they had. Yet the major issue confronting Hungary, and the Monarchy in general became obvious only in 1918–19: it was a multinational kingdom within a multinational empire, in an era of triumphant nationalism. At no time since the French Revolution, since it had become the dominant passion in Europe, did nationalism attain or result in the extremes of destructiveness it attained in the First World War. The multinational kingdom of Hungary was bound to prove an anachronism.

Ethnic and cultural assimilation were resorted to in an effort to solve the "problem" of nationalities, to solve the contradictions among ethnic groups as well as to satisfy the cravings of Hungarian nationalists. But even assimilation was not consistently pursued; official policy was only consistent in disregarding the relatively liberal nationalities law of 1868.

The alternative to assimilation would have been respect for minority rights (to be sure, these rights had nowhere been clearly formulated before the end of World War I), the enhancement of ethnic variety, autonomy or independence for the subject nations. I do no more than mention this alternative (or these alternatives) here, for I shall have occasion to discuss it (or them) when focusing on writers and progressive intellectuals. As for the political parties, they were unable to see alternatives. The Social Democratic Party, insofar as it took cognizance of the problem at all, evaded the issue by rejecting nationalism and referring to the principle of internationalism; hence its program was less progressive than that of Jászi, the leader of the Bourgeois Radicals. And Jászi's program, although relatively advanced, fell short of the expectations of the most progressive minority leaders.

To be sure, the horrors of Hungarianization have been exaggerated at times by third-party historians; witness the arguments of R. Seton-Watson, "Scotus Viator," which were found convincing by subsequent British or American historians.³¹ So was the censure manifest in the publications of such influential writers as Lord Bryce and Lord Fitzmaurice in England, Clémenceau in France, Björnson, or Tolstoy.³² But the issue is not whether the grievances of the ethnic minorities were or were not justified, or how they were seen by third-party historians; the issue is how the members of minority groups themselves felt, and how the Hungarian ruling class and, for my purposes, the progressive writers, reacted to their grievances.

Between 1880 and 1910 the proportion of Magyars to non-Magyars in-

---

³⁰ "Lekésett országok törvénye" [The Law of Retarded Countries] (*Huszadik Század,* 1910), 228.
³¹ For instance, Arthur J. May writes: "British and French writers, too, excoriated Magyar racialism. The most compelling and effective of them was R. W. Seton-Watson, a Scottish intellectual, who spread before the Western world almost incredible evidence of political and social injustices inside Hungary." *The Habsburg Monarchy, 1867–1914* (New York: W. W. Norton, 1968, 1st ed. 1951), 235.
³² Szekfü, *Magyar történet* 5: 579–81.

creased from 46.9 percent to 54.5 percent. The increase was the result of the combination of three factors: a) a relatively high birthrate among the Magyars; b) emigration depleted the Magyar population less than some other nationalities within the kingdom; c) the assimilation or acculturation of other ethnic groups. The latter process accounts for an increase of more than one million speakers of Magyar, mainly former Germans, Slovaks, and Jews.[33] For my purpose, it is particularly important to observe—the *Nyugat* being printed in Hungarian and being mainly a vehicle for urban literature—that while the majority of the population of Budapest had been German-speaking in the middle of the nineteenth century, by 1910 some 86 percent of its inhabitants claimed Magyar as their mother tongue; and the same trend could be observed in the provincial towns.[34] Furthermore, it is also pertinent to note that while 33.3 percent of the country's population was illiterate in 1913, among speakers of Magyar the rate of illiteracy was only 17.6 percent.[35]

Assimilation affected certain ethnic groups more than others. The Germans and the Jews can be considered special cases: they were neither irredentist (at least not at the time), nor did they reside in a single compact area. The acculturation of segments of the Slovak population was relatively successful even though (or because) several violent clashes had occurred between Slovaks and the Magyar authorities (for instance, at Csernova in 1907). The Slovak language high schools had been closed down as early as the 1870s, not long after they were established; only about 16 percent of the Slovak students were receiving instruction in their mother tongue immediately prior to World War I.[36]

The Romanians were particularly neglected. It is true that Prime Ministers Tisza and Lukács had both negotiated with Romanian national leaders from Transylvania, including officials of the Romanian National Party in 1912–13; and this occurred after the Hungarian authorities had ordered the Party's dissolution two years earlier.[37] But the Hungarian effort at assimilation was intermittent, half-hearted, and almost entirely unsuccessful.

On the whole, the political parties that claimed to represent the interests of the ethnic groups achieved their biggest success in 1906 when they managed to send twenty-five delegates to the Hungarian parliament.

There was no such thing as a "German problem" (for reasons which need not be discussed here); but the Jews were a "problem," in a manner quite different from that presented by other ethnic groups. Consequently, anti-Semitism was an attitude and, at times, a political program, that differed from the attitude of Magyar superiority towards minorities in general, or from official discrimination against those who did not speak Magyar. The difference was partly a consequence of the fact that the Jews were often

---

[33] *Magyar történet* 5: 607.
[34] *Magyar történet* 5: 7.
[35] Ibid., 11.
[36] *Magyar történet* 12: 18.
[37] Ibid., 11: 67 ff.

willing and able to assimilate. Unlike other ethnic groups, the Jews were increasing in numbers rapidly, mostly because of immigration on a large scale; there were about five hundred and fifty thousand Jews in Hungary in 1870, and by 1914 their numbers had increased to nine hundred and thirty-five thousand. Even more spectacular was the rate of their concentration in cities; in the period we are dealing with the Jews represented 23.4 percent of the inhabitants of Budapest, and 25.8 percent in the city of Nagyvárad (where Endre Ady did his apprenticeship as journalist and poet).[38]

No Hungarian bourgeois was more Magyar in his outlook and feeling, asserts Arthur J. May, than the assimilated Jew.[39] There were no legal obstacles to such assimilation after 1896 when the Hebrew faith was placed on a footing of official equality.[40] The Hungarianized Jews took an increasingly active role in the development of a bourgeois, anti-feudal society, and oriented themselves towards the professions in disproportionately large numbers. Although literacy among Jews was not higher than literacy among non-Jews (to be sure, statistics are not at all clear on this point, since the concept of Jewish literacy remained undefined), Jews succeeded in enrolling at the universities and constituted about 30 percent of the student body in 1910. In the same period, two-fifths of the lawyers, three-fifths of the medical doctors, and two-fifths of the journalists in Hungary were Jewish.[41] It should be noted, however, that in most cases journalism was far from a "lucrative" occupation, and it would be silly to speak of "conspiracy" or even of "solidarity" among Jewish journalists: those who opted for a career in publishing were certainly not guided by greed.

Although assimilation proceeded at a goodly pace, and seemed to "pay off" for the Jewish minority, my study would not be properly understood if we did not bear in mind that this process of assimilation elicited a reaction. Karl Lueger, and particularly Georg von Schönerer, had their Hungarian counterparts. But even if they had not, their anti-Semitism in the Austrian half of the Monarchy would have been sufficient to inspire fear among Jews within the Hungarian half; for, as I had attempted to show in the introductory chapter, conditions in Austria mirrored, in several respects, those in Hungary. Because of Jewish involvement in banking and industry, it was often the Jew, rather than the capitalist, who drew the ire and resentment of the politically still dominant gentry and aristocracy, especially

---

[38] Szekfü, *Magyar történet* 5: 552–55.

[39] *The Habsburg Monarchy*, 243, 245. For a less positive analysis of the "Jewish Question" see Mary Gluck, *Georg Lukács and His Generation 1900–1918* (Cambridge: Harvard Univ. Press, 1985). 58 ff.

[40] Assimilation did not mean conversion. Between 1896 and 1910 only 6,442 Jews converted to other religions in Hungary. *Magyar statisztikai évkönyv* [Hungarian Statistical Yearbook] 18 (1911): 416.

[41] Ibid., 67. In 1900, according to Szekfü, some 48 percent of the medical doctors, 68.6 percent of the lawyers, and 42.4 percent of the journalists had been Jewish. *Magyar történet*, 5: 553. See also William M. Johnston, *The Austrian Mind: An Intellectual and Social History, 1848–1938* (Berkeley: Univ. of California Press, 1972), 14.

of those elements which felt economically and socially insecure; hence capitalism was referred to in some circles as "Jewish" capitalism. Because of the role played by other Jews in the spread of bourgeois and urban culture, and of bourgeois democratic thought, because of the Jewish receptivity to new ideas and currents from the West, bourgeois culture was referred to in some circles as "Jewish" culture.

The problem of the landless peasant and of the small peasant, the problem of the "people of the pusztas," was quite as basic as the nationalities problem; whether or not these peasants spoke Hungarian had little bearing on their predicament. In addition to the two million peasants who owned a parcel of land, there were another two or three million who owned no land at all,[42] working as day-laborers, as servants, or forced to remain idle.

Yet the issue of land ownership and land distribution was seldom aired, even less often than the nationalities issue, if that be possible. It was no fault of the peasants; for some sectors of the peasantry had become as restless and as politically active as the industrial workers. In the spring of 1897 the harvesters had struck in several provinces (in Hungary spring harvests were and are possible), and the repression was brutal.[43] In June and July 1906 1,581 strikers were sentenced to an average of 25 days each in jail.[44] Vilmos Mezöfi, András Áchim, and István Nagyatádi Szabó had each organized peasant movements whose programs included some variety of land reform. Szabó's party became active in early 1907, and it was also at this time that Mezöfi's movement assumed a more radical stance. Áchim's party was organized a year earlier, and its program included some revolutionary items, such as the compulsory division of estates over 100 *holds.*

The editors of the theoretical journal of the Social Democratic Party had asked Karl Kautsky, the German socialist responsible for the Erfurt program, to write the lead article to the first issue, in October 1906; Kautsky chose to write about the peasantry. He argued that the peasantry had become a factor for reaction in every country of Western Europe. Not so in Hungary: "the peasantry there is still a revolutionary element, much as in Russia."[45]

Statistics on emigration are a fair indication of the condition of the peasantry. At no time in recent history had a country lost so many inhabitants through voluntary emigration as had the Monarchy in the first decade of the twentieth century. The rate of emigration was higher among the non-Hungarian population (except for the Romanians), and this constitutes one of the factors which help explain the relative increase of speakers of Hun-

---

[42] The most recent multivolume history of Hungary writes of one and a half million landed peasants and two million agrarian proletarians, but does not take into account their "dependents." *Magyar történet* 5: 31.

[43] Szekfü, *Magyar történet* 5: 542. For a vivid and sensitive description of such incidents see Anna Lesznai, *Kezdetben volt a kert* [At the Beginning was the Garden].

[44] Zoltán Horváth, op. cit., 317.

[45] Quoted in Süle, op. cit., 148. Another social scientist who saw a parallel in the predicament of Russia and Hungary was Zoltán Ronai in his article on "A Társadalomtudományi Társaság fejlödése" [The Evolution of the Society of Social Science] (*A szociologia elsö magyar mühelye* 1: 129).

garian. Between 1890 and 1910 approximately a million and a half emigrants from Hungary landed in the United States (not all of whom remained, or even meant to remain). In the single year 1907 some 338,452 persons arrived in the United States from Austria-Hungary, and 203,332 of them came from the Hungarian side.[46] Of the Hungarian emigrants 58,739 claimed Hungarian as their mother tongue. Furthermore, there were 37,611 German speakers, 32,739 Slovaks, 26,491 Romanians, 5,088 Ruthenians (i.e. Ukrainians), 16,589 Croatians, and 13,514 Serbs—all these figures being disproportionately large in relation to the size of the respective ethnic group living on Hungarian territory.[47]

Mass emigration worried the big bourgeoisie which felt hampered in its attempt to build up an industrial base under conditions that were not too favorable to begin with. The peasant who left the country depleted the ranks of the reserve army of workers. But the industrialists were not bold enough to clamor for land reform, which was the obvious alternative to mass emigration.[48]

A third important issue which, however, requires no elaboration, was suffrage. Unlike the nationalities problem, or that of land reform, the question of extension or reform of suffrage was constantly on the agenda in the Parliament, and frequently debated in the press. In fact, the division on this issue would allow us to draw certain political boundaries between "liberals" and "conservatives."

Were it not for the issue of suffrage such distinctions might prove problematic. In February 1904, at a debate on political doctrines organized by the Society of Social Sciences, the advocate for liberalism, Gusztáv Grátz, accepted the traditional nineteenth-century definition of the term: all true liberalism is democratic, he argued, but liberalism and socialism remain incompatible, if only because liberty and equality cannot be reconciled.[49] According to an unnamed socialist observer at the debate, Gusztáv Grátz and the advocate of conservatism spoke in almost identical terms.[50] It is not surprising, therefore, that the designation "liberal-conservative" was widely accepted in Hungarian politics. Edward Shils seems to have arrived at a generally valid law which finds confirmation in the Hungarian context: "Modern liberal and constitutional politics have largely been the creation of intellectuals with bourgeois affinities and sympathies, in societies dominated by landowning and military aristocracies."[51] These liberal and constitutional politics, however, did not prevail in Hungary.

---

[46] May, op. cit., 235. For the sake of comparison, in the same year the United States received 285,731 immigrants from Italy, and 258,943 from the Russian Empire. Elek Bolgár, "A kivándorlás" [Emigration], *A szociológia elsö magyar mühelye* 2: 42.

[47] *Magyar statisztikai évkönyv* [Hungarian Statistical Yearbook], uj folyam XVIII (1910) (Budapest: Magyar Mir. Központi Statisztikai Hivatal, 1911), 53.

[48] Miksa Fenyö, "Önéletrajz VIII" [Autobiography], *Uj látóhatár*, 548–49.

[49] *A liberalizmus* (Budapest, no publisher indicated, 1904).

[50] Süle, op. cit., 79.

[51] "The Intellectuals and the Powers: Some Perspectives for Comparative Analysis," in *On Intellectuals*, 35.

The issue was somewhat complicated by the confusion surrounding the notion of liberalism in Hungary; for instance, the so-called "new liberals" were not in sympathy with the notion of universal suffrage.[52] Although they sought theoretical justification for their undemocratic attitude, it is clear that the very notion of liberalism had lost much of its meaning; if anything, it meant not so much economic liberalism, as a fairly consistent stand on the issue of separation between Church and state. As for István Tisza and his regime, while pretending to favor reform, they remained adamantly opposed to any meaningful extension of the suffrage.

While the issue of the right to vote may seem to be a secondary one, in the sense that it was a logical concomitant of the nationalities problem and even of land reform (although the Prussian and other examples might have indicated to the Hungarian ruling classes that universal suffrage need not entail land reform), it was, nevertheless, the issue that led directly to the revolution of October 1918. Radicals and liberals, socialists and democrats, exacerbated by promises of suffrage extension proferred by establishment politicians in the course of a decade and a half, organized various leagues around this issue, at least as of 1905. The logical outcome of this concordance of interest was the Right to Vote Bloc, established on 6 June 1917— a coalition of the Social Democrats, of the Bourgeois Radical Party, of the Party led by Károlyi, of the Party led by Vázsonyi, the Christian Socialist Giesswein, and lesser groups.[53] The Bloc recognized Count Mihály Károlyi as its spokesman. It was largely out of this Bloc that the National Council was carved on 25 October 1918, and it was in the name of the National Council that the revolution was fought and won five days later, on 30 October.

I have deliberately neglected some of the major themes of political history in this period: the controversies regarding the Kaiserliche und Königliche (Imperial and Royal) army, the regulation of customs, the matter of a joint bank, the relationship to the Austrian metropolis in general. The picture I have given of domestic affairs certainly does not reflect the main concerns of the daily press: cabinet meetings, parliamentary debates, the dominating personality of István Tisza. But it was the failure to resolve those three basic problems, that of minorities, of land reform, and of suffrage, that hastened the coming of the revolutions. Yet the revolutions came too late. They could not solve the nationalities issue, for the Habsburg Monarchy, and the "Kingdom of Saint Stephen" had already dissolved or, better said, disintegrated as if by explosion. The revolutions' failure to deal adequately with the perennial land problem has been cited by participants and by historians as the most important internal factor in the collapse of the Republic of Councils. It is true that universal suffrage was introduced by the revolutionary regimes, but the elections of 7 April 1919 could not stem the

---

[52] *Magyar történet*, 68.
[53] *Magyar történet* 15: 124, and 11: 22.

counter-revolution. Long ago György Lukács reached the same conclusion: the three most important factors in the "Hungarian tragedy" had been the "oppression of nationalities," the land problem which the political parties considered taboo, and the exclusion of the masses from parliament.[54] Lukács's analysis is not subjective or arbitrary, but is based on conclusions warranted by the achievements and failures of the revolutions of 1918–19 in which he played a significant part.

Lukács might have added a fourth objective factor (that is, a factor other than consciousness) which hastened the advent of the Great October Socialist Revolution, as well as of the Hungarian revolutions: World War I. The history of the war is a chapter of European and world history. It makes little difference that certain Hungarian leaders, including Tisza who was assassinated by an agent of those who erroneously blamed him for the war, had entered the war reluctantly; but what Hungarian leaders did, or failed to do, hardly affected the outcome. It makes little difference that Hungarian politicians such as Count Albert Apponyi or Count Gyula Andrássy had or had not approved the annexation of Bosnia-Hercegovina in 1908. The annexation was carried out, the Austrian Archduke was assassinated, the Monarchy did provoke a conflict with Serbia, and Hungary fought a war in which her role was unequivocally imperialist. Although all the participants in the war lost, Hungary was by far the biggest loser. It is not necessarily the magnitude of the loss that accounts for the likelihood of revolution; but it is clear that in several respects Hungary was an even more unfortunate loser than the Russian Empire.

Clearly, the war quickened certain social and political processes (while at the same time, at least in the beginning, attenuating certain conflicts).[55] The war and its outcome can be considered a *sine qua non* of radical political change, because other factors that might have proved more basic seemed to work at cross-purposes. I need only mention the workers' disaffection with the Social Democratic Party after 1913, the attitude adopted by the Party vis-à-vis the war (similar to the attitude of Social Democratic parties in other countries), the diminution of strike activity in the first two years of the war, and the pessimism that numbed most radical intellectuals, including Ady.

I do not suscribe to the "catastrophe theory" of revolution; but it is clear, in the Hungarian case, that the revolutions were not sufficiently prepared, the movement did not have a wide enough base, and the socioeconomic conjuncture was not the most favorable. Ultimately, the revolutions failed, whether one takes the short or the long view of history.

---

[54] "Ady, a magyar tragédia nagy énekese" [Ady, the Great Minstrel of the Hungarian Tragedy], in *Magyar irodalom magyar kúltura*, 162. Schöpflin also stresses the issues of general suffrage, the "agrarian-socialist" movement, and the demands of the nationalities. *A magyar irodalom története a XX században*, 148.

[55] Süle, op. cit., 222.

III. THE LITERARY CONTEXT

A book is only a book if it is read, argues a French researcher.[1] It seems fair to assume that an increase in the number of people able to read resulted in the reading of more books, and in a rise in the popularity of literature. By 1910 some 69 percent of the population of Hungary who had reached school age were able to read (as opposed to 44.5 percent in 1870). About two hundred and fifty thousand persons had completed eight years of schooling or more. Between 1876 and 1913 the number of books printed annually increased by about one hundred percent. The number of copies of newspapers sold increased eight or ten times within the same period, the total daily sales of papers reaching close to nine hundred thousand.[2] In 1910 there were altogether 1,603 newspapers and periodicals published in Hungary, twelve of which were officially described as "literary" (and six of these were published in Budapest). That same year thirty-nine dailies were published in Budapest, more than in Vienna, Berlin, or any other European capital.[3] While 199 Hungarian-language periodicals ceased publication in 1910, another 221 got launched.[4] The spread of newspaper consumption is not simply an indication of literacy, or of an interest in current affairs; it is relevant from our point of view because most of the Nyugat writers had earned their living, at one time or another, as journalists.[5]

The figures above confirm the original assumption; literacy was on the rise, and progress in the consumption of printed products far exceeded the rise in literacy. But we must be wary of deriving conclusions regarding the political significance of these data, for there seems to be no correlation between literacy and revolution: only 20 percent of the population of the Russian Empire was able to read in 1917.

It seems reasonable to assume that the rise in literacy contributed to the increase in the popularity of literature, but it may be equally correct to assume that the popularity of certain writers resulted in a rise in literacy; in other words, that certain writers taught the public the habit of reading. Thus the increase in the number of readers in England in mid-nineteenth

---

[1] Nicole Robine, in *Letteratura e società*, ed. Robert Escarpit (Bologna: Mulino, 1972), 187.
[2] *A könyv és a könyvtár a magyar társadalom életében* [Book and Library in Hungarian Society], 2 (1849 to 1945), ed. Máté Kovács (Budapest: Gondolat, 1970): 77.
[3] Béla Dezsényi, György Nemes, *A magyar sajtó 250 éve* [250 Years of Hungarian Press] (Budapest: Müvelt Nép, 1954) 1: 225.
[4] *A könyv és a könyvtár . . .* , 95–96.
[5] Of course, this also applies to the United Kingdom, and a number of other countries. Q. D. Leavis, *Fiction and the Reading Public* (London: Chatto & Windus, 1965, 1st ed. 1932), 185.

century is reflected in, or perhaps the result of, the work of Dickens (more so than any other writer of the period).⁶ In Hungary it was the ultraromantic novels of Mór Jókai that contributed to the increase in readers of literary works.⁷

This extension of the reading public does not necessarily imply a lowering of literary standards. David Daiches points out, using the Soviet Union as an example, that the "ordinary" reader may be as responsive to good literature as he is to bad;⁸ which of the two dominates becomes a matter of guidance and of availability. The increase in the number of readers in Hungary was a process parallel to the increase in the production of dime novels, but also to an increase (qualitative and quantitative) in the production of good literature.

Nor was the increase in the number of readers simply a matter of quality of literature or quantity of publications; it was much rather a component of a general intellectual fermentation that consisted, in part, of a multiplication of styles and theories, of a more favorable reception accorded to currents flowing from abroad. Hungary, being a small country, has an economy that is dependent on trade, particularly imports; by analogy, if for no other reason, it may be said that her intellectual life is also particularly susceptible to influences from the outside. In 1913, to take the last year of general peace as an example, out of a total of 419 literary works published in Hungary, 106 were translations.⁹

The fermentation of the beginning of the twentieth century is known as the phenomenon of "combined development" in Hungary, as it was also in the Russian Empire. Ideas, movements, or trends occasioned by changes in social conditions in the West were somewhat indiscriminately imported or transposed into Eastern Europe where they became assimilated with some delay due, in part, to the backwardness of socioeconomic conditions. What's more, the order of their assimilation did not necessarily follow the order in which these ideas, movements, or trends evolved in the West.

Actually, a variety of currents flowed onto the Hungarian cultural scene more or less simultaneously: symbolism and naturalism, art nouveau and decadence, impressionism and futurism.

Of all these currents symbolism was the most relevant in the context of the literary revolution of the beginning of the century. Like other "isms" and currents, it arrived in Eastern Europe after some delay, although it seems to have affected Czech literature by 1890 (but the Slovak only about 1909). The date mentioned in connection with Hungary is usually 1906,¹⁰

---

⁶ David Daiches, *Literature and Society* (New York: Haskell House, 1970, 1st ed. 1938), 210.

⁷ Lujza Farkas, *A Nyugat és a századeleji irodalomforduló* [The Nyugat and the Literary Revolution of the Turn of the Century] (Budapest: Gyarmati, 1935), 7.

⁸ Daiches, op. cit., 240–41.

⁹ *A könyv és a könyvtár* . . . 2: 92.

¹⁰ See, for instance, László Sziklay, "Le rôle de Pest-Buda dans la formation des littératures est-européennes," *Littérature hongroise, littérature européenne* (Budapest: Akadémia, eds. István Sötér and Otto Süpek), 333.

the publication of Endre Ady's third volume of poetry, when he found his style which, indeed, seemed closer to French symbolism than to any other imported trend. The title of Ady's volume was *Uj versek* [New Poems]; another volume of "new poems" [*Neue Gedichte*] by another great poet from the Habsburg Monarchy, Rainer Maria Rilke, appeared the same year. Furthermore, Ady's symbolism shared certain characteristics with Irish symbolism, especially that of Yeats.[11] Significantly, André Karátson's impressive treatise titled *Le symbolisme en Hongrie* is devoted mainly to Ady and other stars of the Nyugat constellation.[12]

It was the symbolist poetry of Baudelaire, Mallarmé, Rimbaud, and others that was referred to as "modern" or "contemporary" by the Hungarian critics and poets of 1908, even though all three French poets had passed away by the time the *Nyugat* started publication.[13] And the poet Dezsö Kosztolányi was the first to classify Ady as a symbolist poet, although he may have meant it as a term of opprobrium.[14] In fact, in a letter to Babits back in 1904 Kosztolányi had referred to Mallarmé as "empty," and to Verlaine as "miserable": "To hell with them! They spoil our sense of esthetics and, in addition to dirty things, they favor monsters."[15]

Baudelaire, however, would remain popular; the *Nyugat* published six studies on him, and eleven translations of his poems between 1908 and 1918. Verlaine and Albert Samain were also well represented with ten and seven poems respectively.[16]

With regard to a poem he had written back in 1898, Ady claimed that it was the first decadent poem in Hungary.[17] If that is so, we note a lag of some fifteen years; for Huysman's "decadent" novel, *A rebours*, often accepted as the prototype of decadence, had appeared in 1884.[18] Ady's decadent tone is often unmistakable; but even his most "decadent" poems reflect a Hungarian predicament rather than a French or Belgian one. They do serve a purpose: the decadent poems of Ady shatter, to paraphrase Engels, the optimism of the bourgeois world and instill doubts as to the eternal character of the existing order; but they can accomplish this, of course, by merely describing the real world, by breaking down the con-

---

[11] "The Literary Revolution in 1900," *New Hungarian Quarterly*, 18 (1977), No. 67: 128.

[12] Paris: Presses Universitaires, 1967.

[13] It was with some justification that József Pogány, a prominent socialist intellectual, could write in 1910, that "our literature, our art is the copy of foreign literatures and art forms dead decades ago." *Renaissance*, 2 (1910): 259. Regarding the cultural lag of Hungary see also Jenö Robert, in *Figyelö*, 1, No. 8, August 1905, 473 ff. and Oszkár Jászi, in *Huszadik Század*.

[14] Review of "Vér és arany" [Ady's "Blood and Gold"], *Uj idök*, 1 (1908): 144.

[15] Letter of 11 August 1904. *Babits-Juhász-Kosztolányi levelezése*, ed. György Bélia (Budapest: Akadémia, 1959). Kosztolányi's initial view of Ady was equally negative or condescending. See letters of 19 February and 18 August 1906.

[16] Ferenc Galambos, *Nyugat repertorium* [Index to the Nyugat], 1959.

[17] György Rónay, *A nagy nemzedék* [The Great Generation] (Budapest: Szépirodalmi, 1971), 55.

[18] Zsolt Harsányi, *A 'franciás' Nyugat* [The Frenchified Nyugat] (Debrecen: 1942), 6.

ventional illusions about them.[19] "In a decaying society," wrote Ernst Fischer, "art, if it is truthful, must also reflect decay . . . And help to change it."[20] In vain did Jean-Paul Sartre argue that the category of decadence was useless.[21] It was an inevitable category in the Prague of Kafka, or in the Budapest of Ady and Babits; the term simply meant that the social system behind them, the bureaucratism of the Monarchy, the semi-feudal conditions prevailing in Hungary, were themselves in decay.[22]

Hence realism and decadence meet in the Hungarian context, the former comprises the latter; it was naturalism, however, that found a relatively fertile ground in Hungary after the turn of the century. Emile Zola, of course, was the model: he proved more popular, it seems, in Budapest than in Paris, especially after 1897 and 1905, as a result of his interventions in the "Affaire." The pre-Nyugat writer Sándor Brody introduced the term, if not the method of naturalism; the misery of the lower middle-class was one of his favorite themes. Yet the best Hungarian naturalists, such as Zsigmond Móricz or Lajos Nagy, never ceased to be true realists.[23] In any case, it is not clear to me why naturalist writers have become the subject of widespread contempt. It is true that Marx and Engels made some unkind comments about Emile Zola; but then they were probably reacting, on the one hand, to his extraordinary popularity and, on the other, to the strong streak of petit-bourgeois sentimentalism that survived in Zola, but which need not be regarded as an essential ingredient of naturalism. It seems to me, an amateur in matters of literary history, that the mediocre realist writer is often referred to as a naturalist, whereas the good naturalist is certainly a realist.[24] The social function of naturalism, wrote Antal Szerb, who achieved recognition between the two world wars as a historian of Hungarian and of world literature, consisted in consecrating as literature the life-style, language, and ideology of the petite bourgeoisie and the proletariat of the cities, "these new classes."[25]

And there was art nouveau, or *Sezession* as its Hungarian and German versions were called, although (like impressionism, expressionism, and

---

[19] Engels to Minna Kautsky, 26 Nov. 1885. Reprinted among other places in *Marxism and Art,* eds. Forrest Williams and Berel Lang (New York: McKay, 1972), 51.

[20] Ibid., 160.

[21] Sartre added that Kafka, Joyce, and Proust paved his way towards Marxism. *Radical Perspectives in the Arts,* ed. Lee Baxandall (Baltimore: Penguin Books), 238.

[22] Raymond Williams objects to the use of the term decadent when applied to the literature of Western Europe at the beginning of the century; it was anything but decadent, he argues. *Culture and Society, 1780–1950* (Garden City, N.Y.: Doubleday, 1960), 300–301.

[23] Mihály Czine, "Le naturalisme hongrois au tournant du siècle," *Littérature hongroise, littérature européenne,* 108.

[24] Witness Mihály Czine's observation: "L'époque accusait de naturalisme à titre principal ceux qui, dans le but d'un changement équitable de la vie, s'efforçaient de mettre à nu l'homme et la société." *Littérature hongroise, littérature européenne,* 422.

[25] *Magyar irodalomtörténet* [History of Hungarian Literature] (Budapest: Magvető, 1972, 1st ed., 1935), 418.

constructivism) it manifested itself primarily in the visual field, especially the decorative or industrial arts. This did not prevent the poet and critic Aladár Komlos from referring to Ady as the foremost poet of art nouveau, even internationally speaking.[26] It is not surprising, then, that art nouveau was controversial, criticized even in the Hungarian Parliament; or that a perceptive essay on Aubrey Beardsley could not be published in Hungary in 1903—it was too soon.[27] The same Komlós also described the editor of the *Nyugat* Ignotus as a product or disciple of art nouveau,[28] a style about which Ignotus wrote several essays.[29]

This list of literary or art currents might be complemented by another list of individual giants whose influence was powerful enough to alter the course of Hungarian letters; one might mention Freud, Dostoievsky, Zola, France, and Nietzsche as a bare minimum.

"I had not had a reading experience," wrote Ignotus, "which changed my outlook on the world as much as Freud, and later Einstein . . ."[30] The influence of Freud is likewise clearly discernible in the work of Frigyes Karinthy, even before Freud had been translated into Hungarian. In Karinthy's short stories dreams and the notion of the unconscious often assume crucial importance. Mihály Babits's novel *A golyakalifa,* more recently translated into English as *The Nightmare,* is another case in point. Freud's theory of dreams became available in translation by 1913; and in 1917 the *Nyugat* brought out an article by Freud written "expressly for the *Nyugat*."[31] Several studies by Sándor Ferenczi, at that time still one of Freud's foremost disciples, were published in the *Nyugat* from 1912 on. Yet, in a poll inquiring about the favorite readings of prominent Hungarian writers, the only one to mention a work by Freud was Ignotus.[32]

Literary influence need not be direct. It was the distinguished professor of French literature at Yale University, Henri Peyre who, in his lectures, emphasized that influence may be felt or may manifest itself even where there is no direct acquaintance, no direct contact with the works of the agent; and he used to mention Nietzsche as a prime example. It is clear that Nietzsche was important to Ady, although it may have been mostly a matter of second-hand experience.[33] To many, Nietzsche was the hero of the age; and in Hungary it was the "modern" writers who spoke up for

---

[26] Aladár Komlós, *Vereckétől Dévényig* (Budapest: Szépirodalmi Kiadó, 1972), 100.

[27] *Politikai Hetiszemle,* 14, No. 25 (15 Dec. 1907): 14.

[28] *Ignotus válogatott irásai* [Selected Writings of Ignotus], ed. Aladár Komlós (Budapest: Szepirödalmi Kiadó, 1969), 17.

[29] In the journal *Hét,* ibid., 183.

[30] *Ignotus válogatott irásai,* 39.

[31] "A pszihoanalizis egy nehézségéröl" [About One of the Difficulties of Psychoanalysis], 10 (1917), No. 1: 47–52.

[32] Béla Köhalmi, *Könyvek könyve* [The Book of Books] (Budapest: Lantos, n.d. ca. 1918), 8.

[33] György Ronay, *A nagy nemzedék,* 11, 62. *Magyarország története,* 8 (chapter on culture), 716–17. Plekhanov wrote about Nietzsche: "In the civilized world today, there is not a single country where the youth of the bourgeoisie are not in sympathy with the ideas of Friedrich Nietzsche." Quoted in *Marxism and Art,* 94.

him, including Kassák,[34] Babits, Kosztolányi, and particularly Gyula Juhász.[35] Nietzsche had died in 1900, but it was only in the first decade of the new century that his works became available in Hungarian translation. It was most unfortunate, of course, and certainly no fault of Nietzsche, that Hitler was to be among his posthumous admirers. In Hungary, at least one prominent writer, a playwright and president of the society of freethinkers, mentioned Nietzsche in the context of progress in the natural sciences, and of socialism![36]

As for Anatole France, he was probably the foreign author most often mentioned on the pages of the *Nyugat*. The first volume of the journal carried an essay on France by the socialist Pál Kéri: France is "the cleverest man in Europe today," argued Kéri.[37] Gyula Juhász considered him "the greatest intellectual of the age."[38] France was the subject of eleven more articles and reviews in the first ten volumes of the journal.[39] Nor is it entirely irrelevant to remind ourselves that France was an *engagé;* for a long time he wavered between anarchism and Communism, but eventually opted for the latter tendency, and did not hesitate to stake his reputation as a man of letters on his political activity: "it is the writers, indeed, who lead the people, inasmuch as they form and define the spirit of every nation."[40] The *Nyugat* continued to take up the cudgels on behalf of Anatole France, wrote Antal Szerb, at a time when Claudel's Catholicism, and Gide's belligerent Protestantism had already become the literary news in France[41] (not to mention Proust, Apollinaire, and many others). When it came to a broader survey of writers, however, the position of Anatole France was no longer so eminent; in a poll, the Hungarian writers asked to name their favorite authors listed France ahead of Zola, Balzac, and Baudelaire, but behind Tolstoy, Dostoievsky, Heine, and Ibsen (considering only "foreign" authors).[42]

Several of the Nyugat writers developed a particular "elective affinity" for Thomas Mann who, in any case, was their contemporary. The *Nyugat*, however, was not the first Hungarian periodical to take notice of him. Some of Mann's writings had appeared in the *Hét* in 1908; and he first visited Hungary in 1913, under the sponsorship of the radical bourgeois daily *Világ*. Nevertheless, Mann was in contact with the Nyugat. He paid

---

[34] Lajos Kassák, *Egy ember élete* 2: 206.
[35] Ferenc Kiss, *A beérkezés küszöbén* [On the Threshold of Success] (Budapest: Akadémia, 1962), 19–34.
[36] Samu Fényes, quoted in *A magyar irodalom története* [The History of Hungarian Literature] 5: 40, 244–45, 275, 306.
[37] "A szocialista Anatole France," [France the Socialist], *Nyugat* 1 (1908): 195.
[38] *Juhász Gyula összes müvei* [The Complete Works of Juhász] (Budapest: Akademia, 5, 1968), 146.
[39] Galambos, *Nyugat repertórium*.
[40] *Les matinées de la villa Saïd; propos d'Anatole France,* recueillis par Paul Gsell (Paris: Bernard Grasset, 1921), 299–303.
[41] *Magyar irodalomtörténet*, 433.
[42] Köhalmi, *Könyvek könyve*, 8.

a visit to Zsigmond Móricz (although their conversation must have been awkward, since Móricz spoke hardly any German), and developed a lasting relationship with Kosztolányi. Moreover, it seems by now well established that György Lukács was the model for Naphta of *The Magic Mountain*, written during World War I.[43] Mann's public reading, on 6 December 1913, attracted a large audience, in spite of Ady's rather lukewarm preview of the occasion, and was to be repeated four times during the coming decades.[44]

Having listed Western currents and Western writers who played a role in the Hungarian literary revolution of the beginning of the century, let me open a parenthesis. To be sure, it would be quite laughable to speak of mutual influences, of Hungarian influence on the course of Western literature; it is worth noting, however, that some Nyugat writers were given publicity abroad, in fact considerably more publicity than older or non-Nyugat writers. Lajos Hatvany was as well known in Germany as in Hungary. The plays of Sándor Brody, Lajos Biró, Ferenc Molnár, and Menyhért Lengyel were performed abroad, particularly in the two German-speaking countries, and earned fame for Hungarian drama in general. Ignace Kont's book, *La littérature hongroise d'aujourd'hui*, published in 1908, already mentioned Ady, Kaffka, and Ignotus among the eminent modern poets and novelists of Hungary.[45] In a series of volumes dealing with "exotic" literatures translated into German, the poetry of Ady, Juhász, and Kosztolányi from the Nyugat was represented, along with five Hungarian poets of the previous generation, and this as early as 1907.[46] In an anthology of German translations from the Hungarian published in 1918, in two thousand copies, all the great poets of the Nyugat were represented, along with some older poets, but Babits and Ady lead in the number of poems included. Among the poems of Babits was a translation of "Fortissimo," his most vehement anti-war poem, which had not been published in Hungary because of the intervention of the censors.[47] All this is merely a sample of modern Hungarian literature available in translation; nevertheless, this literature remained almost totally isolated and unrecognized to the present day.

Zola, Nietzsche, Anatole France, Baudelaire, Freud, the symbolists, the naturalists, the impressionists, were the foreign protagonists of the battle for modern literature in Hungary; but if their Hungarian admirers had been

---

[43] *Magyarország története*, manuscript version, 12: 651. Thomas Mann stayed with the Lukács family during his visit to Budapest.

[44] For a monograph on the subject see Judit Györi, *Thomas Mann Magyarországon* [Mann in Hungary] (Budapest: Akadémia, 1968), 7, 18. An expanded German version of this study has been published under the title *Thomas Mann und Ungarn*, eds. Antal Maile and Judit Györi (Budapest: Akadémia, 1977). Admiration between Mann and the Hungarian writers of the Nyugat movement was not always mutual. Mann's comment on an early novel by Móricz was: "boring." Thomas Mann, *Diaries 1918–1939*, (New York: Harry N. Abrams, 1982), entry for 22 Sep. 1921, p. 120.

[45] Paris: E. Sansot & Co., 15, 19.

[46] Hans Bethge, ed., *Die Lyrik des Auslandes in neuerer Zeit* (Leipzig, Max Hasses Verlag, 1907).

[47] *Neue ungarische Lyrik in Nachdichtungen* by Heinrich Horvath (München: Georg Müller, 1918).

mere imitators, the battle for modern literature would have been lost from the start. Endre Ady and the other members of the Nyugat were far from imitators. They did not allow French or Western currents simply to flow onto Hungarian territory. "We were rebels and revolutionaries," wrote Babits, "even when, especially when we held onto the roots of Hungarian traditions most tenaciously . . ." Indeed, the literary revolution of the beginning of the century did not break with the traditions established by the first great reform generation.

Literary historians satisfy the technical requirements of their profession by dividing the literature they are particularly concerned with into epochs, periods, ages, or styles. They draw demarcation lines, discover turning points, and seem to have a predilection for round numbers, especially for century marks. The more discriminating talk about "periods of transition" (as if, to quote Robert S. Lopez, all historical periods were not periods of transition). Hungarian literary scholars may not attach much importance to the year 1900, but they do concur in referring to 1905 or 1908 as turning points. Yet was there a year, a moment, when literature could be said to have become modern? (Quite apart from the fact that "modern" is of all ages.) Can modern Hungarian literature be said to begin at a specific time? Would it not be more appropriate to talk about "beginnings," and about the time when a certain literary trend or trends prevailed, carried the day?

It is at least clear that the Nyugat movement did not begin on 28 December 1907, when the maiden issue of the periodical hit the stands (and even less on 1 January 1908, as generally assumed). For one thing, that first issue went practically unnoticed by the press and the public. For another, a literary "fermentation" had been going on for a number of years. One might reasonably argue (although I have even better reasons for rejecting that interpretation) that by the time of the *Nyugat*'s appearance, the battle for modern literature was in full swing, the battle lines had been drawn.

If we must chose a first, the first document pertaining to the new literature was the appeal for subscribers formulated by Ernö Osvát, Miksa Fenyö, and others, in the summer of 1901: they announced a new review, "the contributors to which would be alien to all interests except an interest in the beautiful and in social justice."[48]

Nothing came of the appeal, but Osvát did take on, as editor, the *Magyar Géniusz* on 1 June 1902, and remained its editor until 8 March 1903.[49] Its October 1902 issue already carried a one-act play by Ady, "A mühelyben" [In the workshop]. Many of its contributors were to participate in the Nyugat movement. Other members of the Nyugat, such as Babits, Kosztolányi, Juhász, and Aladár Kuncz were still attending the seminar of Professor Négyessy at the University of Budapest, whereas Árpád Toth, Milán Füst,

---

[48] Lajos Pók, "A Nyugat elözményei (négy folyóirat)" [The antecedents of the 'Nyugat'—four periodicals], *Irodalomtörténet* (1957) 45, No. 3: 286.

[49] After which the journal declined, according to Oszkár Gellért, who took over as its editor.

Józsi-Jenö Tersánszky, and Frigyes Karinthy had not yet graduated from high school.[50]

The next attempt to create a journal devoted to the propagation of modern literature and of western bourgeois values resulted in the *Figyelö*, actually launched on 1 January 1905, three years before the *Nyugat*. In that issue the editor Osvát overcame his writer's cramp, amounting to something of a phobia: "nowhere do talents perish as they do in Hungary . . . We have seen a hundred promising starts, and one literary career in a hundred."[51] Whatever may have been his grounds for making such an unverifiable statement, here was a program of sorts, with implications that went well beyond the purely literary.

The *Figyelö* was printed by a book-dealer on condition that the editors contribute 160 crowns towards the cost of publication; eight persons contributed 20 crowns each, namely the editors and authors of the journal.[52] The story goes that it was their girl friends who subscribed to it and kept the journal going, but eventually the writers married their girl friends, the journal was sent out as courtesy copies, and the venture went bankrupt. Nevertheless, during its eleven issues the group of writers who rallied around the journal made a conscious effort to modernize Hungarian literature.[53] This group was essentially identical with the team that was to constitute the Nyugat movement; and the first number of the *Nyugat* actually bore the inscription "the new series of the *Figyelö*."

Other journals helped fertilize the soil on which the new literature was to feed. One might mention the short-lived *Szerda* (edited by Ignotus and Zoltán Ambrus in October and November 1906), or the weekly *Hét* which had a long life, beginning as early as 1890. *Hét* had a cosmopolitan approach, strove to popularize French letters, and gave Ignotus a chance to develop as writer and critic. The *Budapesti Napló* was the daily organ of the progressives until the creation of the *Világ*; it printed some of Ady's most glorious poetry and employed him as a correspondent.

Clearly, many felt some kind of change was imminent. The September 1907 issue of the political weekly *Politikai hetiszemle*, which had hardly bothered with good literature until then, printed an editorial stating: "In the past few years a peculiar liveliness is manifesting itself in our rather poverty-stricken literary life . . ." The editors vowed that henceforth they

---

[50] Oszkár Gellért, *Egy iró élete* [A Writer's Life] (Budapest: Bibliotheca, 1958), 1: 8.

[51] *Osvát Ernö összes irásai* [The Complete Writings of Osvát], ed. Kálmán Osvát (Budapest: Nyugat, 1945), 195.

[52] Miksa Fenyö, *Följegyzések a 'Nyugat' folyóiratról és környékéröl* (Pátria: Niagara Falls, 1960), 21. Also Lujza Farkas, op. cit., 18. But in a letter to Hatvany, December 1911, in *Levelek Hatvany Lajoshoz* [Letters to Hatvany] (Budapest: Szépirodalmi, 1967, 140), Fenyö speaks of a contribution of 30 crowns per person. In a letter to Babits he claims that the editors had to pay 60 crowns a month (Babits Papers, III/437 Széchenyi Irratár).

[53] Julius von Farkas, *Der Freiheitskampf des ungarischen Geistes, 1867–1914* (Berlin: Walter de Gruyter, 1940), 226.

would make room for the literary products of the youngest generation of writers.[54] They kept their word: the subsequent issues carried several poems by Mihály Babits,[55] as yet an almost unknown entity, followed by a number of contributions by Ady.

Ady's poetry and politics had stirred a storm long before the appearance of the *Nyugat*. By 1908 the literary polemics were well under way; in fact, it seems the controversy surrounding Ady had subsided by then, at least for the time being, and the literati who still looked upon Ady with hatred or contempt were definitely in a minority.[56] To be sure, the controversy had been, in part, the by-product of Ady's life-style: venereal disease, daily bouts with large quantities of alcohol, veronal and (100 to 120) cigarettes, created an image of the *poète maudit* calculated (for the image he projected was not void of intentionality) to shock the *bien-pensants*. But the real issue was Ady's politics, rather than his life-style; and that pertains to another chapter.

Although this chapter is meant to give the reader an idea of the literary context, I must mention here, as I will several times in the course of this study, a journal devoted to the social sciences, the *Huszadik század*. Launched in 1900, its name, meaning "twentieth century," was entirely appropriate; Hatvany called it the "first eye-opener."[57] Through the volumes of this journal, and even before 1908, we meet with authors who were to achieve international distinction: György Lukács, Sándor Ferenczi, the disciple and companion of Freud, Jenö Varga the economist, Ervin Szabó, Oszkár Jászi who, after twenty years of intense political activity, was to become a distinguished historian in exile, Károly and Mihály Polányi, eventually Károly Mannheim, and others. It should be noted that neither the *Huszadik század* nor the *Nyugat*—periodicals which, as will be seen, shared a number of contributors—rallied all the brilliant minds who were to exert, singly and collectively, such an impact on science and scholarship in the twentieth century; rather, both periodicals, as well as these "minds," were the product of the same fertile spiritual soil.[58]

The circumstances surrounding the appearance of the *Nyugat* itself have never been adequately elucidated or investigated. As we have seen, the periodical came about and survived only after repeated attempts. The most recent attempt and failure had been an appeal for subscribers sent out by

---

[54] "A legfiatalabb irodalom; felhivás a legfrisebb irói generációhoz" [The Youngest Literature; Appeal to the Most Recent Generation of Writers], *Politikai hetiszemle*, 14, No. 19.

[55] For instance, "Olvasás közben" [While Reading], "Anyám névnapjára" [For My Mother's Name-Day], and "Tájkép" [Landscape] in the 22 September issue; furthermore "Aliscum éjhaju leánya" [The Night-Haired Daughter of Aliscum] in the next issue.

[56] See, for instance, János Jakó's review of Ady's "Sápadt emberek és történetek" [Pale People and Stories], in *Politikai Hetiszemle*, 14, No. 21: 20.

[57] "Az úri hölgyhöz" [To the Noble Lady], *Nyugat*, 3 (1910), No. 2: 1132.

[58] György Litván, "Aspects de la vie intellectuelle et culturelle en Hongrie au début du XXe siècle," *Arion* 10 (1977): 26–27.

Fenyö, in the name of Lajos Hatvany, in the spring of 1907. Neither Fenyö nor Osvát had the necessary social contacts; Hatvany, however, was the scion of a noble family, albeit Jewish, which had made a fortune in sugar refineries and other industrial ventures. Furthermore, Hatvany was himself a man of letters whose literary career, as we have seen, unfolded in Germany as much as in Hungary. "We will have no difficulty," wrote Fenyö to Hatvany, "in collecting 600–650 subscribers, and then we will be lacking only 300–400 more . . . [The review] would be a piece of culture or, let us say, a cultural topic. Something for those who have no use for the *Uj idők*. Our Nile, too, will some day reach the sea, have no doubt . . ."[59] Obviously, the goal must have been to collect a thousand subscribers. Only about twenty-five persons sent in their subscriptions. But Fenyö's over-optimistic estimate of the situation was calculated to encourage Hatvany in his role as patron. Actually, the first issue of the *Nyugat*, when it did appear a few months later, contented itself with considerably fewer than a thousand subscribers.

On 12 December 1907, Ignotus, Osvát, and Fenyö applied at the city hall of Budapest for authorization to publish the *Nyugat* in time for Christmas, the 20th of the month. By that time the journal had already found its name, and was described in the application as a bi-monthly dealing with the arts, with social and economic matters, but with emphasis on literature.[60] The journal missed the Christmas market, but did appear on the stands in the last days of December. There was not the least bit of fanfare. The dailies commented on the prolonged parliamentary debate regarding the status of Croatia within the kingdom, the continued Japanese occupation of Manchuria, the preparations for another Hague peace conference, the activities of anarchists in Hungary and elsewhere, the trial of Harden in Berlin, accused as he was of defamation of character (the character of the chief of the German general staff), the wave of suicides—apparently always a current topic in Hungary—and the rent-strike by seventy thousand tenants in the slums of New York City. Even Ady's paper, the *Budapesti Napló*, made no mention of the new literary journal for a while.

All other details surrounding the beginnings of the journal are the subject of (mild) controversy. According to Fenyö, Osvát and himself had thought up the Nyugat some time in 1907 at the Café Royal.[60] Further on in the same series of reminiscences Fenyö writes that the *Nyugat* got under way from the Bristol coffeehouse.[61] In another collection of reminiscences Fenyö writes that he and Osvát used to meet at the Café Hangli, planning a new review, a "new methadone era." Osvát's pocket was filled with scraps of

---

[59] 9 April 1907, MTA Akadémiai Irattár, Ms 380/j.
[60] *Följegyzések a Nyugat folyóiratról és környékéről*, 8; also Lujza Farkas, op. cit., 22.
[61] *Följegyzések . . .* , 42–43.

paper bearing meaningful titles for the review—"but the one that appealed to me most was Nyugat [Occident], a tribute to the French spirit."[62]

If I have sufficient energy remaining, I should like to write a chapter on the literary function of the Budapest coffeehouses. For the time being it may suffice to note that the Café Bristol did become the headquarters, practically the editorial office, of the *Nyugat*.

What were the considerations that led to the founding of a new review (or to the revival of the *Figyelő*)? Partly the conviction that the era of great Hungarian poetry had not come to an end with János Arany, and that Mór Jókai, Kálmán Mikszáth, and Géza Gárdonyi were not the last great virtuosi of Hungarian prose, the "last of the buffaloes";[63] the conviction that literature could not flourish in isolation, that it must not regard the great political, social, and economic issues as taboo. Such were the considerations, according to Fenyö, that led to the establishment of the *Nyugat*;[64] as for the review's program once it was launched, I shall discuss that in a subsequent chapter, in connection with the political attitudes of the members of the movement.

One measure of the success of the *Nyugat* could be the imitators it bred, obviously not because of profits, but rather because of the high quality of its literature, and because of its viability, its ability to survive. Thus the *Renaissance* was launched on 10 May 1910, the *Aurora* in 1911, the *Május* in 1913.

The conviction that there was literary fermentation, literary innovation in search of an adequate outlet, was not altogether new; what, then, was the new ingredient, precisely in late 1907, that seemed to warrant another attempt to create such an outlet? An improved prospect for financial support, I should think. Unfortunately, the finances of the *Nyugat* are yet another issue that has been entirely neglected by historians and literary historians. One of the most distinguished among them, Erzsébet Vezér, called my attention to it: "It would be a worthwhile task . . . to compile the history of the *Nyugat* publishers, including its economic and financial aspects."[65]

---

[62] "Önéletrajz VIII" [Autobiography], *Uj látóhatár*, 554.
[63] Péter Nagy's introduction to the *Móricz Zsigmond válogatott elbeszélései* [Selected short stories of Móricz] (Budapest: Szépirodalmi, 1951), viii.
[64] *Följegyzések a Nyugat folyóiratról és környékéről*, 37.
[65] ". . . on the basis of the pertinent records of printing shops, publishers, banks, and large enterprises . . ." adds Vezér, in *Följegyzések és levelek a Nyugatról* (Budapest; Akadémiai, 1975), 23.

IV. THE FINANCIAL CONTEXT[1]

Almost from the beginning the review found support among certain well-to-do bourgeois, partly through their subscriptions, partly through the peddling of their influence, but mostly by means of direct contributions and capital. The diligence of Fenyö made the *Nyugat* financially possible and viable; it not only resulted in adequate funding for the review but even provided a livelihood for Endre Ady and, to a lesser extent, for Babits and other members of the movement: "the financial secret of the Ady problem was Fenyö's constant flurry of activity on behalf of Ady, and Hatvany's role as patron of the arts."[2] Ady received a monthly stipend of 500 crowns, and became the first Hungarian poet able to live off his earnings as poet (however strait his circumstances). Babits received 400 crowns.[3] In neighboring Prague Jaroslav Hašek had to content himself with a monthly 180 crowns, and two pitchers of beer a day, as editor of a journal called "Animal World."[4]

The first important supporter of the journal was a young member of the most powerful family of industrialists in Hungary, the owners of the Manfréd Weiss works at Csepel, namely Ferenc Chorin Jr., who had played an active and progressive role as a student at the University of Budapest and as a member of the Society of Social Sciences.[5] The other Maecenas was the above-mentioned Hatvany, the scion of a noble family, albeit Jewish, which had made a fortune in sugar refineries and other industrial ventures. Unlike Chorin, Hatvany was himself a man of letters, in Germany as much as in Hungary. It was no mere coincidence that Fenyö had been

---

[1] A different version of this chapter appeared as "Big Business and the Nyugat" in *Acta Historica,* 21 (1979), No. 2: 36–45.

[2] Aladar Schöpflin, *A magyar irodalom története a XX, században* [The History of Hungarian Literature in the 20th Century] (Budapest: Grill, 1937), 110. Lóránt Hegedüs, *Ady és Tisza* [Ady and Tisza] (Nyugat 1940): 34–35. In one of his letters, dated 30 December 1913, Fenyö claims that he and Ignotus were not only working "free" for the *Nyugat,* but were actually contributing to it from their own pocket (To Babits, Babits Papers, III/438, Széchenyi Irattár). Both Fenyö and Ignotus, however, admit a personal debt to Hatvany, whereas Ignotus was also receiving a salary as president of the Nyugat Publishing Company. Osvát, too, received regular wages as editor of the *Nyugat* (in fact, his main source of income). In 1912 Ignotus offered to take over the *Nyugat* if Hatvany would cancel his personal debt (Letter to an unnamed friend of Hatvany, June 10, Ms 383/b, Akadémiai Irattár).

[3] Fenyö to Hatvany, 25 June 1910, *Levelek Hatvany Lajoshoz* [Letters to Hatvany] (Budapest: Szépirodalmi, 1967), 96.

[4] László Dobossy, *Hašek világa* [The World of Hašek] (Budapest: Europa, 1970), 66.

[5] Márta Tömöry, *Uj vizeken járok* [I sail on New Waters] (Budapest: Gondolat, 1974). Ignotus hailed Chorin Jr. as the "bourgeois version of the great and eternal Hungarian Széchenyism . . ." in the *Nyugat,* 4 (1911): 73.

an employee of the national association of manufacturers since 1907, and that the top officials of this association were the elder Hatvany and the elder Chorin. In fact, Fenyö became co-editor of *Magyar gyáripar*, the official bulletin of the association, when it was launched in February 1911. It was the younger Chorin whom he recommended, in October 1909, as executive director of the Nyugat corporation then in process of formation.[6] It may be, as Fenyö claims, that the *Nyugat* got on its way with only minimum support from the big bourgeoisie; but the fact remains that members of this stratum began to assume the main burden of support soon after its start, as soon as the journal was able to prove its literary worth.[7]

In June 1910 Fenyö proposed the launching of a series of books, the "Nyugat Library," which would "bring plentiful returns by the third year!"[8] On 18 August 1910, barely two years after the start of the journal, its editors opened a publishing house under the name of Nyugat Book Publishing Company. The "founders" of the company were Chorin, Hatvany, Fenyö, and Andor Miklós, editor-in-chief of *Az Est*, a daily with a circulation of over 100,000. Perhaps it was felt that the talents of Miklós as organizer could be put to good use in an attempt to expand the circulation of the *Nyugat*. The largest number of shares, 60 out of a total of 150, were purchased by Lajos Hatvany, and another 20 by his father.[9]

At the beginning, the enterprise seemed successful in a variety of ways. Ignotus went so far as to claim that the company, of which he was president, not only proved that literature (as opposed to non-literary publications) could become the basis of a publishing venture, but also that it was not bad business to publish good literature.[10]

The records themselves are less convincing. It is true that the works published by the Company were usually of a high literary value. It is also true that for the most part they sold well. Between 1910 and 1914 the company published at least 113 works,[11] including twelve volumes by Ady (some of which were second and third editions).[12] The publishing house worked in grand style, despite its limited capital. Menyhért Lengyel, the playwright employed as "overseer" of the company noted, around 1911, that the company operated "like a Parisian publishing house. Thousands of manuscripts in the works. And they sell, too . . ."[13] In December 1910,

---

[6] Fenyö to Hatvany, October 1909, Ms 380/j, Akadémiai Irattár.
[7] Lujza Farkas, *A Nyugat és a századeleji irodalom—forduló* [The *Nyugat* and the Literary Revolution of the Turn of the Century] (Budapest: Gyarmati, 1935), 22–23.
[8] Fenyö to Hatvany, 14 June 1910, *Levelek Hatvany Lajoshoz*, 92.
[9] Project dated 1 July 1910, Archives of the Cégbiroság, Cg 628.
[10] *A Nyugat almanachja* [The Almanach of the Nyugat] (Budapest: Nyugat, 1912), 5. See also, the unpublished thesis by Márta Ruszinyák, "A Nyugat könyvkiadó" [The Nyugat Book Publishers] (University of Budapest, 1962), 16–17.
[11] Marta Ruszinyák, ibid., appendix.
[12] János Szilágyi, "A Nyugat könyvkiadó" [The Nyugat Book Publishers], *A könyv*, 4, No. 10 (October 1964): 356.
[13] Lengyel to Hatvany, no date, Ms 385/f, Akadémiai Irattár.

during "the Christmas season," the Nyugat books became best-sellers.[14] According to another witness, they "practically dominated the market" in the winter of 1910–11.[15] It is no less remarkable that these successes were achieved without exploiting the authors, in fact, were to benefit them first of all: Ernö Szép and Mihály Babits received two hundred and two hundred and fifty crowns of royalties respectively for a volume of poetry (there being at least that much difference in the esthetic worth of their poetry), to be printed in two thousand copies.[16] Margit Kaffka received eight hundred crowns, plus ten percent of the sales, for one of her shorter novels.[17] The price of a copy on the market was indicated as a mere thirty fillérs. At one time, unofficially, Babits was offered as much as fifty percent of the income on an anthology of his poetry.[18] It is true that considerations of supply and demand were not neglected; the directors of the Book Publishing Company, i.e. the editors of the *Nyugat*, felt they had to compete in order to obtain the rights to publish Babits's poetry.[19] Yet competition or not, the poetry of Babits did not sell particularly well,[20] although I have grounds for believing that poetry in Hungary has far more currency, in general, than poetry in Western countries.

In spite of successful sales, the Nyugat Company operated at a deficit from the start. The minutes of the meeting of 1 June 1911 already record a loss of about 50,000 crowns. One explanation is that the Company had grown bigger "than its base capital warranted."[21] Indeed, the capital was not too impressive. Originally it amounted to 150,000 crowns but, on 1 June 1911, the shares were devaluated by one-third, hence the capital would have diminished to 100,000 crowns; at the same time, however, 300 new shares were issued, so the capital increased to 400,000 crowns.[22] Simultaneously, the company changed its name from Nyugat Book Publishing Company to Nyugat Literary and Printing Co., Inc. For the sake of

---

[14] Ferenc Molnár to Hatvany, incorrectly dated 30 December 1909 (*Levelek Hatvany Lajoshoz*, 81).

[15] Ferenc Kende, "Miként fokozható a könyvkereskedelem által a közönség könyvásárlási és olvasási kedve" [How the Book Business may Increase the Public's Yearning to Buy and Read Books], *Csak szorosan* 10, No. 5 (May 1910): 4.

[16] Artur Elek, "A magyar iró és kiadója" [The Hungarian Writer and his Publisher], *Nyugat*, 6 (1913), No. 1: 17, 46. The cost estimate on three volumes of poetry, by unspecified authors, in 1909, was 800 crowns (Fenyö to Hatvany, *Levelek Hatvany Lajoshoz*, 63). Elsewhere, the cost of producing a volume of the Nyugat Library is given as about 700 crowns. Fenyö to Hatvany, 11 March 1911, ibid., 118–19.

[17] Kaffka to Schöpflin, 23 March 1917 (Schöpflin Papers, Széchenyi Irattár).

[18] Fenyö to Babits, 8 February 1909, Babits Papers, III/438, Széchenyi Irattár.

[19] Fenyö to Hatvany, 3 December 1910, Ms 380/j Akadémiai Irattár.

[20] Fenyö to Babits, 27 November 1910, Babits Papers, III/438, Széchenyi Irattár. For instance, a cheap edition of Petofi's collected verse, published by Athenaeum, sold 50,000 copies in 1898–99. *A könyv és a könyvtár a magyar társadalom életében* [The book and libraries in Hungarian social life], II, ed. Máté Kovács, Budapest: Gondolat, 1970, 82–83.

[21] Nyugat records, Cégbiroság Archives, Cg 628.

[22] Minutes of meeting, 1 June 1911, Cégbiroság Archives, Cg 628. The idea was already brought up in a letter from Fenyö to Hatvany, 4 March 1911 *Levelek Hatvany Lajoshoz*, 116.

comparison, the largest publishing house in Hungary, the Athenaeum, had a base capital of 2,200,000 crowns in 1910.[23]

The changes were to no avail. The series known as the Nyugat Library, comprising contemporary Hungarian and foreign works of literary value, had to be sold by October 1911. The volumes in stock were sold to Athenaeum at 0.10 crowns apiece, or one-third of the retail value, according to an order of transfer signed by Mór Magyar, the Company's new executive director under Ignotus, on 9 January 1912. The duel between Osvát and Hatvany, as a result of which Hatvany definitely withdrew his support from the journal, had taken place three days earlier. On the 12th of January, Magyar committed suicide.[24] The personal fortune he had invested in the company had gone down the drain.

Ignotus blamed the failure of the venture on the limited capital, and on the pressures applied by Viktor Ranschburg, the executive director of the Athenaeum, and a shareholder in the Nyugat Company.[25] It is true that Athenaeum continued to float loans to the Nyugat in 1913, but withdrew these in 1916, when the account books of the Nyugat Company indicated disastrous losses.[26] True enough, the Nyugat Company, despite Fenyö's initial optimism, was never meant to make huge profits; it was designed to play a role subordinate to the journal. But handled in such a half-hearted manner, complained Ignotus, the company could never have become an effective way of promoting the journal.[27] This new venture had simply compounded the losses. According to Balázs, the Nyugat operated with an annual deficit of around 11,000 crowns, at least up to 1912.[28] Yet there could be no question of mismanagement; the staff of the journal consisted of a single typist, and the editorial offices of the journal were (during the first few years) Osvát's *Stammtisch* at the Bristol café, rented at the cost of a cup of coffee a day.

According to Fenyö, the annual budget was 61,800 crowns, including 16,800 crowns for royalties, whereas revenues were about 50,000 crowns, thus confirming the estimate of Balázs.[29] But by 30 June 1912, the losses suffered by the review amounted to a total of 93,343 crowns.[30] Clearly, the losses of the *Nyugat* had to be made good by loans or donations.

The Nyugat Library series nevertheless proved a "moral" success. By

---

[23] These figures, suggested in part by Márta Ruszinyák, have to be taken with caution. She states, erroneously, that the Nyugat publishing house operated with a capital of 110,000 crowns. Op. cit., 17.
[24] Records of the Athenaeum, No. 1267, Országos Levéltár.
[25] Letter Ignotus to Hatvany, 24 October 1911, Ms 383/b Akadémiai Irattár.
[26] Letter from Athenaeum to Nyugat publishers, 13 March 1916, Records of the Athenaeum, No. 1432, Országos Levéltár.
[27] Ignotus to Hatvany, No. 1432, Országos Levéltár.
[28] Diary of Béla Balázs, Ms 5023/17, Akadémiai Irattár.
[29] Fenyö to Hatvany, 15 July 1913, *Levelek Hatvany Lajoshoz*, 177–78. It is not true, then, that royalties and printing costs—some 40,000 crowns all told—were covered by the sale of one-third of the copies, as Márta Ruszinyák claims. Op. cit., 17.
[30] Cégbiroság archives, Cg 628.

the time of its demise the series consisted of twenty-eight volumes,[31] which sold for as little as thirty fillérs apiece, a record low that may have contributed to the failure of the enterprise. To be sure, this philanthropic venture, if that is what it was, was not altogether unique within the context of Western civilization. Other companies in other countries had experimented with cheap editions; in England around 1907 clothbound editions of good novels could be purchased for seven pennies.[32]

Incidentally, the copies of the journal were not particularly inexpensive. The cost of a yearly subscription to the twenty-four issues had been twenty crowns in 1908, raised to thirty-two crowns by 1918. The cost of a single issue in the early years was one crown, later raised to one crown twenty, and eventually to two crowns. The cost of an issue was "the equivalent of two balcony tickets to the theater," wrote Gyula Juhász. More to the point, it was the equivalent of the average daily wage of an agricultural worker (one crown sixty-two), which may have been one of several reasons why the journal was not widely read in the countryside. And one crown was the equivalent of one French franc.

Between 1912 and 1916 the Nyugat Literary and Printing Company, Inc. continued its precarious existence, and even published some additional volumes. In 1916, however, the Company had not paid corporate taxes for, as it informed the royal court of justice, "it was not possible to compute business accounts because almost all the clerical staff had been drafted into the army." In any case, the Company was officially dissolved in October 1916, its losses having amounted to more than half of the capital.[33] Once again the remaining assets were sold to Athenaeum. The explanation of the bankruptcy was "lack of work" occasioned by the World War.[34] Contemporary observers, however, testify that never had there been such a boom in literary production, and in the sale of good and bad books![35]

For a few years the Nyugat had functioned as a regular publishing house, almost as a species of capitalist enterprise, the journal representing one of its ventures. If I am reluctant to refer to it as out and out capitalism, it is for a fundamental reason: the enterprise made no profits. The likelihood of success was small; and the businessmen who supported the Company by purchasing shares must have had enough experience and acumen, for the most part, to know that it was not a promising venture, hardly the means to get rich. It would be foolish to argue that a Leo Lánczy, the director of the Hungarian Bank of Commerce and one of the country's

---

[31] János Szilágyi, op. cit., 356. Archives of the Cégbiroság, Cg 628. It should be noted, however, that the Nyugat continued to publish occasional volumes even after 1916.

[32] Malcolm Bradbury, *The Social Context of Modern English Literature* (Oxford: Basil Blackwell, 1971), 207.

[33] Archives of the Cégbiroság, Cg 628. It should be noted, however, that the Nyugat continued to publish occasional volumes even after 1916.

[34] Minutes of meeting, 4 April 1916. Archives of the Cégbiroság, Cg 628.

[35] For instance, Margit Kaffka, *Az élet utján* [On the Road of Life] (Budapest: Szépirodalmi, 254). Also K.L., "Az olvasó Magyarország" [The Hungary that Reads] (*Magyarország*, 30 December 1917, 6).

most experienced bankers, or prominent industrialists like Ferenc Chorin and Moritz Kornfeld (who occasionally contributed essays on economic policy to the *Nyugat*) had invested in the company for the sake of increasing their assets, that they had a "vested interest" in the prosperity of the journal. The *Nyugat* was a financial liability all along, and these prominent capitalists knew it well. Endre Ady, who was no capitalist and no businessman, seems to have been the only one who showed genuine interest in acquiring stocks, and exhibited impatience when he did not receive his allotment of shares at the expected time; and he was flattered when, in June 1911, he became a member of the board of directors.[36] As for Zsigmond Móricz, he rather deplored the fact that the *Nyugat* was "raising such a storm," that it was becoming a business, rather than remaining content with the happy few.[37] Indeed, Móricz was no businessman either, and when he took over as editor-in-chief around 1930 the journal did worse than ever.

An examination of the list of shareholders may provide some valuable information. In addition to the Hatvany-Deutsch family, the names of some of the best known and some of the less well-known industrialists appear on it. Most of them were members of the GyOSz, the national association of manufacturers. All of them, Ady being the sole exception, had a trait in common, a trait which historians and others had either overemphasized, particularly during the Horthy regime and the Second World War, or had neglected to mention altogether: all the shareholders were Jewish, or of Jewish background. Yet Oszkár Gellért's accusation, himself a member of the Nyugat and of Jewish extraction, appears ill-considered. In one of his autobiographical writings he wrote that it was "typical" that Fenyö and Ignotus had seated, at a reception in 1917, Ady and Babits between two well-known industrialists.[38] Fenyö deeply resented the charge, and protested that Gellért's memory had betrayed him.[39] The line of defence was ill-chosen, for the crux of the matter lay elsewhere. The connection between the Nyugat movement and emergent, culturally aware capitalism is undeniable. Even the most radical of the Nyugat, even Ady had fought for modernization and for capitalism, as much as he fought against them. The point was that the relationship between the *Nyugat* and capitalism was not a sinister one, not even a concealed relationship; the *Nyugat* could not become prey to pseudo-literary vested interests. In fact, time and again, literary considerations prevailed over financial ones; opportunities to publish works by best-selling authors, even the works of better than mediocre popular writers such as Ferenc Molnár (perhaps on the grounds that he had no difficulty finding publishers), were passed up to make room for

---

[36] Ady to Fenyö, 5 March 1910, in *Föjegyzések és levelek a Nyugatról* [Notes and Correspondence about the *Nyugat*], ed. Erzsébet Vezér (Budapest: 1975), 283.

[37] Virág Móricz, *Apm regénye* [A Novel about my Father] (Budapest: Szepirodalmi, 1953), 122.

[38] *Egy iró élete* [A Writer's Life], 1: 9. The two industrialists were supposed to have been Ferenc Chorin and Móritz Kornfeld.

[39] *Föjegyzések és levelek a Nyugatról*, 155.

works of greater literary value. To be sure, the editors' decisions were not always clear-cut, not always unanimous, as the infamous Hatvany-Osvát affair was to prove; but there again literary considerations, esthetic considerations eventually prevailed.

The real reason for the financial involvement of elements of the big bourgeoisie could not have been the profit motive, that much is clear. Nor was it the fact that the *Nyugat* could be considered, as often as not, a propaganda organ advocating industrialization, industrial capitalism. Nor was it in general, as one of the contributors claimed, a "matter of sport, of fancy . . ."[40] The most important reason was simply that the *Nyugat* was an effective tool to promote assimilation, integration, pro-Semitism. The right-wing critics of the Nyugat were hardly mistaken: the most eminent writers of the movement were not Jews, in fact, their background was purely "Aryan," but they had nevertheless been "coopted" on behalf of the cause of Jewish assimilation. They set the example. And this assimilation, the creation of a more open, more cosmopolitan, more receptive, and urban culture, the acceptance of modernism, of progress at various levels—the creation of a bourgeois culture, in short—was clearly in the personal and class interest of the Jewish stockholders.

Thus a stratum of the big bourgeoisie could identify with the *Nyugat* (even though it had to take exception to certain manifestations of the Nyugat movement). The very fact that the Nyugat became a stock company, at a time when such companies were still only one-quarter of all industrial enterprises in Hungary,[41] is indicative of the advance of the spirit of capitalism and modernization.

* * *

The Nyugat bred imitators. Obviously not because of financial success, but rather because of its high literary quality, and because of its viability, its ability to survive. The *Renaissance* was launched on 10 May 1910, the *Aurora* in 1911, the *Május* in 1913, the two avantgarde journals, the *Tett* and the *Ma*, in 1915–16, and Lajos Hatvany's *Esztendő*, a sort of literary supplement to his daily paper, in 1917.

The *Renaissance*, allegedly financed by the Archduke Francis Ferdinand, carried essentially the same authors, the same brand of literature as the *Nyugat*. The editors of the *Nyugat* were concerned about the competition. In a letter to Hatvany, Fenyö actually hinted at the need for more financial support on the grounds that "the Nyugat did not have the means to settle financial matters with its contributors, hence several of them were writing for other reviews."[42] It was the first issue of *Renaissance* that carried Ady's

---

[40] Henrik Gonda to Hatvany, 2 April 1908 (*Levelek Hatvany Lajoshoz*, 28). Incidentally, the "owners" of the *Nyugat* were as follows: from July 1908 to 4 August 1909, Gonda; from August 1909 to July 1911, Zsigmond Thein; from July 1911 to June 1912, the Company; subsequently, Miksa Fenyö (The Mayor's Office, Fövárosi Levéltár, I 7875/907).

[41] In 1913 (Magyarország története [in manuscript], volume 7, chapter 4: 125).

[42] Fenyö to Hatvany, 14 June 1910, *Levelek Hatvany Lajoshoz* (1967): 92.

sally in defence of Petőfi ("Petőfi nem alkuszik"—Petőfi does not compromise), as well as the short story by Lajos Nagy that Osvát had rejected for reasons that were not strictly literary or esthetic.[43] Lajos Kassák thought of the *Renaissance* as politically to the left of the *Nyugat* or, at least, as a forum more open to the left; in his memoirs he quotes a friend who told him this journal had come about in opposition to the *Nyugat*, and would have a socialist tendency—and so, notes Kassák, "we too will be allowed to have our say in it."[44]

The *Aurora* was also an epigone of the *Nyugat* presenting literature, art, etc., in a rather more appealing format than its model. Yet it too, like the *Renaissance*, had to close after a few issues.

The journals founded by Kassák were rather different in both content and format; they were the first avantgarde reviews in Hungary. The maiden issue of *Tett* carried the translation of a poem by Guillaume Apollinaire. Its second issue ran afoul of wartime censorship,[45] although the journal was allowed to continue and survived for a total of seventeen issues, in spite of its artistic, literary, and even political radicalism. *Ma* was actually a continuation of *Tett*, the latter having been finally forced to close down in 1916. This second avantgarde journal outlived not only the war, but also the two revolutions, and Kassák even managed to find support for the journal in exile, in Vienna. Both the *Tett* and the *Ma* relied heavily on foreign models; and this very fact, their high regard for Western literary and artistic currents and stirrings, would have been much more controversial had not the *Nyugat* prepared the way. By the same token, Kassák's two reviews far outdid the *Nyugat* in their leftist and politicized orientation—an orientation that was typical of most avantgarde movements, including cubism, expressionism, constructivism, and even, at its beginnings, of futurism.[46] All these debts were recognized by the writers around the *Ma*: while their own Béla Révész was declared the "harbinger" (I suppose, of social change) in prose, the same function was conceded to Ady in poetry. Furthermore, they gave credit to the *Nyugat* for its long and "respectable cultural work," and for "having swung into motion paralyzed brains . . . and forever-compromising feelings."[47] On the other hand, Kassák and his companions rebelled against the Nyugat because it had become a kind of establishment within the counterculture. Jean Cocteau's remark applies

---

[43] See following chapter.

[44] *Egy ember élete* 2: 107. Kassák, however, was disappointed when, by way of preface to his poems in the journal, the editors felt it necessary to note that he was a twenty-three-year-old smith. Ibid., 183.

[45] The charge against the review was "deprecating religion and stirring class conflict." *Egy ember élete* 2: 597, 631 ff. The seventeenth issue, on 1 August 1916, would have presented an international cast: Libero Altomare, Kandinsky, Leo Rubiner, N. Kubin, Arcubasev, Ivan Mestrovič, Emil Verhaeren, George Duhamel, Paul Fort, Bernard Shaw.

[46] Leszek Kolakowski, *Marxism and Beyond* (London: Pall Mall, 1968), 182.

[47] Reprint of a speech Kassák delivered to the Galilei Circle on 3 December 1916, in *Ma*, 1 (1916): 20–21; and Kassák's review of the ten-year-old *Nyugat* in *Ma*, 1: 46.

equally to the rebellion of the Nyugat against the literary establishment, against the academicians, and to Kassák's rebellion against the "bourgeois" literature propagated by the Nyugat: "It is the dictators of art who make possible the disobedience without which art would die."[48]

The *Nyugat* nevertheless proved more successful, both from a literary standpoint, and financially. The reasons can be surmised. The *Nyugat* was the first-comer, the journal with the longest experience. It was also the journal which had attracted and well-nigh preempted sources of financial support among the literate bourgeoisie, the amount members of that class were willing to sacrifice for "the cause of culture." The *Nyugat* had found the tone which, while never making it popular, nevertheless catered to the esthetic needs of a segment of the population, a segment that was relatively well-endowed.

The right-wing opposition to the Nyugat also found some financial support, if not literary distinction. This opposition consisted of the "literary and critical" Catholic weekly *Élet*, founded in 1909, mildly progressive in tone; the *Magyar Kultura*, founded in 1913, unabashedly clerical and reactionary; and the more significant *Magyar Figyelő*, established in 1911. The *Magyar Figyelő* was the *porte-parole* of Count István Tisza, under the editorship of the playwright and novelist Ferenc Herczeg, who was also the editor of the genteel literary magazine *Uj idők* (which at times attained a circulation of 40,000 copies per issue). *The Magyar Figyelő* evidently enjoyed official support; for instance, the Ministry of Defence subscribed to 25 copies of the journal right from the beginning.[49] By 1916, however, the number of its subscribers had declined to 1,537.[50] Nevertheless, for a number of years the journal was considered the most powerful adversary by Jászi and the bourgeois radicals, as well as by the Nyugat.

The intellectuals of the ruling class are not invariably the ruling intellectuals;[51] to be sure, the ruling class had found allies among the intellectuals, but it was only among certain categories of non-intellectuals that their hegemony was undisputed. It may be argued that the Nyugat prevailed against conservative intellectuals (insofar as such a stratum existed), even in the period preceding the revolutions. One concrete indicator of the triumph of the Nyugat, as we shall see in a subsequent chapter, was the circulation figures: while the *Magyar Figyelő* sold only 1,500 copies per issue in 1916, the circulation of the *Nyugat* reached more than double that number.

Actually, the turn in the "reception" of the *Nyugat* and in its attitude towards political forces in the country seems to have occurred already

---

[48] Merle Fainsod, "The Role of the Intellectuals in the Soviet Union," *The Intellectuals in Politics* (Austin: University of Texas, 1966), 89.

[49] Minister of Defence to Prime Minister Károly Khuen Héderváry, 2 February 1911, Miniszterelnökség ME 856 (1911), Országos Levéltár.

[50] Actually, the number of copies sent through the mails; Miniszterelnökség, K-26-1916-V-540, Országos Levéltár.

[51] Frédéric Bon and M.-A. Burnier, *Les nouveaux intellectuels* (Paris: Cujas, 1966), 28.

around 1912. Many critics agree that there was a turning point of some kind, but I have found diametrically opposite descriptions of it. A present-day literary historian has argued that "socialist" manifestations in the periodical became increasingly frequent after 1912, and especially after 1917.[52] A literary historian from the previous generation claimed that while at the beginning the Nyugat had no political tendency, it was to acquire an increasingly radical hue during the war.[53] The evidence does not bear out their contention; rather the opposite. After 1913 articles by Socialist authors become a rarity. Bresztovszky, for one, complained in the Socialist periodical *Szocializmus*, of the renunciation, if not betrayal, of the cause of progress, of the cause of the worker.[54] Zoltán Horváth does not fail to note that the glorious age of the *Nyugat* had lasted only until about 1913, in part because "the public grew up to its level."[55]

But the change was a matter of degree rather than of essence; the Nyugat did not really cease to serve the cause of progress even in 1913 or 1914 and, during the war, it once again assumed a role that can only be described as directly political (in addition to its indirectly political function). Nevertheless, around 1912, the Nyugat movement, having successfully maintained its independence against onslaughts by the establishment, felt it necessary to guard its independence from the left, and felt strong enough to achieve both.

The relative popularity of the *Nyugat*, however, was due in part to circumstances which were not directly related to its literary standards, nor even to the financial support it enjoyed; I have in mind incidents which placed members of the movement in the limelight.

Of course, Ady was perennially in the limelight, partly because of the attacks he was subjected to, and partly because of his life-style. According to the statistics, Ady was read rather widely, but even more was published about him in the dailies and reviews.[56] On the other hand, the public gradually became conscious of his ties with the Nyugat and, it may be presumed, this awareness did not hurt sales of the journal. The popularity of Ady and, to a lesser extent, that of the *Nyugat*, was in part a *succès de scandale*.

The most notable personality conflict in the history of the journal was the one that pitted the art patron Hatvany against the penurious Osvát. In vain Ignotus and Fenyö marshaled all their diplomatic skill to pacify the antagonists. In vain did Ignotus argue that, though there was internal dissension, the journal "must show the greatest calm and harmony . . . We

---

[52] József Farkas, ed., *Mindenki ujakra készül*, 1: 6.
[53] Antal Szerb, *Magyar irodalomtörténet* [Hungarian Literary History] (Budapest: Magvetö, 1972, 1st ed. 1935), 435.
[54] Ernö Bresztovszky, "Vissza az öserdöbe" [Back to the Jungle], *Szocializmus*, 8 (1912-13), No. 9: 474-77.
[55] Zoltán Horváth, *Die Jahrhundertwende in Ungarn*, 410.
[56] Bodog Halmi, "Ady Endre," *Máramaros* (1910, 6 February-3 March).

must not spoil its market value by any unpleasant scandal."[57] Osvát, as we shall see, was the most directly responsible, the most directly involved of the three editors of the journal. Lajos Hatvany had decided to challenge this position back in 1911. The challenge led to an anachronistic episode, a duel fought until "first blood drawn" on 6 January 1911, at one of the fencing *salles* of Budapest.

I would need considerable space just to sum up the arguments of the antagonists; but I will refrain from doing that, as it might stir up the controversy, which is far from settled. I will mention but one or two of its aspects.

Perhaps the controversy would have been cleared long ago, perhaps literary historians, especially nowadays, would all have argued on the side of Osvát, whose attitude was clearly more progressive in this instance, had it not been for the fact that Ady had taken the side of Hatvany, at least for a while. If Ady was on Hatvany's side, was that not sufficient guarantee of the rectitude of his cause? It was, the critic György Bélia seems to argue; and he quotes a letter from Ady to Aladár Schöpflin, to the effect that Osvát ought not to give Hatvany a hard time merely because the latter happened to be a millionaire.[58] But Ady had written in defence of Hatvany, in defence of a friend, rather than in defence of a cause.

Although Ady was on Hatvany's side, it does not follow that Hatvany was on Ady's side, nor that the cause was right. For one thing, Hatvany had recognized Ady's talent relatively late in comparison to Osvát and many other members of the Nyugat. During the "affair" with Osvát he considered running the periodical with Ady alone but, upon reflection, rejected the idea as unfortunate.[59]

As Ady's stance shows, personal feelings played an important role in the controversy, perhaps the most important. Margit Kaffka also came to Hatvany's support, and she was no mean ally; clearly, however, her former intimate relationship with Osvát and the ensuing resentment had a bearing on her sympathy for Hatvany. One is inclined to suspect vindictiveness may have been a motive.[60]

The disagreement, it seems, was mainly (but certainly not exclusively) over financial viability versus the task of bringing to the fore new, hitherto unrecognized talents. The editors of the journal were agreed that purely financial considerations should not prevail. When the *Nyugat* was given an opportunity to publish short stories by the popular Ferenc Molnár (known in the West as the author of comedies that are part of the repertory of theater companies around the world), Fenyö rejected the opportunity, explaining that "we are reluctant to deprive the *Nyugat* of good short stories,

---

[57] Ignotus to Hatvany, 1 March 1911, Ms 383/b, Akadémiai Irattár.
[58] György Bélia and Anna Sándor, "Schöpflin Aladár hagyatékából," [From the Papers of Schöpflin], *Irodalomtörténeti Közlemenyek*, 57 (1953): 334. Belia also argues that the direct cause of the split between Hatvany and Osvát was the latter's refusal to publish certain manuscripts in the *Nyugat*. Ibid., 329.
[59] Undated letter, Hatvany to Schöpflin, Schöpflin Papers, Széchenyi Irattár.
[60] See diary of Béla Balázs, Akadémiai Irattár.

even if this should mean good business,"⁶¹—a sarcasm implying that Molnár's stories were mediocre in comparison with those stories which would have to be left out. This shows that the standards were not primarily commercial, but rather exacting, for Molnár's writings certainly do not lack literary merits.

Since Hatvany and members of his family were the most important financial contributors to the journal, it is only reasonable that they should advocate sound business practice to balance a sound literary policy, in particular the reliance on tried and proven writers of talent. Somewhat unjustly Móricz even accused Hatvany of meaning to make the journal suitable for a petit-bourgeois public and for daughters of "good families."⁶² But since Osvát had created the periodical, among other reasons, so that "talents would not have to perish before they have a chance to develop" in Hungary, it was equally reasonable that he should advocate the discovery of further talents, at whatever cost. Osvát was not dissuaded by Ady's boast, that "it is impossible, even from the point of view of the laws of natural science, that a better and truer poet than I should come about within the next thirty or forty years." In this, as in so many other things, Ady's prophecy proved entirely accurate.

The quarrel is, of course, of little moment to Hungarian literature viewed from an international perspective. Only two things are of real concern: 1) Osvát won the controversy, even though the duel was a draw. Hatvany felt compelled to withdraw from the Nyugat altogether, although he maintained friendly relations with a number of Nyugat writers. He also resigned from the board of directors of the Nyugat Literary and Printing Company, Inc. (as did, soon afterwards, Ignotus, Osvát, and Fenyö).⁶³ Osvát, on the other hand, remained as editor of the journal until his death, although his name was replaced on the cover of the journal in July 1912, and for a number of years thereafter, by that of Endre Ady.⁶⁴ 2) The controversy, particularly the duel, did not redound to the credit of the Nyugat, and the Socialist daily *Népszava* even denounced it as a disgraceful episode.⁶⁵ Yet the airing of the arguments in the daily press undoubtedly attracted attention. Ignotus was wrong. The market value of the journal was not spoiled by the unpleasant scandal. The support the *Nyugat* lost as a result of the pique felt by Hatvany, its principal patron, may have been compensated by a rise in the number of subscribers. As Móricz had noted, the Nyugat was becoming "business" because of the storm it stirred.

The controversy surrounding the Nyugat did not abate with the resolution

---

⁶¹ Fenyö to Hatvany, 14 June 1910. *Levelek Hatvany Lajoshoz*, 93.
⁶² Móricz to Artur Elek, 15 February 1911, *Móricz Zsigmond levelei*, ed. Dóra Csanák (Budapest: Akadémia, 1963), 105.
⁶³ Letters from Dr. Viktor Veigelsberg (brother of Ignotus and attorney for the Company) to Court of Justice, March 1912 and May 1913, Cégbiróság Archives, Cg 628.
⁶⁴ Prior to the duel, Osvát and Fenyö had announced their resignation, at least to Babits. Babits Papers, III/437, Széchenyi Irattár.
⁶⁵ "A disgraceful episode not worthy of progressive thinkers . . . Those who argue with the sword in hand should feel ashamed." *Népszava*, 7 January 1912.

of the Hatvany-Osvát affair. Furthermore, controversies were constantly arising between the Nyugat and its individual members: many of the collaborators ceased to collaborate for a shorter or longer period (Béla Balázs, Dezsö Szabó, Dezsö Kosztolányi, Milán Füst, and others). But the conflicts with the establishment, as we shall see in a subsequent chapter, were deeper, and had more serious repercussions, and probably resulted in greater attention being focused on the periodical, especially during the war, than the internal conflicts.

The names on the cover of the journal changed, although infrequently. Few of these changes were significant. Osvát's name was replaced in 1912 by that of Ady, as we have seen. There was no other change until 1917, when Fenyö was replaced by Mihály Babits.

In the fall of 1916 the *Nyugat* applied for and was granted authorization to become an explicitly political journal in addition to its other endeavors. This administrative action was likewise of minor significance; the profile of the journal did not change in practice, as it had carried political articles all along.

More significantly, year after year the *Nyugat* worked on behalf of modernization. The new literature was becoming increasingly palatable. In the struggle between new and old forms of art, between *les anciens* and *les modernes*, once again the new was winning out.[66] The process was readily apparent even to the participants, first of all to Ady: while Hungary was still "a feudal, stupid, and beggarly province, in art and in literature we have become beautifully bourgeois . . ."[67] This does not mean, however, that the new art, the new literature, must be labeled bourgeois; good literature taken collectively is heterodox, polyphonic, even dissonant—hence it defies labels, or at least elicits debate whenever some eager critic attempts to stick one on it. In any case, the greatest art of the bourgeois period is the least bourgeois.[68]

---

[66] Umberto Barbaro, "Materialism in Art," *Marxism and Art*, eds. Berel Lang & Forrest Williams (New York: David McKay, 1972), 167–68.

[67] Draft of an article reprinted in *Földjegyzések a Nyugat folyóiratról és környékéröl* (Pátria, 1960), 109.

[68] Arnold Kettle, in *Radical Perspectives in the Arts*, ed. Lee Baxandall (Baltimore: Penguin, 1972), 167.

V. THE POLITICAL ATTITUDES OF THE NYUGAT WRITERS

How did the writers around the Nyugat relate to the issues I had discussed in a previous chapter: the nationalities question, the peasant problem, suffrage, and the war? "Did the writer reach into the fundamental issues determining social change, or was he merely moving on the surface?" queried György Lukács in 1949, debating the tasks of Marxist criticism.[1] What prescriptions, what advice did they receive from the organizers of the review? To begin with, what were the political attitudes of the editors themselves?

There was truth in the remark of Zsigmond Móricz, that the encounter of the three founders and editors of the review, Ignotus, Ernö Osvát, and Miksa Fenyö, was a fortunate event; fortunate because their tastes were in harmony, their cultural background congenial,[2] their social background, their social environment, their education, their apprenticeship largely homogeneous. What was their literary taste, what were their political attitudes, and how did the three editors differ?

Ignotus, whose title as editor-in-chief was warranted by his seniority, his prestige, and his abilities and experience as a writer, has been accused of inconstancy and inconsistencies in his political views. He was a supporter of the Compromise of 1867—of the Dual Monarchy, that is—of the alliance with Germany, but also of bourgeois radicalism, and of a liberalism mingled with Bernsteinian reformism.[3] At times, he considered himself a socialist pure and simple, and regarded the dissenting socialist thinker, Ervin Szabó, as the man of the moment.[4] On another occasion he referred to the "iron discipline of Marx's logic."[5] In the autobiographical short story "Literature, or the Little Boy and the Little Old Man," he described himself as a Communist in his teens, around 1885, who had but contempt for the compromises of the Social Democrats (meaning, I suppose, precisely the Bernsteinian socialists).[6] In between his boyhood and his old age, however, he

---

[1] *Magyar irodalom—magyar kultura*, 535.
[2] "Huszonöt év" [Twenty-five years], *Nyugat*, 25 (1932): 2.
[3] *Ignotus válogatott irásai* [Selected Writings of Ignotus] ed. Aladár Komlós (Budapest: Szépirodalmi, 1969), 14.
[4] In his review of Szabó's study *Töke és munka* [Capital and labor] in *Nyugat*, 4 (1911): 2. 423.
[5] *Ignotus válogatott irásai*, 306. As regards Szabó some of his best work is available in English in *Selected Writings of Ervin Szabó*, ed. by György Litván and János Bak (London: Routledge & Kegan Paul, 1982).
[6] Ibid., 127.

had supported the two economic liberals and advocates of the Monarchy, Count Gyula Andrássy (Junior) and Count János Hadik, and even acted as their *homme de plume*. Later, during his exile in Vienna, he attempted to formulate a new creed, a synthesis of capitalism and socialism![7] So much for his politics.

His views regarding literature were rather more consistent; hence a sample or two will suffice. Already in 1908, while commenting on Ady's poem "The Black Piano," Ignotus asserted that "art is ruled by no other law than one: you must be able to express yourself."[8] A Rabelaisian formula he was to repeat and rephrase a number of times: "Do what you please, as long as you are capable of doing it well."[9] Literature can only become politically and socially useful if it has no other intention than to be, commented Ignotus in another of his didactic essays (but is it not a paradox to prescribe precepts according to which everything is permissible?)[10] Hence political or social goals should be neither deliberately included, nor deliberately excluded from the work. Yet within the same essay, only a few pages further on, Ignotus had already forgotten the lesson he had taught: in addition to literary matters, he asserts, the *Nyugat* is justified in dealing with social and political issues as well.[11]

Furthermore, Ignotus claimed, it was not necessary to subordinate literary policy to economic interest. In 1912, after the Nyugat Publishing Company had attained some rather mixed successes, Ignotus wrote: "We know that it is possible to make literature, meaning good literature, the foundation of a publishing house in Hungary, and it might not even be bad business!"[12] Can this be the answer to the academic question Lenin addressed to the writer functioning in a bourgeois society: are you free in relation to your bourgeois publisher, are you free in relation to your bourgeois public?[13]

Ernö Osvát was the most apolitical of the three editors, the one least inclined to express political opinions. The superlative loses some of its significance, however, if we recall that Osvát was very reluctant to express himself in writing on any subject at all; when he had to communicate with distant friends or relatives, including his wife, he much preferred to send a short cable. But no man is totally apolitical, or completely and exclusively

---

[7] Letter Ignotus to Fenyö, 18 Sep. 1921, *Feljegyzések és levelek a Nyugatról* [Notes and Letters about the Nyugat], ed. Erzsébet Vezér (Budapest: Akadémia, 1975), 377. Some of these notions had already been aired in "Polgári szocializmus" [Bourgeois socialism], *Nyugat*, 9 (1916): 629–31.

[8] *Nyugat*, 1 (1908): 146.

[9] *Ignotus válogatott irásai*, 13.

[10] Introduction to *A Nyugat almanachja* [The Almanach of the *Nyugat*] (Budapest: Nyugat, 1912), 6.

[11] *A Nyugat almanachja*, 10.

[12] Ibid., 5. See also Márta Ruszinyák, "A Nyugat könyvkiadó" [The Book Publishing House Nyugat] (thesis, University of Budapest, 1962), 16–17.

[13] From "Party Organization and Party Literature," reprinted in *On Literature and Art* (Moscow: Progress Publishers, 1970), 26.

political—*homo politicus* is an abstraction; and there are clues to be gleaned even from Osvát's sparse publications. In a review of a work around the turn of the century Osvát commented to the effect that its author was conservative "as all intelligent people are," and liberal "as all honest people are."[14] (We have seen, however, that the antinomy conservative-liberal is not particularly meaningful in the Hungarian context.) Osvát was well aware that literature, including poetry, may have a function: "The poet is best able to express the conscience of his time," he wrote in 1898.[15] In 1911 Osvát was accused of being "petty" for having published a radical poem by Frigyes Karinthy ("Martinovics"—the only political poem he ever wrote) precisely at a time when the *Magyar Figyelő*, the counter-Nyugat, was scheduled to be launched; in other words, Osvát was accused of having exposed the Nyugat and himself to attacks from the right.[16] But he was attacked from the left as well; for instance, for his refusal to publish a naturalistic short story by Lajos Nagy, on the grounds that "merely spitting in the face of society does not constitute art . . ."[17] Witness also the denunciation by György Lukács, delivered long after Osvát's death; Lukács complained that those articles in which he had stated his social views too clearly were rejected by Osvát outright.[18] It is a pity, to be sure, that the two did not arrive at a higher opinion of one another.

The third editor, Miksa Fenyö, was not entirely consistent, either in his political liberalism, or in his advocacy of literature for its own sake. He claimed that the very objective in establishing the *Nyugat* was to lift the taboo from political, social, and economic issues:

We did not have a point by point program of reforms in mind. We did not have a clear conception of how to create a truly urbane and urban bourgeoisie, how to liberate the country from the yoke of the provinces, how to establish a truly parliamentary form of government . . . But the *Nyugat* saw as its main task the creation of a favorable intellectual atmosphere . . .[19]

All this is evidence of political awareness, to be sure; yet a lack of awareness of those issues that were truly fundamental, an explicitly, consciously bourgeois program, that was not a means to further changes (as, for instance, Oszkár Jászi's program claimed to be), but was an end in itself.

---

[14] *Osvát Ernö összes irásai* [The Complete Writings of Osvát], ed. Kálmán Osvát (Budapest: Nyugat, 1945), 189.

[15] Quoted by Miklós Lackó, "Osvát Ernö," *Uj irás*, 16 (1976): 95.

[16] Zsigmond Móricz to Artur Elek, 15 February 1911 in *Móricz Zsigmond levelei* [Letters of Móricz], 104–105.

[17] Pál Kardos, *Nagy Lajos élete és müvei* [The Life and Works of Nagy] (Budapest: Bibliotheca, 1958), 32. It seems to me Osvát never finished reading the manuscript—which was published later in a rival review, the *Renaissance*—for at the end of this long short story the capitalist "villain" relents.

[18] Review of "Osvát Ernö összes irásai" (1947), reprinted in *Magyar irodalom—magyar kultura*, 377.

[19] *Följegyzések a Nyugat folyoiratról és környékéről* [Notes about the Periodical Nyugat and its Environs], (Niagara Falls: Patria, 1960), 37, 42.

Fenyö recognized that the review had brought together different, even conflicting tendencies.[20] He insisted, however, that the *Nyugat* was essentially revolutionary, because the freedom of thought it advocated "brought about, of iron necessity, an ideological revolution . . . For all true writers are revolutionaries, because nothing that is, is well enough, and everything that is, deserves to be changed."[21] These are indeed strong words on the part of someone who was to remain aloof from the revolutions of 1918 and 1919.

In his history of modern Hungarian literature, Aladár Schöpflin, himself a member of the Nyugat movement from its very beginnings, states inaccurately, yet revealingly, that the editors of the *Nyugat* wanted to create a literature that was above social class, just as the editors themselves stood "apart from all social class; they were the free citizens of a republic of letters."[22] This is the process the philosopher Ágnes Heller describes as the tendency of the bourgeois class to anthropological generalization, its tendency to consider itself the party of humanity. The editors of the *Nyugat* and its writers did not stand above social class (if such a thing be possible). They were not free-floating intellectuals, as Karl Mannheim may have suggested, but were, like most writers at the turn of the century in Europe and elsewhere, unmistakably members of the petite bourgeoisie whose political views coincided with those of a given social stratum. Yet Schöpflin's observation would have been shared by most members of the movement, as my analysis will soon make clear.

It was not only Ignotus, Osvát, and Fenyö who held views in common. Apart from a few scandals, a certain harmony was maintained within the ranks: there was a minimum consensus. If pressed about their literary views, if compelled to opt for a "philosophy" of literature, most members of the movement would have made some reference to *l'art pour l'art*. To give but one example: the hero of Babits's epic novel *Halálfiai* [Sons of Death], admittedly the author's alter ego, sings the praises of art for art's sake in his university days, for it meant not rigid constraints but, on the contrary, a liberation from all constraint.[23]

The editors themselves were wont to make some reference to art for art's sake in discussing their theories of literature; but the label did not quite fit. The principle of nonintervention, at least at the beginnings of the movement, was essentially a defensive measure to protect themselves and the journal from attacks by the establishment.[24] If literature was to abstain from politics, it was only fair that politics should not interfere with literature. Nor were the Nyugat people the first to hit upon this defense mechanism.

---

[20] Ibid., 44. See Ady's well known description of the Nyugat crowd: "Fall, winter, summer, spring, all run together . . ."

[21] Ibid., 60.

[22] *A magyar irodalom története a XX. században* [The History of Hungarian Literature in the Twentieth Century] (Budapest: Grill Károly, 1937), 110.

[23] Budapest: Szépirodalmi, 1972, 485.

[24] Miklós Lackó, op. cit., 97.

Pushkin had already thought of it, as had the Romanticists, and the Parnassiens, argues Plekhanov:

> The tendency towards art for art's sake arises and develops where an insoluble contradiction exists between the artist and his social environment. This contradiction exercises a favorable effect on the work of the artist to the extent that it enables him to rise above his social environment.[25]

And the Marxist critic Ralph Fox, compatriot and contemporary of Christopher Caudwell, contrasts art for art's sake not with academic art, or with an art that is socially and politically committed, but with art for money's sake. Art for art's sake is a "banner" and a "war-cry" not so much against political intervention, but "against a civilization which denies any value to art at all, save that of money."[26]

Hence some inconsistency between literary theory and practice is to be expected. Lajos Hatvany, although not one of the editors, but nevertheless playing an important role in the elaboration and application of editorial policies during the first three or four years of the review, pointed to one of these inconsistencies.

> Our purpose is to disturb and dissolve the unhealthy esthetic relationship between life and literature, and to bring life directly into literature. We would be pleased to concede the sleepy realm of esthetics to the Kisfaludy Society [an academy of letters]. Our new literature is as much a manifestation of life as are the political and economic developments in the city, in the country . . .[27]

he remarked in a speech to members of the printers' union in 1910, and his remarks were received with frenetic applause. Hence Hatvany was advocating an *engagé* literature, a literature involved in life. The circumstances of the speech are perhaps symbolic: a baron, albeit Jewish, speaking to and pleasing an assembly of workingmen, amounts to a political act in itself.

It was precisely in a review of a novel by Hatvany that Ignotus, who had come close to advocating estheticism and art for art's sake, felt compelled to admit that novels inevitably had a political content: there could be no Hungarian novel without politics, for life itself had become politicized. So it had been already in the previous era, the era of Jókai and Kálmán Mikszáth.[28] Art for art's sake was hardly possible, declared Ignotus during

---

[25] Gyorgii Plekhanov, "Art and Society" (1912), reprinted in *Marxism and Art*, eds. Berel Lang and Forrest Williams (New York: David McKay, 1972), 88. Ervin Szabó wrote, with regard to the principle of science for the sake of science: "The search for truth becomes the self-goal of the scientific function, independent of all other goals and interests." *Mutatis mutandis* this was applicable to the literature sponsored by the Nyugat, taken in a positive sense. "A Társadalomtudományi Társaság feladatai" [The Tasks of the Society of Social Sciences], reprinted in *A szociológia elsö magyar mühelye*, 1: 40.

[26] Ralph Fox, *The Novel and the People* (London: Cobbett, 1944, 1st ed. 1937), 50.

[27] Lajos Hatvany, "Uj irodalom, uj könyvkereskedés" [New Literature, New Bookdealing], *Csak szorosan*, 10, Nos. 3–4 (April 1910): 2.

[28] *Ignotus válogatott irásai*, 268.

a debate over the function of literature in 1912: the prime mover of literary works, their ultimate determinants, are those same needs, those same factors which determine political developments![29] Elsewhere Ignotus quoted Lassalle, to the effect that the meaning of politics is "to say that which is." Thus, when Zsigmond Móricz could see, clairvoyantly enough, what Hungary was actually like, and had the courage to write down his observations, "he was carrying out politics of the highest order."[30] Indeed, Ignotus was the first of the Nyugat to disregard the principle of abstention from political matters. In a letter to Hatvany on 11 April 1910, he revealed his intention to reserve a column for himself in order to "smuggle politics into the journal, gradually, imperceptibly."[31]

Yet Ignotus and his fellow editors had no lucid awareness of the function of the literature they sponsored with so much devotion; again and again they would return to the notion that politics and literature were domains apart. "Politics may be socialist," Ignotus argued in the same speech in which he had asserted that art for art's sake was hardly possible; "but literature will always be the province of the Manchesterian doctrine: laissez passer, laissez faire . . ."[32] What is the explanation of these contradictions? Perhaps a dim awareness that the freedom advocated by the Nyugat would result not only in the demise of the ancien régime, for which they would shed no tears, but contained the seeds of destruction of bourgeois liberalism itself. At any rate, they perceived, not dimly, but clearly, that socioeconomic forces were beyond their power to control, perhaps even beyond their power to influence.

Part of the *Nyugat*'s program was contained in its very name: its western orientation. On this, as on so many other issues, the Nyugat was in accord with other progressive forces, the review *Huszadik Század* for instance. In an assessment of his own review Oszkár Jászi wrote:

All our thoughts turned towards the West . . . But we must pay even closer attention to the West in the future. It is from that direction that we have received, over a thousand years, all our objectives, all our principles, all our aspirations . . .[33]

The editors of the *Nyugat* might have professed the same.

For the *Nyugat* the West implied primarily France. We know what role France, and Paris in particular, played in Ady's private, literary, and political life, in his poetry as well as his polemics. But francophilia was not peculiar to Ady: was Paris not the Mecca of all Bohemians, of painters, composers, and poets alike? Zoltán Ambrus's first journey had been to Paris, and French literature became his life-long companion.[34] Dezsö Szomory spent fifteen

---

[29] *Ignotus válogatott írásai*, 520.
[30] Ibid., 394.
[31] *Levelek Hatvany Lajoshoz* [Letters to Hatvany] (Budapest: Szépirodalmi, 1967).
[32] *Ignotus válogatott írásai*, 520.
[33] *A szociológia elsö magyar mühelye*, 1: 100, 105.
[34] "Ambrus Zoltán emlékezete" [Remembering Ambrus], *Ignotus válogatott írásai*, 409. Also Valèria Korek, *Hangulat és valóság* (Munich: Aurora, 1976).

years in France, partly in order to avoid being drafted into the *Kaiserliche* and *Königliche* army; and the products of his prolonged contact with France were a handful of unimpressive poems and short stories in French, and his autobiographical masterpiece, the *Párisi regény* [Novel of Paris]. Aladár Kuncz was to pay dearly for his devotion to France: caught in Paris at the outbreak of the war he was deported and eventually interned in a fortress on the island of Noirmoutier, where he spent three miserable years—an experience recorded in another masterpiece, *A fekete kolostor* [The Black Cloister]. Dezső Szabó, who had occasionally proferred racist views before he joined the Nyugat, and who was to indulge in racism after he left the review, nevertheless claimed to be West European, and especially French, "with a thousand moistures and secret fluids of my ancestral soil."[35] Paris affected not only writers and artists, but progressive individuals in general: Oszkár Jászi, for one, was to describe his trip of January 1905 to Paris as the most sensational event of his life.

In 1942 there appeared a monograph under the title "The Frenchified Nyugat," and the subtitle "The French Connections of the Nyugat during the Thirty Years from 1908 to 1938."[36] In addition to an analysis of the contacts with France, the monograph lists, in an appendix, all translations, articles, and reviews pertaining to French literature. Their numbers diminished somewhat during World War I, but not as much as wartime circumstances might lead one to believe; the Nyugat stayed in contact with "the enemy." Collating these data with the list compiled by Galambos in his Nyugat "repertory," we find that in the period 1908 to 1918 the review published 56 translations and 137 articles and reviews dealing with some aspect of French literature or literature written in French: Anatole France, Charles Baudelaire, Henri Bataille, and Maurice Maeterlinck lead the list.[37]

The *Nyugat* was cosmopolitan, yes. But cosmopolitanism had its drawbacks, its limitations; it did not include concern for the nations of Eastern Europe, for Hungary's neighbors, for the culture and predicament of the nationalities within the boundaries of the kingdom. So far I have discussed the attitudes of the editors of the review; but how did the writers who formed the Nyugat movement deal with the fundamental issues, particularly the issue of nationalities?

Perhaps we can accept as fairly typical the attitude of Viktor Cholnoky, a politically conservative member of the Nyugat, towards the Serbs of southern Hungary:

The best of the Serbs live in our country. There is no hardier, more fortunate, more beautiful, more energetic offspring of miscegenation anywhere in the world, than

---

[35] This is the best I can do to render his imagery into English. Dezső Szabó, *Életeim* [My Lives] (Budapest: Szépirodalmi, 1965) 2: 10.

[36] Zoltán Harsányi, *A 'franciás' Nyugat; francia vonatkozások a 'Nyugat' harminc esztendejében, 1908-1938* (Debrecen, 1942).

[37] Ferenc Galambos, *A Nyugat repertorium* (Budapest: MTA Irodalomtörténeti Intézet, 1959).

the offspring that results from the mingling of Magyar and Serbian blood. I am speaking of the gentry of the Bácska, and of our own Serbian aristocracy.[38]

To be sure, Cholnoky's remarks date from 1903; by 1917–18 even the blindest, most insensitive observers could not fail to perceive that the policy of Magyarization or, more exactly, the policy of neglect of the nationalities, was leading, or had already led, to disaster from the Hungarian nationalist point of view. In December 1918 Móricz was to write in the daily *Pesti Hirlap:*

The people do not want to fight, the nations do not want to fight against one another. The Hungarian peasant had never intended to subjugate the Slovak peasant, nor his Romanian, Serbian or Croatian brother, and the hands of the Hungarian people have not been polluted by fraternal blood for the last thousand years.[39]

Gyula Juhász was to write, with the wisdom of hindsight in January 1919: "there are no little nations, and no great nations, only nations."[40] Too late.

The Nyugat writers either ignored the issue, assumed an attitude of superiority which barely differed from that of the gentry, or evinced an ambiguous stance; witness the contradictions, the ambiguities in the attitude of Mihály Babits. When assigned as teacher to faraway Fogaras, a county deep in the Transylvanian Alps, inhabited mainly by Romanians, Babits took it as punishment, as a place of exile; he compared himself to Ovid at Tomi far removed from the excitement of the Roman cosmopolis, from the centers of cultural activity. "Thus I go among the Romanian barbarians . . ." he complained to his friend the poet Gyula Juhász.[41] In his novel *Halálfiai,* the protagonist teaches under similar circumstances in a similar area of Transylvania and expresses similar thoughts (even though in the meantime Babits might have learned the lessons of a lost war, of ethnic resentment, of revolutions that failed—since the novel appeared in the mid-twenties). This protagonist speaks of educating "the half-savage and pale children of the Balkans into citizens of a modern cultural state [i.e. Hungary]." But in the same novel and almost on the same page Babits refers to the Romanians as "this virgin and talented race."[42] Indeed, Babits's compliments could not have been more ill-timed; to speak well of the Romanians, or even half-well, after the Treaty of Trianon, was to rub against the grain of popular prejudice misguided by the chauvinist press. But Babits went further; in an episode of the novel he denounces the repressive meth-

---

[38] Cholnoky to Oszkár Gellért, 27 February 1903, quoted by Gellért, *Egy iró élete* [A Writer's Life] (Budapest: Bibliotheca, 1958) 1: 65.
[39] Ibid., 1: 330.
[40] *Egy iró élete,* 2: 318.
[41] Letter of 24 July 1908, *Babits-Juhász-Kosztolányi levelezése* [The Correspondence between Babits, Juhász, and Kosztolányi], ed. György Bélia (Budapest: Akadémia, 1959), 172.
[42] *Halálfiai,* 715–16. In the 1913 volume of *Huszadik Század* there appeared a model sociological study of a Romanian village in which the author, Robert Braun, describes the inhabitants as particularly receptive to music, song and poetry. "A falu lélektana" [Psychology of the Village], *A szociológia elsö magyar mühelye,* 2: 312.

ods employed by Hungarian officials against Romanian nationalists and against the entire Romanian ethnic group.[43]

It was again Babits who (along with Ignotus) wrote sensitive lines about Gypsies, the most consistently despised and neglected minority group in Hungary:

And like a stray seed from the branch
you will fall from your mother;
no father,
nor mother,
nor country, nor camp . . .[44]

in the poem "Cigánydal" [Gypsy song], anticipating the famous lines of Attila József in "Tiszta szívvel" [With a Pure Heart]: but that would be another chapter of literary history.

The postwar situation and the resentment occasioned by the partition of Hungary at the Treaty of Trianon should not be read into the conditions prevailing in the period 1908–18. True enough, to assume a humanist attitude required courage before the revolutions, as well as after. It was hardly possible, wrote Lajos Biró, one of the most radical and most politically concerned among the Nyugat, for a Hungarian daily to write the simple truth about the ethnic "problem" without jeopardizing its circulation, without provoking a flood of letters of protest.[45]

After 1919 the Romanians were often regarded as the archvillains, the archenemies by the counterrevolutionary regime bent on the revision of the Treaty of Trianon. During the preceding decade, however, it was precisely with the Romanians that the Nyugat established, or at least attempted to establish, close ties. In any case, certain cultural links between the two nations had already come about in the immediate past. Octavian Goga had published translations of Petőfi and Madách in *Luceafarül*, and Károly Révai had translated poems by Eminescu and Cosbuc at the turn of the century.[46] Ady's intervention on behalf of Goga in early 1912, when the Romanian poet was jailed in Szeged, Hungary, because of his nationalist (i.e. pro-Romanian) activities, is probably the most memorable episode of this contact of cultures.[47] One consequence of Ady's intervention was a meeting be-

---

[43] *Halálfiai*, 716, 724–25.

[44] S mint röpke mag az ágrul
ugy szakadsz majd le anyádrul
se apád,
se anyád,
se országod, se tanyád . . .

[45] Quoted by Zoltán Horváth, *Die Jahrhundertwende in Ungarn* (Budapest: Lüchterhand, 1966), 308.

[46] "Endre Ady war ein aufrichtiger Freund des rumänischen Volkes, das ihm seine Wertschätzung und ein unauslöschliches Gedenken bewahrt." *Die nationale Frage in der Österreichisch-Ungarischen Monarchie 1900–1918*, ed. Peter Hanák (Budapest: Akadémia, 1966), 66.

[47] Indeed, this was not the first time Octavian Goga had been imprisoned in reprisal for

tween the two poets, and a subsequent "caucus" in some tavern in Buda, involving Goga, Móricz, Babits, and Ignotus. Unfortunately the session had no further repercussions; in fact, Goga soon disappointed his new friends by giving vent to anti-Semitic and chauvinistic sentiments.

When Ady felt compelled to denounce the Romanian poet, it was in order to defend another minority group, the Jews:

> I have no intention of coming up with explanations regarding the so highly evolved anti-Semitism of the Romanians . . . Aside from the dose of anti-Semitism that is proper and necessary, and which I harbor towards a number of Aryans as well, my creed is that God has created only one people for the benefit of the Hungarians, and those are the Jews. For they are the antidote to our turbid, sleepy blood, to our dark orientalism . . .[48]

As for Babits, he was no less outspoken and brave. In 1923, at a time when a pro-Semitic pronouncement could only be interpreted as defiance of the counterrevolutionary regime, he confessed publicly that his own race had painfully misunderstood him, whereas the Jews had understood and appreciated him from the very beginning.[49] The Jews included the editors of the *Nyugat*.

Next to Ady, Ignotus was most inclined to deplore manifestations of Hungarian chauvinism. He neglected few opportunities to come to the defense of slighted ethnic groups and denounce all forms of injustice (including the exploitation of children by their parents).[50] He commented favorably on the political activity of the young Goga and of another Romanian writer, Emil Isac,[51] one of whose short short stories (altogether one page) appeared in the *Nyugat*.[52] In 1913 the *Nyugat* also published a two-page essay on Romanian literature by Pavel Konstantin, with a footnote to the effect that the review intended to publish further articles on the literatures and cultures of each ethnic group living or represented on Hungarian territory.[53]

This project came to nought,[54] although it is difficult to say what might have happened had the war not intervened within a year or so after these encounters and publications. In comparison with current programs of cultural exchange, and the still half-hearted efforts reciprocally to introduce

---

nationalist activities. He had previously been arrested in December 1909 in Budapest, taken to Kolozsvár, and released on 9 January 1910.

[48] Quoted by Fenyö, *Följegyzések* . . . , 89.

[49] Zoltán Éder, *Babits a katedrán* [Babits on the Podium] (Budapest: Szépirodalmi, 1966), 87.

[50] *Ignotus válogatott irásai*, 433.

[51] "Az uj magyar irodalom" [The New Hungarian Literature], *Nyugat*, 6 (1913), No. 1: 496–98.

[52] "A szerecsen" [The Moor], *Nyugat*, 7 (1914), No. 1: 212. The story exploits a stereotype view of the Black male as sex symbol.

[53] "Hatások a román irodalom fejlödésében" [Influences in the Evolution of Romanian Literature], *Nyugat*, 6 (1913), No. 2: 723–24.

[54] Sámuel Domokos, *A román irodalom magyar bibliográfiája, 1831–1960* [The Hungarian Bibliography of Romanian Literature] (Budapest: Irodalmi Könyvkiadó, 1966), 23.

the literatures of the East-Central European nations, contacts at the beginning of the century were practically nonexistent; though Hungary probably "exported" more literature to its neighbors than it imported. During the entire decade from 1908 to 1918 the *Nyugat* published altogether four items pertaining to Romanian literature, three to Polish, and one item pertaining to Croatian literature (Ivo Voinović).[55] The only plausible excuse for this neglect, that the Nyugat's program was explicitly "western," is a rather weak one; that the record of most other Hungarian periodicals, literary or political, was even worse could be adduced as a mitigating circumstance.

The sensitivity of the establishment to any criticism of its nationalities policies can be gauged from the following incident. In 1913 Ignotus wrote a brief but sarcastic account of an incident involving a Hungarian policeman and the Romanian Minister of the Interior. The Minister happened to be traveling through Arad, in southern Hungary, in an official vehicle displaying the Romanian flag. The policeman stopped the car and removed the flag, enforcing some law prohibiting the "unauthorized" display of foreign banners. Ignotus noted, prophetically as it turned out, that similar incidents would occur again and again until such time as "the law was laid down in Bucharest" rather than in Budapest, and heeded in Arad.[56] The response to Ignotus's attack came in the reactionary clerical journal *Magyar Kultura*, where he was crucified as unpatriotic and un-Hungarian.[57]

Aladár Kuncz, one of the "French experts" of the Nyugat, was also in contact with Romanian intellectuals, particularly Emil Isac. The two of them elaborated a project which would have consisted in the simultaneous performance of plays by Isac and Caragiale in Budapest on one hand, and of Ady's one-act play "A mühelyben" [In the Workshop] in Bucharest on the other hand. Like other projects of Hungarian-Romanian cultural collaboration, this one came to naught, possibly on account of Caragiale's sudden death.[58]

Bartók's activities were more effective. While it is true that his letters contain nothing that is even remotely political, it seems that almost everything he did was nevertheless political, in the best sense of the word. The analysis of his scientific work on folk music would be beyond my competence; but it may suffice to mention that the beginning and end of that work was the building of bridges, of understanding among nations and cultures. By 1918 he had collected something in the region of 2,700 Hungarian, 2,500 Slovak, and 3,500 Romanian melodies—in other words his research was not in the least ethnocentric.[59] It is equally pertinent to mention

---

[55] Ferenc Galambos, *Nyugat repertorium*, passim.
[56] "Disputa," *Nyugat*, 6 (1913), No. 2: 600.
[57] 2 (1914): 53ff.
[58] Béla Pomogáts, *Kuncz Aladár* (Budapest: Akadémia, 1968), 32.
[59] Paul Griffiths, *Bartók* (London: J. M. Dent & Sons, 1984), 26. Mihály Babits had written somewhere that "much like the explorers of folk art and folk music I peered with awe, as a

Bartók's efforts to introduce modern Hungarian literature, Ady and Móricz in particular, to outsiders. Thus he sent his Romanian friend, Janos Buşiţia, a book by Móricz and a volume of poems by Ady. The latter, wrote Bartók to Buşiţia, "says that Hungarians, Romanians and Slavs in this country should all be united, since they are kindred in misery. We've never had a poet who would dare write such things."[60]

The Romanians were not the only ethnic group whose fate seemed to preoccupy some of the Nyugat writers; but the ambiguous expressions of concern emanating from a number of them do not allow for a systematic, well-organized analysis. Margit Kaffka, the daughter of fairly typical gentry parents, who claimed that one of her forefathers had arrived in Árpád's train (that is, with the very first Hungarians—a distinction akin to having arrived in America aboard the *Mayflower*), nevertheless wrote with equal pride, in her short autobiography, of her Czech ancestor.[61] The fact that her second husband, Ervin Bauer, the brother of the Nyugat writer Béla Balázs, was a Jew, and an object of her worship, may account in part for her militant pro-Semitism (or vice versa). In a letter to the critic Aladár Schöpflin, dated 23 March 1917, Kaffka wrote: "It is interesting that I must argue not only with my good friend [i.e. Schöpflin] but with my husband as well and I must defend his own sect against him . . ."[62] She also wrote with basic sympathy about the aspirations of the Croatians, exacerbated by the recently promulgated Railway Service Act which required a knowledge of Hungarian on the part of all railwaymen, including those working on Croatian lines.[63] Reporting from Zagreb she deplored the fact that Hungarians knew so much more about London, New York, or Paris than they did about the Croatian capital which lay within the kingdom of Hungary. She compared the Croatian literary review *Savremenik* with the *Nyugat*: both belonged to the young, the progressive; yet the *Savremenik* was "about twenty years behind," and had but two thousand subscribers.[64]

Here and there the writers found some good words for the Serbians, too; witness Cholnoky's remark about the superiority of the Serbo-Hungarian gentleman I quoted a few pages earlier. Béla Balázs had the good

---

child, into the depths where cultures had not as yet set nations apart, but rather have brought them together, with songs, stories, memories in common; and where, in the shade of their snow-capped mountains, Szekely and Romanians still preserve something as good neighbors and brothers, something we had lost long ago." Zoltán Eder, op. cit., 63.

[60] *Béla Bartók: Letters,* ed. János Demény (London: Faber & Faber, 1971), 113 ff. The relevant letters are dated from January 1912 and September 1917.

[61] *Az élet utján; versek, cikkek, naplójegyzetek* [Along the Road of Life: Poems, Articles, Diary Notes] (Budapest: Szépirodalmi, 1972), 401.

[62] Schöpflin Papers, Országos Széchenyi Irratár. Although it may seem from Kaffka's letter that Schöpflin had made some uncomplimentary remarks about Jews, it should be noted that he boldly defended the Jews as the most worthy readers and supporters of the *Nyugat*, and this at a time when anti-Semitism was in ascendance. *A magyar irodalom története a XX. században.*

[63] Arthur J. May, *The Habsburg Monarchy,* 383.

[64] *Az élet utján,* 285, 288.

fortune to have some of his works translated into Serbo-Croatian, before the outbreak of the war; as a result he was prompted to write in his diary his "declaration of Slav faith," that contact with the Slavs could prove truly productive for the Hungarians.[65] This faith, however, did not prevent Balázs from hailing the news of the outbreak of war between Serbia and the Monarchy with shameless enthusiasm.

As for the Ruthenians—that is, the Ukrainians living in what was then the northeastern corner of Hungary—they encountered sympathy in the writings of Ady and of others. Imre Csécsy, a minor member of the Nyugat movement, and later an active participant in the revolution of October 1918, wrote of the exploitation of the Ruthenian people. The occasion for the article was the trial of some Ruthenian nationalist "agitators." To solve the problem of nationalities, wrote Csécsy, "all we need is a politics of humanity."[66]

All in all, a consistently progressive attitude with regard to the nationalities was exceptional; the exceptions were Oszkár Jászi, Endre Ady and Béla Bartók.[67] Ady's attitude is best summarized by Fenyö (who himself perceived the "problem" in a somewhat different light): "Of all the current issues it was the problem of the nationalities which exacerbated Ady first and foremost."[68] Or let me quote Ady himself who, as early as 1902, declared: "It is a patriotic thing, in Hungary, to blame the German, the Serb, the Romanian, the Slovak. Is it not so? If it is so, I hereby declare that I am no patriot."[69] Similarly, Bartók and Kodály attempted and achieved a basic understanding of the diversity and unity of cultures in East-Central Europe and the Balkans, and even beyond, in the spirit of Herder, in a spirit of respect for all cultures.[70] But it would be misleading to dwell on Ady and Bartók; more typical was the lack of understanding displayed by others.

Their record remains disappointing if we make comparisons with other progressive movements, in other countries, at other times. Thus in the 1960s and early 1970s few American writers could disregard the pleas or demands of minority groups in the United States, not even those writers who generally managed to remain aloof from contemporary issues. If noth-

---

[65] Diary of Béla Balázs, entry for 19 April 1913. Ms 5023/17, Magyar Tudományos Akadémia Irattára.

[66] *Nyugat*, 7 (1914): 222–23. The politician Miklós Bartha had been equally outspoken in defending the Ruthenians. Magyarország története (manuscript), XII, 43.

[67] The meeting of Bartók and Ady is described as somewhat anticlimactic. It took place at the 1912 exhibition of the Eight: Ady and Bartók shook hands, exchanged some trivialities, and departed. Ady preferred gypsy music, whereas Bartok knew little about the plastic arts. See Krisztina Passuth, *A nyolcak festészete* [The Art of the Eight] (Budapest: Athenaeum, 1967), 91.

[68] *Följegyzések . . .* , 88.

[69] Quoted in *Irodalomtörténet*, 5: 92.

[70] György Lukács claimed that the only persons who could understand the nationalities problem in Hungary were Ady and Bartók. "Ady jelentösége és hatása" [The Significance and Influence of Ady], 1969, reprinted in *Magyar irodalom—magyar kultura*, 606. See also his "Demokrácia és kultura" [Democracy and Culture], 1946, in the same anthology, 318.

ing else, they sooner or later began to refer to the minorities as Blacks, Native Americans, or Chicanos, instead of Negroes, Indians, and Mexican-Americans. The best of contemporary American literature was and is aware of an impending crisis.

To be sure, manifestations of racial or ethnic prejudice were rare among the Nyugat, as they are rare in great modern literature anywhere. Sartre is undoubtedly correct in stating he does not know of a single good novel the express purpose of which was to serve oppression; not a single good novel written against the Jews, Blacks, workers or, I might add, the Slovak people.[71]

If the Nyugat's contribution to the struggle against the exploitation of nationalities and ethnic discrimination was spotty and ambiguous, the other basic problem, that of the peasant, was greeted with almost complete silence. To be sure, the literature of the Nyugat tended to be urban and cosmopolitan rather than rural and provincial; but was land reform not originally a Western, and even French notion?[72]

The provincial writers, the "folk-national" school as they were wont to refer to themselves, the epigons of the great nineteenth-century poet János Arany, wrote about village life from the point of view of the "gentry." If they condescended to write about peasants it was to record the *puszta*—the arid zones of the great Hungarian plain—the peasant homes, the crates adorned with arabesques and tulips in red and green, the mirages on the plains, the "folksy" objects.[73] Or they would stress some trait traditionally ascribed to the Hungarian peasant: his foxiness, his sense of humor, his conservatism, his imperturbability.

Zsigmond Móricz did all of this, but added realism and naturalism. He added a concern for the existential circumstances of the Hungarian peasant. He added an understanding of the compensations of a seemingly hopeless existence, the rewards of "the culture of poverty," the peasant's sensuality. Instead of idealizing the peasant, Móricz described his brutish life, rendered brutish by the misery to which he was often confined, by the treatment to which he was subjected. Móricz was quite unlike the *narodniki* novelists; the condition of the peasantry became readily apparent to the reader not because Móricz described him in pathetic terms but, on the contrary, because

---

[71] Jean-Paul Sartre, *What is Literature?* (New York: Harper & Row, 1965, 1st French edition, 1949), 58.

[72] Some of the "allies" of the Nyugat did pay heed to the issue. Members of the Galilei Circle argued that the peasant must be given land as his personal property, and without regard to his ethnic background. Márta Tömöry, *Uj vizeken járok* [I Walk on New Waters] (Budapest: Gondolat, 1960), 65.

[73] I am paraphrasing a critic's description of the themes presented by Móricz: "The *puszta*, the peasant-house, the tulip crate, the mirages. A peculiar combination of the Hungarian peasant and the man of Western culture." Dénes Ficzay, "Ady, a 'Holnap,' és a 'Nyugat' Aradon" [Ady, the Holnap, and the Nyugat at Arad], *Nyelvi és irodalomtudományi közlemények*, 11 (1967), No. 2: 254. The original of the text quoted is to be found in the 23 November 1909 issue of the *Függetlenség* of Arad.

his descriptions amounted to demystification. One of his earliest short stories, titled "Tragédia," may be cited as an example of Móricz's approach: its protagonist is a peasant who bears a grudge against a certain landowner, his employer, but accepts the latter's invitation to a feast; his intention is to eat so much that his host will go bankrupt. Instead, the peasant dies of apoplexy. Móricz himself was not too proud of his own peasant background; he would not forgive the indiscretion of Lajos Hatvany, who once took the liberty of reminding the reading public of Móricz's origins.[74]

At any rate, the picture painted by Móricz was convincing. True, his readers generally lacked the kind of social background that might have enabled them to verify these descriptions first hand; for he was read not by the peasants, nor even by the hardly more literate gentry,[75] but rather by those who subscribed to the *Nyugat*. But whether his stories were authentic or not the reader was bound to grow more sensitive to the predicament of the people on the land. "In the revolutionary army," complimented Ady, "Móricz alone would be worth a whole battalion of volunteers."[76]

As might be expected, Ady was likewise conscious of the agrarian problem. "There is trouble with the peasant," he wrote in October 1907. "That he should go to America, big deal! But he comes back! He becomes unruly and spoilt. America and the socialists rendered him unruly and spoilt."[77] A few days later Ady editorialized about the village of Mezöcsát, the entire population of which marched through the streets of Budapest, on their way to the New World.[78]

Ady was in correspondence with András Áchim, the radical peasant leader and founder of the Independent Socialist Peasant Party, the program of which included redistribution of land. Áchim appealed to Ady: "My dear old man, singing bird of my soul, do compose the tune, do sing us

---

[74] Miksa Fenyö, as quoted in *A magyar irodalom története*, 5: 151. But in a letter to Schöpflin on 4 December 1911, Móricz wrote: "Among my ancestors by blood you can find some representatives from every social stratum from the lowest serfs to the *noble d'épée*. That is why I feel entitled to judge everyone from the Count Károlyis to the lowest peasant . . ." *Móricz Zsigmond levelei*, 109.

[75] It would not be accurate, however, to assert that the provincial gentry was entirely impervious to modern literature. A good many of the writers of the movement came from precisely this background. Aladár Schöpflin, as one of the editors of the *Vasárnapi Ujság*, a Sunday weekly widely read in the provinces, assumed the role of propagandizer for the Nyugat. The conservative readers knew and appreciated Schöpflin; their faith in him was confirmed by his membership in the conservative Kisfaludy literary society. Thus Schöpflin was in a position to "smuggle in" the works of Ady, Moricz, Kaffka, and others, among the kitsch and the literary junk of purely entertainment value. György Bélia and Anna Sándor, "Schöpflin Aladár hagyatékából" [From the Papers of Schöpflin], *Irodalom.*

[76] Quoted in *Móricz Zsigmond válogatott elbeszélései* [Selected Stories of Móricz] (Budapest: Szépirodalmi, 1951), 10.

[77] *Ady Endre összes prózai müvei*, 9: 26.

[78] Ibid., 9: 44. The item originally appeared in the 5 November 1907 issue of the *Budapesti Napló*.

the tune which, not so very long ago, set the churches and lordly castles ablaze in this land . . ."[79] A couple of years later, on 14 May 1911, Áchim was murdered by the Zsilinszky brothers, members of the gentry, in reprisal for an "insult." Subsequently the Zsilinszky brothers were acquitted of all charges (but in fairness, it should be noted that one of the brothers, Endre Bajcsy-Zsilinszky, became a hero of the Hungarian resistance against the Nazi occupation in 1944—the only Hungarian politician to have opened fire on the German invader).[80]

According to an unverified family tradition Ady was a descendant of György Dózsa, the leader of a widespread peasant uprising that had seriously threatened the rule of the nobility in 1514, a few years before the battle of Mohács. "I am the grandson of György Dózsa," he proudly proclaimed.[81] In one sense or another, it was true. In several of his poems he makes reference to the "hot summers," the strikes of the agrarian workers, the repression and violence that ensued, and the inability of the landless peasant to obtain meaningful or lasting redress:

I walk the fields, I keep walking/I anxiously spy at those yoked by thousands of summers,/and their ancient sorrow/but in vain do I wait to hear their songs . . .

Thus wrote Ady in "Uj magyar bukolika" [New Hungarian Bucolics] of 1911.[82] Here too, under the ironic title, he expressed his disappointment at the revolution delayed, at the perpetuation of the condition of serfdom two generations after its official abolition.

Ady was the prophet rather than the leader; his concern for the fate of the peasant was not generally shared by the Nyugat movement. In the first ten volumes of the journal I found only one article dealing specifically with the predicament of the peasant. The argument of this article runs: there is no longer time to await peaceful, gradual change, improvement will come about only as a result of aggressive, revolutionary action. But the article appeared in 1917, rather late in the game.[83] By that time the author's thesis was hardly new. The Russian events, if nothing else, had awakened Hun-

---

[79] Áchim to Ady, 23 March 1908, quoted by József Domokos, *Áchim L. András* (Budapest: Kossuth, 1971), 196.

[80] Mario D. Fenyo, *Hitler, Horthy, and Hungary* (New Haven: Yale University Press, 1972).

[81] "Dózsa György unokája vagyok én,
Népért siró, bús, bocskoros nemes.
Hé, nagyurak, jó lesz tán szóba állni
Kaszás népemmel, mert a Nyár heves . . ."
From the poem "Dózsa György unokája" [Grandson of Dózsa] in the volume *az Illés szekerén* (1908).

[82] "Járom a mezöt, járva-járom,
Ezernyi nyár leigázottját,
Ös bánatát esengve lesem,
De a notáit csupán várom . . ."
First appeared in the *Nyugat*, 4 (1911), No. 2: 102.

[83] Ernö Éber, "A magyar mezögazdaság átalakulása" [The Transformation of Hungarian Agriculture], *Nyugat*, 10 (1917), No. 2: 730.

garian public opinion to the possibility of radical change, including the redistribution of land; the Nyugat dared not claim credit for the awakening.

When the war broke out, the Nyugat did not present a united antiwar front; if anything, the war met with tacit or explicit approval. I have found no trace of disapproval, of scepticism, of pacifism in the issues immediately following the outbreak of hostilities.

On the contrary, several Nyugat writers expressed their approval of military action, even beyond the call of patriotic "duty," beyond the consent that may have been prompted by official pressure or by fear. The most notorious cases of war fervor were those exhibited by Ignotus and Béla Balázs. The attitude of Balázs, in particular, may seem surprising. Here was a distinguished writer, playwright, and poet, who was to achieve an international reputation by his pioneer work in film theory, in the sociology of the cinema; a man, moreover, who was to become politically committed in 1919 and would remain, from that time on, a member of the Communist Party to the end of his life.

> There is war . . . I volunteered, but was refused. For two days I was completely beside myself. I, the athlete, who had avoided the draft [in 1908] only by cheating, who had always sung the praises of war . . .

wrote Balázs in his diary.[84] What he confessed to his diary he also proclaimed in public, on the pages of the *Nyugat*: this war was sacred.[85] His glorification of the war was not unlike the *vivere pericolosamente* of Gabriele d'Annunzio (and of Benito Mussolini).[86] Jolán Kelen writes that she and her young companions within the Galilei Circle were thoroughly dismayed by the attitude of Balázs, and even more so by that of Lukács, who undertook to defend Balázs.[87] It is true that Lukács had admired Balázs to an excess, and for a long time considered Balázs his best friend; but we know that Lukács himself objected to the war from its very beginning, and was not reluctant to say so even in Germany, face to face with his German acquaintances.[88]

Ignotus found sensible political arguments to justify the war: "There can be no doubt that the Hungarians need the Austro-Hungarian Monarchy, hence they also need the present war . . ."[89] Miksa Fenyö, although he turned from the war with a feeling of personal revulsion, and nearly ran into trouble with the mob chanting "let the dog Serbia perish!" when he refused to join in, nevertheless felt duty-bound actively to support the war

---

[84] No date, Ms 5023/17, Magyar Tudományos Akadémia Irattára. For a more understanding view of Balázs's initial enthusiasm see Mary Gluck, *op. cit.*, 177–78.
[85] "Páris-e vagy Weimar?" [Paris or Weimar?], *Nyugat*, 7 (1914), No. 2: 200.
[86] Ferenc Fehér, "Balázs Béla és Lukács György szövetsége a forradalomig" [The Alliance of Balázs and Lukács until the Revolution], *Irodalomtörténet*, 51 (1969), Nos. 1–2: 558.
[87] *Eliramlik az élet*, 71.
[88] Ferenc Fehér, op. cit., 554. Also Éva Fekete, "Lukács György az elsö világháború éveiben" [Lukács during the Years of the First World War], *Valóság*, 1977, No. 2: 33.
[89] "Háború" [War], *Nyugat*, 7 (1914), No. 2: 131.

effort on the pages of the review; the war, he claimed, provided a "thousand new opportunities" for the evolution of "our national life."[90]

Both Dezsö Kosztolányi and Aladár Schöpflin wrote items for the *Nyugat* about their younger brother who had gone to war. "I fear for you and I envy you," said Schöpflin.[91] Kosztolányi expressed similar sentiments in his poem "My Younger Brother."[92] In the dailies Kosztolányi was more political and explicit; he welcomed the war and argued against the Entente with verve, even enthusiasm, especially against what he called the "Muscovite spirit." But his enthusiasm abated as the war proved anything but jolly, and after a year or two he actively, if timidly, denounced it.[93]

Others had denounced the war long before Kosztolányi. The first glimmers of a pacifist attitude can be detected by the end of the 1914 volume of the journal. One of these glimmers was the translation of a poem by Edmond Rostand (the author of *Cyrano de Bergerac*) deploring the destruction of the cathedral of Rheims by the invading German "hordes"; but lest the publication of the poem be taken for an anti-German gesture on the part of the *Nyugat*—which it most likely was—the editors felt compelled to add a footnote to the effect that, although the poem deplored the so-called barbarism of the Germans, "Tyrteus would have sung it better . . ."[94] In other words, the poem was not particularly good. But then why publish it? In any case, the apology had been in vain, for the *Nyugat* came under fire from the clerical and reactionary press for having shed tears, "crocodile tears," over the destruction of a French cathedral.[95]

Beginning with 1915 antiwar items appear with increasing frequency, whereas pro-war items become subdued. Among the antiwar items we find some free verse by Lajos Kassák;[96] the first installment of a running commentary from the front with strong pacifist overtones by Menyhért Lengyel;[97] the apocryphal "Letters from the Front Lines by Harry Russel Dorsan" written by the generally apolitical Dezsö Szomory; Dezsö Szabó coming to the defense of the "national character" of the French people;[98] Zoltán

---

[90] *Nyugat*, 7 (1914), No. 2: 254.
[91] "Katona öcsémnek" [To My Soldier Brother], *Nyugat*, 7 (1914), No. 2: 197.
[92] "Öcsém," *Nyugat*, 7 (1914): 194.
[93] There is a detailed analysis of Kosztolányi's progress and hesitations by Ferenc Kiss in his as yet unpublished manuscript on Kosztolányi, 48–53.
[94] *Nyugat*, 7 (1914), No. 2: 440. The editors had access to Western journals and newspapers throughout the war, as can be surmised from a letter by Bartók thanking Fenyö for letting him peruse such publications regularly. *Bartok Béla levelei*, 229.
[95] *Magyar Kultura*, 3 (1915): 414.
[96] "1914–15," *Nyugat*, 8 (1915), No. 1: 4. According to Miksa Fenyö, these were "the first moving antiwar poems. Perhaps they sprang from the soul of the poet when the boulevards were still resounding from the crowd's 'Down with dog Serbia!' " "Az olvasás gyönyörüsége: spiritus fiat ubi vult," *Irodalmi ujság*, 18, Nos. 16-16 (15 Sept. 1967): 6–7.
[97] "Egyszerü gondolatok" [Simple Thoughts], *Nyugat*, 8 (1915), No. 1: 77–82. According to the Socialist József Pogány, this was the first piece of pacifist writing; and he urged all workers' libraries to acquire it and make their members read it. *A tudás*, No. 1, March 1918.
[98] Szabó was reacting to an anti-French article by another French "specialist," Géza Lackó, also in the *Nyugat*. "Disputa," *Nyugat*, 8 (1915), No. 1: 168.

Ambrus attacking Thomas Mann who had published a blatantly chauvinist statement in some German magazine—"en chauvinisme," wrote Ambrus, "tous les peuples se valent";[99] and so forth.

An item by item enumeration of antiwar publications is hardly necessary; I must mention, however, the outstanding contribution Móricz made to the cause, in 1916, with his short novel, *Szegény emberek* [Poor Folk]. It should have earned its author, writes Fenyö, both the Nobel Prize for literature, and the Nobel Prize for peace.[100]

I must also include Ady, although the tone of his wartime poetry was generally mild, perhaps because several times he was on the verge of being drafted and the harassment—for that is what it amounted to—worried him considerably. But he did not remain silent. He denounced the conflict even before it broke out.[101] Campaigning as a candidate of the Radical Party in the district of Szatmár, he told his constituents, on 28 June 1914 (the day the shots were fired at Sarajevo): "In this world war the Hungarian nation will perish whether the Entente wins or loses. Hungary will be divided . . . reaction will take over . . ." And Ady wept in the middle of his speech.[102] Assuming that he had indeed pronounced such prophetic words, Ady's arguments were rather similar to the ones his archenemy, Prime Minister Tisza, was to use shortly thereafter at the secret deliberations of the Austro-Hungarian cabinet in June and July 1914. During the actual conflict Ady wrote a number of poems deploring the war in unmistakable terms, beginning with "Cifra szürömmel betakarva" [Covered with My Fancy Hide-Jacket].[103] We cannot always know when a certain poem was actually written; it is possible that some of Ady's most forceful protests against the war, for instance his famous "Emlékezés egy nyár-éjszakára" [Remembering a Summer Night], published in 1918, were conceived earlier, at its beginning.

Like Ady, Mihály Babits denounced the war before it even broke out. Witness his article "Children and the War" in the August and September issues of the *Nyugat* (1914).[104] The first antiwar poem to appear in the *Nyugat*, preceding even the poem by Kassák already mentioned, was likewise the work of Babits; titled "Fiatal katona" [Young Soldier] it concluded with the lines ". . . and whether we are triumphant, he will never know, for he must die, must die."[105]

---

[99] "Háborus jegyzetek" [War-time notes], *Nyugat*, 8 (1915): 117.

[100] *Föjegyzések* . . . , 117, 124. The short novel itself appeared in the *Nyugat*, 9 (1916), No. 2: 850–73.

[101] Great artists or writers are prophets by definition, argued Leon Trotsky: "Works of art are embodiments of presentments; therefore, pre-revolutionary art is the real art of the Revolution . . ." *Literature and Revolution* (Ann Arbor: University of Michigan Press, 1960), 110.

[102] Cited by Lóránt Hegedüs, *Ady és Tisza* (Budapest: Nyugat, n.d. about 1940), 90–91.

[103] *Nyugat*, 8 (1915), No. 1: 220.

[104] Zoltán Éder, *Babits a katedrán* [Babits on the Podium], 152.

[105] "S gyözünk-e, meg sem tudja soha, mert halni kell neki, halni." *Nyugat*, 7 (1914), No. 2: 347–49. See also his incidental poem "Prologus" written for a concert performed in November 1914.

Indeed, Babits was a dedicated pacifist, although he protested against the label, and would have preferred to be called simply a humanist. In the manuscript of an article composed in the late thirties and titled "The War and I" Babits wrote: "They say I am a pacifist. I do not recognize myself under this designation. I am not a pacifist: I was born a fighter! I do not yearn for eternal peace . . ."[106] Babits might have admitted a justification for the Second World War (he died in 1941, before Hungary joined the conflict); but in World War I he became a fighter for the cause of peace. He lost his job as a high school teacher after his poem "Játszottam a kezével" [I played with her Hand] was published in the August 1915 issue of the *Nyugat.* The poem was innocent enough, but it ended with a romantic (and not too original) conceit: "I would rather spill gushing blood for the little finger of my sweetheart, than for a hundred kings, a hundred flags . . ."[107] In vain did he follow up, in the next issue of the *Nyugat,* with a poem titled "Poem, in Answer to Attacks" which could be considered a kind of retraction; the retraction, if indeed it was that, convinced no one, and only served to elicit doubts as to Babits's steadfastness in face of criticism and adversity. At any rate, thanks to some influential friends (or rather, thanks to the influential friends of Ignotus and Fenyö), Babits was able to obtain another teaching position.

Momentarily daunted, Babits kept on publishing antiwar poems. At a Nyugat matinée held in Budapest in March 1916 Babits recited a poem titled "Husvét elött" [Before Easter]. It had a rousing effect on the audience (who, it may be presumed, sympathized with the cause of peace to begin with). They picked up the refrain of the poem:

Let there be peace! Peace! Peace!
Let the war be done with! Let there be peace!
Peace! Peace![108]

Then, in 1917, an entire issue of the *Nyugat* was confiscated on orders of the police, because of another poem by Babits. The order of the district police chief read:

On the basis of ordinance B.P. paragraph 567 I confiscate issue no. 5 of periodical published under the title *Nyugat,* and which appeared in Budapest on March 1 of the current year . . . On pages 494–95 of the issue ordered confiscated there appeared a verse publication under the title Fortissimo and with the signature of

---

[106] Babits Papers, III/1544, Országos Széchenyi Irattár.
[107] " . . . nagyobb örömmel ontanám
 kis ujjáért a csobogó vért,
 mint száz királyért, lobogoért!"
Nyugat, 8 (1915), No. 2: 884–85.
[108] "Hogy béke! béke!
 béke! béke már!
 Legyen vége már!"
Nyugat, 9 (1916), No. 1: 392–94. The matinée is described by Jolán Kelen, *Eliramlik az élet* (Budapest: Kossuth, 1976), 77.

Mihály Babits as author . . . Because of his attack against religion, particularly where he writes that if the prayer and cries addressed to God should remain without effect, we men still remember how to curse; we tear and beat the deaf God with our curses—God, like the landlord snoring inside his burning house. . . . March 1, Budapest 1917, Judge Margalits . . .[109]

The title of the poem, "Fortissimo," was indicative of its content; it was strong, indeed, the strongest possible protest against the war and against God who allowed it to rage. All the stronger, since Babits was a believer, a Catholic poet, a Catholic writer, to the end of his life (not quite the same as being a poet or a writer who is also a Catholic).

Babits thus became the most "exposed" member of the Nyugat movement during the war. It would have been expedient for the editors of the review to "play him down," especially since it had taken them a while to realize their moral mistake in supporting the war; instead, they appointed Babits co-editor of the journal, in the middle of 1917, when Fenyö resigned to become an executive with the National Association of Manufacturers (GyOSz).

While some women writers favored the war at the beginning (for instance, the Nyugat poetess Sarolta Lányi, who published some well-nigh blood-thirsty poetry in late 1914),[110] perhaps no one was as horrified by the conflict, as mentally and physically repelled by it, as Margit Kaffka. "I had not seen her for a while," wrote Fenyö in her obituary,

but I can well imagine that she would passionately approve of the revolution, and of every revolution to come . . . as long as she felt there was someone left on earth whose interest it might serve to instigate masses of humanity against one another.[111]

It might be added that Kaffka most likely did approve of the revolution of October 1918, and she would have approved of the revolution of March 1919 (she died on 1 December 1918, a victim of the "Spanish" flu), and not only because she hated war.

All the Nyugat writers turned against the war, sooner or later. I might have mentioned Ernö Szép or Frigyes Karinthy, who were no less passionate in their denunciation, or Lajos Nagy who, in a private letter to a friend expressed his feeling of repulsion towards the war as early as 3 September 1914.[112]

It is entirely possible that the *Nyugat* owed its increasing popularity—if we can judge from the circulation figures—to its courageous, albeit intermittent and inconsistent, stand against the war. The Social Democrats had compromised; while their organ, the *Népszava*, bravely denounced the war

---

[109] Babits Papers, III/1581, Országos Széchenyi Irattár.
[110] By 1918, however, she was to publish "Socialist poetry" in the *Népszava*. See József Farkas, "Forradalmi magyar irodalom," 26.
[111] *Nyugat* (1918) reprinted in *Mindenki ujakra készül*, 2: 207–08.
[112] "Nagy Lajos levelei Nagy Zoltánhoz" [Letters of Lajos Nagy to Zoltán Nagy], *Kritika* (June 1977), 4.

preparations in the summer of 1914, it executed an abrupt about-face the day the war broke out: prosecution must be avoided, the press organ must be maintained at any cost, its editors believed.[113] It was not until a year or so later that the *Népszava* spoke out again against the war. The *Nyugat* was not so timid, but behaved rather well under the circumstances, complimented Kassák.[114] "Compliments" can also be found in the "establishment" papers. In 1916 the *Magyar Kultura* charged that the *Nyugat* was "scared stiff by the prospect of the victory of the Central Powers which would signify, by the same token, the triumph of Christian Conservatism; all this is apparent from what they publish, but even more so from what they don't publish."[115] Only the *Huszadik Század*, Kassák's two reviews, the *Tett* and the *Ma*, and the feminist weekly *A nő* edited by Rózsa Bédy-Schwimmer, maintained a stronger, or equally strong pacifist stand.

The Nyugat movement's position on the issue of universal suffrage was unanimous and unequivocal. Of course, universal suffrage was a liberal issue, and it remained a liberal issue in Hungary long after it had ceased to be one in Western Europe. "Apolitical" intellectuals took part in the struggle. Jenö Heltai, not strictly speaking a member of the Nyugat, but rather an older writer who had contributed to the literary revolution, wrote in the *Népszava*, in response to an informal poll of writers:

> I have always carefully avoided political questions, because my opinion is that a writer should be a writer and nothing else. The issue of suffrage, however, is not a political issue, but an issue concerning general human rights.[116]

Even certain conservative, or "liberal-conservative" elements supported the cause; the "establishment" writer and editor Ferenc Herceg was one of the founding members of the League for the Right to Vote.

On the other hand, universal suffrage was also the major political objective of the Social Democrats, their minimum program to which all other goals had to be subordinated. Hence, universal suffrage was both a liberal and a "radical" issue. It would be next to impossible to assess the contribution of the Nyugat movement to this cause. The front was too ample.

The front was much less ample with regard to the other three issues discussed. As far as the antiwar effort was concerned, in general the Nyugat writers were effective and courageous. On other issues the Nyugat writers were timid. Nevertheless, a handful of them, and the most outstanding at that, were indeed concerned: Ady, Móricz, and Bartók if we accept the latter as part of the movement. The credit they deserve redounds to the credit of the Nyugat as a whole.

---

[113] Magyarország története (manuscript), 15: 28.
[114] Lajos Kassák, *Egy ember élete* [A Man's Life] (Budapest: Magvetö, 1957), 510–11. See also Ruszinyák, op. cit., 31, and Kelen, op. cit., 71, 73.
[115] 4 (1916): 180–85.
[116] 9 January 1913.

If we are to assess the political influence, the political function of the Nyugat, these are some of the factors we have to bear in mind; but we also have to bear in mind that it was not the direct political involvement, not the political attitude of the writers within the movement that primarily determined the political function of this literature. There is no "one-to-one" relationship between politics and literature. The Socialist writer is seldom the most effective "propagandist" for the cause of Socialism, or even for the cause of progress. Marx, Engels, and Lukács have repeatedly recognized the shattering effect of the novels of Balzac on the illusions of the bourgeois world, in spite of Balzac's own political conservatism.[117] Lenin shows greater appreciation for the work of Tolstoy than for that of any of the truly progressive writers of contemporary Russia. Sartre claims that it was the influence of Freud, and of the "decadent" writers Kafka and Joyce, that led him towards Marxism (insofar as he was a Marxist).[118]

Finally what matters to us is not so much the Nyugat movement's political profile, but to what extent was it able to feel, perceive, and reveal the trends of the times. Rather than do a sociological analysis of the texts themselves, as Lukács or Goldmann might have done, I opted for an easier course: the analysis of the impact of this literature on the public.

---

[117] In particular, see György Lukács, *Balzac et le réalisme français* (Paris: François Maspéro, 1969).

[118] Roger Garaudy, J.-P. Sartre, Ernst Fischer, Eduard Goldstücker, *Estética y marxismo* (Barcelona: Martinez Roca, 1969), 58.

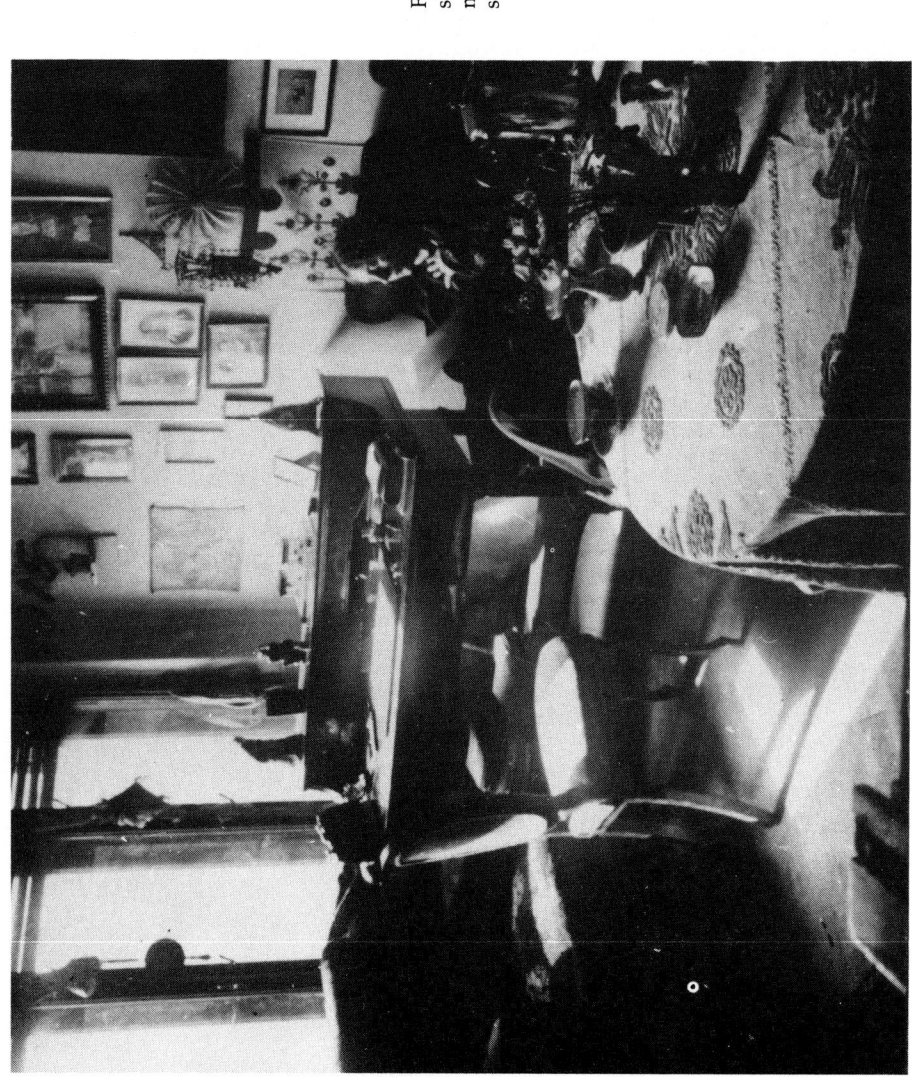

Fig. 1. Margit (Margaret) Kaffka, outstanding member of the Nyugat Literary movement (poet and novelist), in her study.

FIG. 2. Ernö (Ernest) Osvát, founder and editor of the *Nyugat*.

FIG. 3. View of Budapest and the Danube with the Parliament building in the center.

FIG. 4. A scene from the revolution of October 1918, the "Chrysanthemum Revolution."

Fig. 5. Endre Ady and Mihály Babits, the two most outstanding poets of Hungary and of the Nyugat (around 1916).

FIG. 6. Bèla Bartók, Hungarian composer, friend of the Nyugat.

FIG. 7. View of Budapest, Kálvin (Calvin) Square, with the National Museum in the background. The building now houses the main public library.

FIG. 8. Budapest, the Andrássy on Andrássy Street, 1911.

FIG. 9. Miksa (Max) Fenyö, an editor and founder of Nyugat, in front of the Hotel Gellért ca. 1910.

Fig. 10. Portrait of Frigyes (Frederick) Kariuthy, by Jozsef Rippl-Ronai, who painted the portraits of several members of Nyugat.

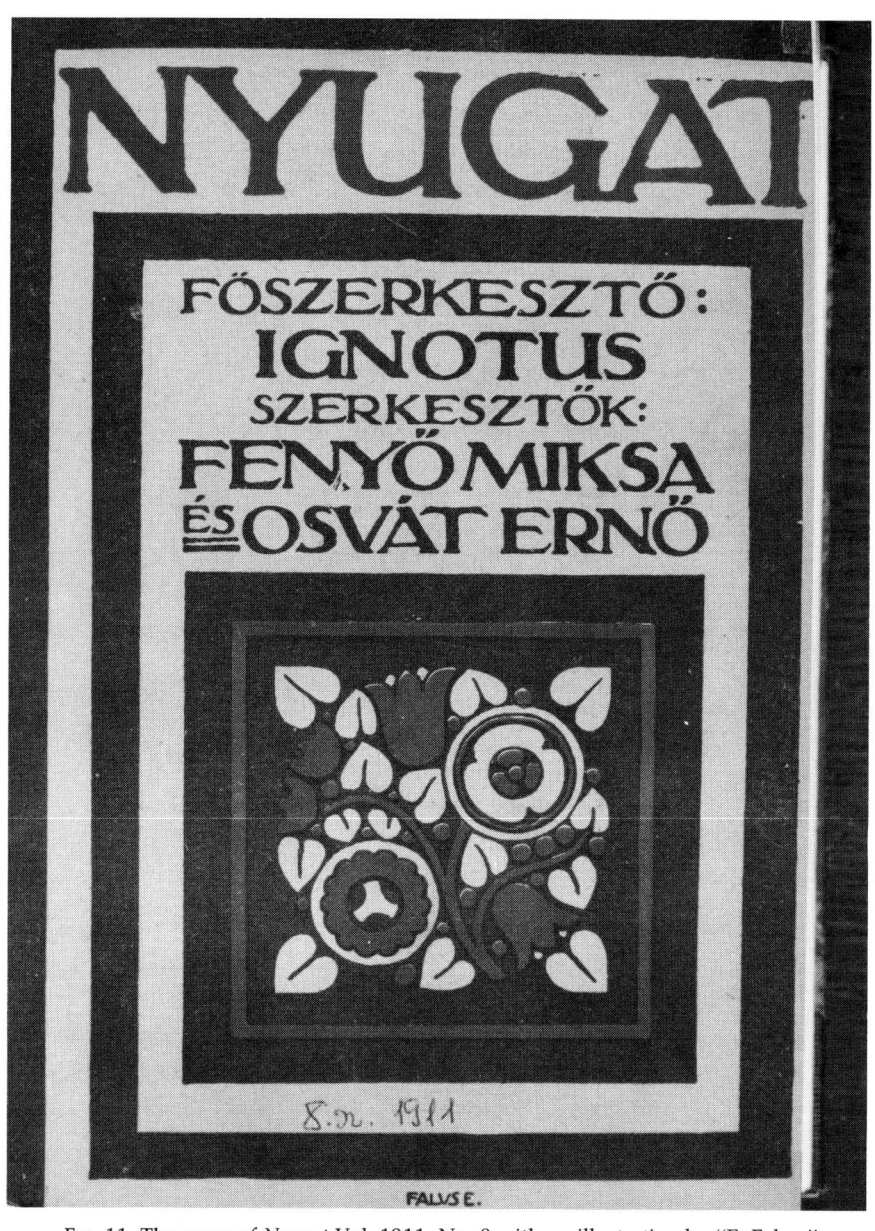

FIG. 11. The cover of *Nyugat* Vol. 1911, No. 8 with an illustration by "E. Falus."

FIG. 12. Pál (Paul) Igustus, the first editor-in-chief of *Nyugat*.

FIG. 13. Inside the Café Central at the turn of the century.

Fig. 14. The cover of *Nyugat*, July, 1911.

VI. NUMBERS AND LITERATURE[1]

The goal I had set for myself some years ago was to determine the relationship between the literary revolution of the turn of the century—in the Hungarian context—and the political revolutions of 1918 and 1919; more specifically, to measure the impact of that literature on the reading public, or some elements of it. Of course, the term "measure" need not imply the use of a yardstick; nevertheless, quantitative data, or statistics, are available and, if appropriately used, could minimize the subjective factors involved in this kind of analysis.

The following discussion is meant mainly as an illustration of what types of statistics can be marshaled to provide a modicum of "scientific objectivity" for the discussion of the topic. In particular, I have been able to gather four sets of statistics that seemed relevant.

The simplest of these, but also the least complete, refers to the circulation of the *Nyugat*, the periodical of the literary revolution. Systematic data pertaining to the first decade of the periodical, from 1908 to 1918, have not been found. By 1935 the account books could no longer be located.[2] It is still possible, however, that this kind of study might evoke some response, perhaps a more intensive search for the missing documents.

As the graph shows, there are but six or seven "facts" at our disposal, and even these are only estimates, the recollections of a few writers from within the Nyugat movement.[3] Nor is it possible to compare these figures, or control them against one another. The only exceptions here are the earliest figures, which do tend to confirm each other, and the datum provided by the daughter of the great novelist Zsigmond Móricz, which is not necessarily valid, inasmuch as Móricz himself was not yet involved in the editorial work. Thus we have to depend on the memory of a few witnesses; and I happen to know, better than anyone in the case of Max Fenyö, and

---

[1] This chapter is a revised version of "A viharmadarak; a haladó magyar irodalom és olvasóközönsége 1908-tól a forradalmakig" [The Stormy Petrels; Progressive Literature in Hungary and its Public from 1908 to the Revolutions], *Könyvtári figyelő*, 1977, nos. 3–4: 340–49.

[2] Lujza Farkas, *A Nyugat és a századeleji irodalomforduló* (Budapest: 1935), 42–43.

[3] The only figure that is not a "recollection" is taken from a letter of Fenyö to Hatvany, *Levelek Hatvany Lajoshoz* [Letters to Louis Hatvany], letter of 15 July 1913, 177. The sources for the other figures are: Oszkár Gellért, *Egy iró élete* [A Writer's Life] (Budapest: 1958) 1: 18, and *Kortársaim* [My Contemporaries] (Budapest: 1954), 63. Miksa Fenyö, *Följegyzések a Nyugat folyóiratról és környékéről* [Notes on the Journal Nyugat and its Environs] (Budapest: 1960), 63. Milán Füst, "A Nyugat születese" [The Birth of the Nyugat], *Irodalomtörténet*, 1959, nos. 3–4. Virág Móricz, *Apám regénye* [The Novel about My Father] (Budapest: Szépirodalmi, 1953), 122. Lujza Farkas, op. cit., 42–43. Márta Ruszinyák, "A Nyugat könyvkiadó" [The Nyugat Publishers], thesis, 1962, 5.

1. *Circulation of the* Nyugat *from 1908 to 1918.*

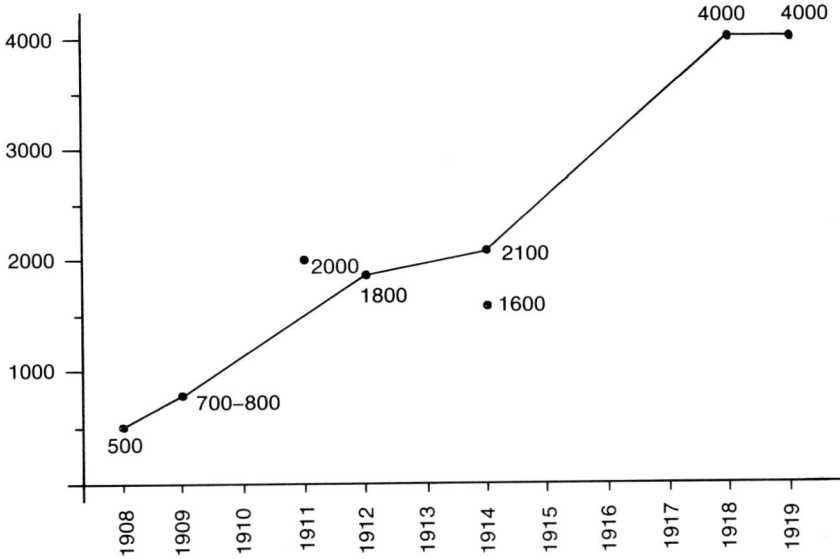

according to his own avowal, that memory is far from reliable, that, indeed, it may play us tricks.

Thus the data provided by the graph are not necessarily valid; such as they are, however, they tend to indicate that the influence of the *Nyugat* was growing, that it was being more widely read as the revolutions were approaching. It might even be argued that the periodical had become almost popular—by Hungarian standards, that is. For the reading public at the turn of the century was small, even in relation to the Hungarian-speaking population.

Subjective testimonies regarding circulation bear out the conclusion that it was rising. I have found several remarks to the effect that the number of subscribers was "on the increase,"[4] whereas I have met with no remark to the opposite effect (although ups and downs became the rule subsequent to 1919).[5] Witnesses assert that the journal had attained its widest circulation

---

[4] "The Nyugat people are doing the journal busily, though it always comes out with some delay—but they do claim that the number of subscribers is rising." Menyhért Lengyel to Hatvany, 18 May 1908, Akadémiai Irattár, Ms 385/f. "The subscribers keep gathering, every day we gain one or two . . ." Fenyö to Hatvany, 5 April 1908, *Levelek Hatvany Lajoshoz,* 30. On the other hand, Zoltán Horváth's statistics are pessimistic, but unwarranted: "In den Jahren vor 1914 würden von den Nyugat Nummern nur ausnahmweise mehr als 1,000 gedruckt, in der Regel begnügte man sich mit sieben bis achthundert Exemplären, von denen Teil unverkauft blieb oder als Freiexemplâre, die kein Mensch las, verschickt würden." *Die Jahrhundertwende in Ungarn* (Budapest: 1966), 409.

[5] Virág Móricz, op. cit., passim.

in the years 1917–18, not merely with regard to the first decade of its existence, but to its entire career, up to the end in 1941.[6]

For the sake of comparison: the *Huszadik század*, a progressive journal concerned with the social sciences, circulated in three to four thousand copies.[7] Among the forerunners of the *Nyugat*, the *Magyar géniusz*—"a tame family journal," according to Fenyö, "may have had up to 400 unsuspecting subscribers . . ."[8] The short-lived rival of the *Nyugat*, the *Renaissance*, launched in 1910, sent 468 copies of each issue through the mails by the end of that year;[9] to be sure, it had to stop publication shortly thereafter, presumably for lack of funds.

Bearing in mind that the population of Hungary decreased considerably in 1918, and that even the numbers of those speaking Magyar have diminished, the numbers of literate persons, and of those who actually read serious literature have increased over the past sixty or seventy years. Hence it is not surprising that recently, in 1973, the literary journal *Elet és irodalom* circulated in twenty-six thousand copies on the average, *Nagyvilág*, which carries translations of foreign literary products, in twenty-one thousand copies, and other literary periodicals, such as *Uj irás* and *Kortárs*, in well over ten thousand copies each, and that all these issues normally sell out in a matter of days.

If we look at other countries, in 1814 the *Edinburgh Quarterly* boasted of a circulation of thirteen thousand. It was rather the exception. In 1908, the year of the *Nyugat*, Ford Madox Ford also launched a periodical, called the *English Review*, but he was none too optimistic about its popularity: "to imagine that a magazine devoted to imaginative literature and technical criticism alone would find more than a hundred readers was a delusion I in no way had."[10] Across the Channel, the *Mercure de France*, perhaps the most important periodical of the ancien régime, rarely sold more than two thousand copies.[11]

Our second set of statistics refers to the reception accorded the works of Nyugat writers. My original intention was to pore through the dailies and periodicals published in Hungary to determine in what way, or to what extent these reacted to the works of the Nyugat writers from year to year, and to what extent they devoted space to literary events in general; in other words, to establish some kind of ratio between the reception of the Nyugat movement, and that of other literature, to works not produced by the Nyugat writers, in the press at large. I soon realized, however, that to pore

---

[6] Oszkár Gellért, *Kortársaim*, 170, and *Egy iró élete*, 1: 18.
[7] According to Tibor Süle, in 4,000 copies. *Sozialdemokratie in Ungarn: Zur Rolle der Intelligenz in der Arbeiterbewegung 1899–1910* (Köln: Bohlau, 1967), 170.
[8] Max Fenyö, op. cit., 12.
[9] State Archives, Budapest; ME 576 V (1910).
[10] Quoted by Malcolm Bradbury, *The Social Context of Modern English Fiction* (Oxford: Basil Blackwell, 1971), 183–84.
[11] Daniel Mornet, *Les origines intellectuelles de la révolution française* (Paris: Armand Colin), 147.

through more than eight hundred dailies and reviews printed in Budapest alone was likely to prove an overwhelming task. Fortunately, I discovered that the review *Irodalomtörténeti közlemények*—Bulletin of Literary History—while not a publication of the Academy of Science, nevertheless had a semi-official character, and included a regular column, called "repertory," or bibliography of Hungarian literature. This "repertory," published on a quarterly basis, retained a consistent format over the decade we are concerned with, for it was compiled by the same individual. It listed recently published literary works, reviews of these works, and articles or essays about particular authors, including the essays that appeared in the *Nyugat* itself. The same work is likely to be listed several times according to the number of reviews in the press, thus providing an indication of the degree of "receptivity" or "recognition."

These data, however, are also deficient. For one thing, the staff member in charge of this repertory could not search through every single daily or periodical any more than I could have. The fact that the same person was responsible for this information throughout the decade may make for consistency, but it also implies that the same criteria of selection, the same biases prevail. Furthermore, the tallying of reviews is purely a numerical analysis, a "numbers game." The repertory says nothing about whether a given review was favorable or unfavorable, long or short, worthy of its object or not. On the other hand, whether a review is favorable or unfavorable need not be a factor of crucial importance. There is evidence to show that even an unfavorable review may help in the dissemination of a given work, certainly more so than an indifferent review, or a review that has nothing interesting to say.[12]

Our second graph offers capricious evidence. It does not confirm the assumption that the popularity of the Nyugat movement rose steadily between 1908 and 1918, neither does it corroborate the evidence provided by the first graph, that the *Nyugat* as a periodical reached a peak of popularity in the two years immediately preceding the revolutions. At best, one may conclude that the press was most inclined to deal with modern Hungarian literature in the years 1909–10, and again in 1917. But here we must consider another factor which may considerably reduce the significance of these numbers: it is entirely possible that "acceptance" or "reception" is to some extent commensurate with publication statistics; it is entirely possible that it was precisely in 1909, 1910, and 1917 that the Nyugat writers were most prolific.[13]

---

[12] Q. D. Leavis, *Fiction and the Reading Public* (London: Chatto & Windus, 1965, 1st ed. 1932), 281. Also, Manó Mautner, "A kritika befolyása a könyvek kelendöségére" [The Influence of Reviews on Book Sales], *Csak szorosan,* 9, nos. 8 and 9 (September 1909): 3.

[13] But K. E. Rosengren has shown, in the case of Sweden in the 1880s and in the 1960s, that the change in the number of reviews is not commensurate with the number of books published. *Sociological Aspects of the Literary System* (Stockholm: Natur och Kultur, 1968), 37 ff.

2. The percentage of reviews dealing with the works of Nyugat authors, as reflected in the compilations of the *Irodalomtörténeti közlemények*.

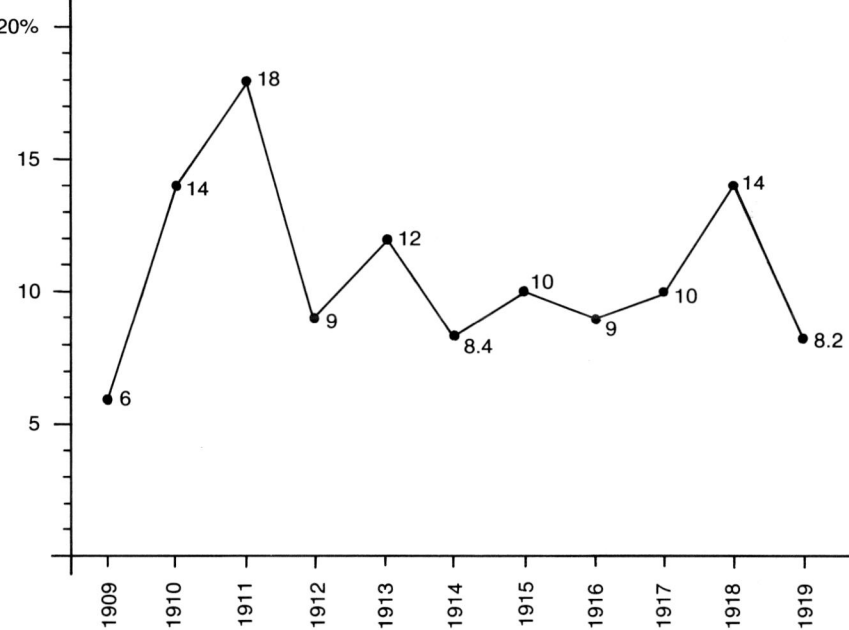

Our third set of statistics refers to the holdings of libraries. Here it is impossible to infer any kind of development, any historical trend in the period 1908 to 1918 on the basis of the available statistics. Yet we are fortunate in that printed catalogues happened to be the vogue at the beginning of the century, albeit more so in small libraries than in larger ones. These catalogues were printed mostly in the years between 1908 and 1913, and were printed but once. I have found only a few from the war years, perhaps because the manpower needed to compile them was not available. Even for the years 1908 to 1913 it is not possible to detect trends, since the catalogues refer to libraries where acquisition was particularly slow.[14] Five to ten years were needed until librarians would grow aware of the most modern literary products and began to acquire them. Thus, theoretically, we might expect the works from the beginning of the Nyugat era to appear on the shelves of libraries by 1918, but not much earlier. I was unable to check this hypothesis, however, because of the small number of catalogues from the last few years, and because the few catalogues that I

---

[14] With respect to the years 1907 to 1911 Béla Köhalmi writes that while the books and the libraries increased, reading did not, because the books "had been read already . . . The decisive factor in the decrease in reading was the neglect of the systematic acquisition of new works." *A Magyar Tanácsköztársaság könyvtárügye* [The Library Policies of the Hungarian Republic of Councils] (Budapest: Gondolat, 1959), 92.

3. *Holdings according to types of library in 1913, and in 1916–21.*

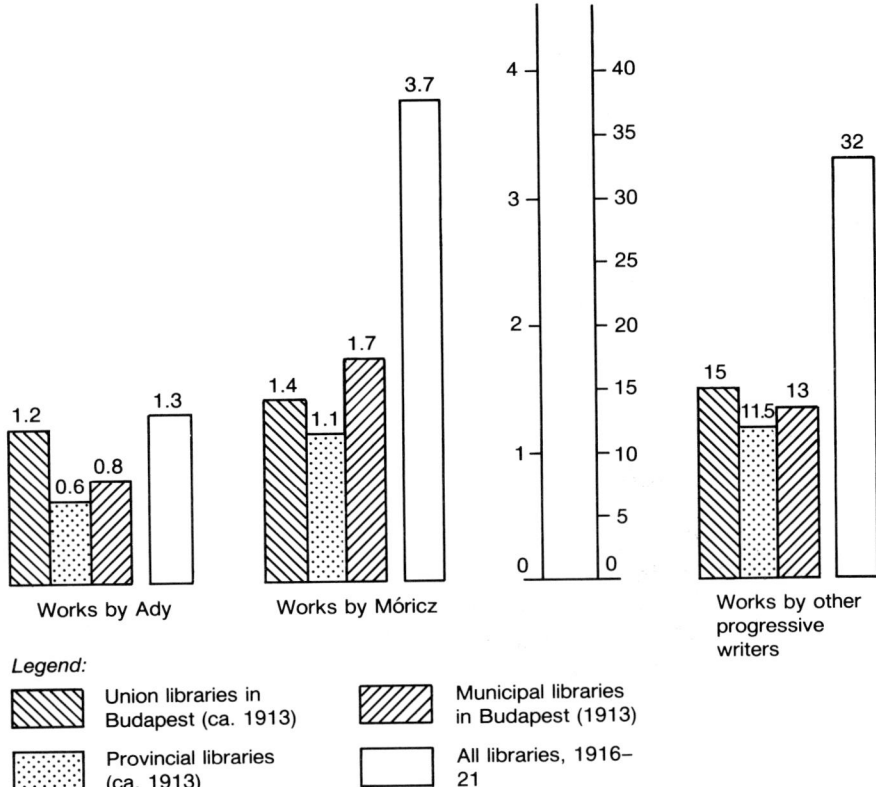

was able to find did not originate with the same libraries as the earlier ones.

I had a fairly wide choice of catalogues from the year 1913. For the sake of comparison I grouped the libraries into three categories: 1) labor union and "workers' libraries" in Budapest; 2) provincial libraries of all types; 3) miscellaneous libraries in Budapest, except workers' and union libraries.[15] In the first category the results are based on data from twenty-one libraries, and for the miscellaneous Budapest libraries on data from only six. In the case of the second category I performed a "random selection," since there was a large quantity of material available: in the case of each community (city or town), taken in alphabetical order, I selected the first catalogue printed in 1913. As regards the period 1916 to 1921, the graph is based on the data provided by eight catalogues, the sum total in the holdings of the Széchenyi National Library.

---

[15] The budget for libraries was not quite 0.01% of the municipal budget of Budapest, less than in most cities in Western Europe. Ervin Szabó, "Községi nyilvános könyvtár Budapesten" [Community Public Library in Budapest], *Városi szemle*, 3 (1910): 449.

The graph shows the frequency of distribution of the works of certain writers according to types of libraries and at two different dates.

Whenever data could be found regarding the number of times a given book was borrowed, these data tend to indicate that the taste of the reading public was by and large in harmony with the taste of librarians. To put it differently, library holdings and the preferences of librarians seem to have exerted a powerful influence over the readers' choice. For instance, in the year 1911 the novels of Mór Jókai and of Kálmán Mikszáth (two distinguished writers from the second half of the nineteenth century) were in the lead, both as regards the number of their volumes present in the libraries, and as regards the number of times these were loaned out.[16] The third favorite of the reading public was Géza Gárdonyi, although the number of his works on the shelves of libraries was far less, no doubt because he was much less prolific than the other two authors. As regards the number of volumes held, third place was occupied by Jules Verne; and had I taken children's libraries into account, Verne might well have come in first. Incidentally, Verne may not be as innocuous as he seems; Edward Teller, the nuclear physicist and "father of the hydrogen bomb," born in Hungary, claims that the works of Verne carried him "into a world of excitement. The possibilities of man's improvement seemed unlimited. The achievements of science were fantastic, and they were good."[17] It might be added that, in addition to the authors mentioned above, Miklós Jósika, Emile Zola, Ferenc Herczeg, and Sándor Brody seemed to enjoy the greatest vogue.

Thus it may be concluded that the reception accorded the progressive Hungarian writers, Ady and Móricz in particular, was none too encouraging; they were not among the most widely read, the most frequently sought authors. Ady had published ten volumes by 1913, mostly poetry, but only one or two of these was generally available in the libraries, and those were collections of short stories. According to our tabulation, union libraries were more likely to include volumes by Ady, and a slight increase in the dissemination of his works may be noted towards the end of the war. The works of Móricz—perhaps because they were novels—enjoyed somewhat greater popularity and, by the end of the decade 1908–18, they became almost three times as popular as they had been in 1913. This conclusion is supported by the data from Móricz's own records, according to which large quantities of his books had been printed by 1917 and, though they did not sell out, they sold quite well.[18] The third part of the tabulation indicates that the works of other progressive writers were again more frequently to be found in "workers' libraries," especially towards the end of

---

[16] István Kamarás, "Olvasóportrék 2000-ben" [Portraits of Readers in the Year 2000], *Könyvtári figyelő*, 1974, no. 6: passim.

[17] Quoted in William McCagg, *Jewish Nobles and Geniuses in Modern Hungary* (Boulder: East European Quarterly, 1972), 164.

[18] Móricz Virág, op. cit., 198.

the war. Among these the most popular were the works of those writers whose literary career began before the *Nyugat,* and who achieved relative popularity independently from that journal, although they can be said to be in general sympathy with the movement: first of all Zoltán Ambrus, followed by Gyula Krudy, Lajos Biró, and Jenö Heltai. All four were prose-writers who felt most at home in the "novella," the short story, the croquis. Their works offer no great complexities, and make for enjoyable reading to this day.

The public needed time to catch up with the "progressive writers," and with their critics. It should hardly surprise us that a generation or two had to pass before Ady, Babits, and Móricz could be appreciated at their true worth by the public at large. That is practically a tautology; and the lag in the acceptance by, let alone the enthusiasm of, the public is, indeed, proof enough that these writers and poets were the leaders of a literary revolution, were truly "in advance of their time!" At any rate, their works seem to have found but a faint echo even in the minds of those contemporaries who took the trouble to read them.

Among the less prolific modern writers it was the works of Ignotus that were most commonly available in the libraries, particularly his anthology, *Olvasás közben* [In the Course of Reading]. Once again, although Ignotus was at least the nominal editor-in-chief of the *Nyugat,* it should be noted that his writings were already known in the 1890s. Two volumes of pastiche by Frigyes Karinthy, best known to the public as a humorist, were printed in forty thousand and thirty thousand copies respectively, and sold out. It was possible to find, however scattered, one work or another by Margit Kaffka, Gyula Szini, Dezsö Szomory, Menyhért Lengyel—all stalwarts of the *Nyugat*—and even by György Lukács[19] in the various types of libraries.

Since Ady deserves more extensive treatment, both because of the power of his poetry and because of his political activism, let us take a closer look at the publication figures pertaining to his volumes. The friends of Ady, in their eagerness to come to his defence, have at times exaggerated the scorn heaped upon him. The fact is that Ady had become relatively popular even before the two political revolutions, before his death. Margit Kaffka, who considered Ady "crazy" in the colloquial sense of the term, testified that his books, "thank God, have always sold, and always sell, even in several editions: and they have their effect . . ."[20] A provincial journalist confirms Kaffka's appraisal: "If we are to believe the statistics issued by the publishing houses, Ady is being widely read in Hungary."[21] Unfortunately the journalist neglected to give the source of his information; I have found no relevant statistics from publishing houses. Ady himself testified that one of his collections of short stories had been printed in ten thousand copies, and one of his anthologies of poetry in twenty thousand. His volume

---

[19] *A lélek és a formák* [The Soul and the Forms].
[20] *Az élet utján* [Along Life's Path], Budapest: Szépirodalmi, 1971, 310.
[21] Bodog Halmi, "Ady Endre," *Máramaros,* 1910, no. 11 (6 February): 1.

of poetry, *Vér és arany* [Blood and Gold], first published in 1908, had reached its third edition by 1910, altogether three thousand copies.[22] Ady may have underestimated the number of copies, since we know that volumes of poetry by some other poets of the Nyugat, by no means more popular than Ady, were normally printed in fifteen hundred or two thousand copies each.

By the mid-fifties the works of Ady had gone through about five hundred editions. Today Ady is still among the three most popular Hungarian poets, although he is most appreciated, as he was in his lifetime, by the urban professional stratum. The best known and most appreciated poets today all died before the end of the Second World War, which shows that it takes a while for lyrical works to become familiar.[23]

Our fourth set of data concerns the rate of sale of works by Nyugat writers (Ady and Móricz not included). These data are derived from two inventories I have found among the records of the Révai Brothers publishing house.[24] The inventories had been compiled by the Nyugat Literary and Printing Company, Inc., with a view to selling their stock of books, at 13.5 percent of the regular retail price. The first inventory is dated 30 December 1915, the second was taken some time in May 1917, or about seventeen months later. The books in overstock had been published at different times and in various numbers of copies, but most often around two thousand copies for the first edition.[25] At any rate, by comparing the two inventories we can compare the rate of sale of particular works or particular authors within that period.

The best-selling work from the inventory was a volume of short stories by Gyula Szini with the luring title *Profán szerelem* [Profane Love]. Next came a rather difficult novel by Margit Kaffka, *Mária évei* [The Years of Mary], which sold 535 copies during this period. In third and fourth place we find two collections of short stories by Heltai, which sold 489 and 414 copies respectively. All six volumes by Heltai sold relatively well. The same can be said of the only volume by Karinthy, a collection of short short stories titled *Esik a hó* [It is Snowing], which sold 340 copies. Still relatively popular were a volume by Krudy, *Szindbád ifjusága* [Sindbad in his youth], with 303 copies, two volumes of poetry by Babits with 279 and 225 copies, a volume of short stories by Dezsö Szomory with 251 copies, a volume of poetry by Ernö Szép with 227 copies, another volume by Kaffka with 209 copies, and the *Taifun* [Typhoon] of Menyhért Lengyel, with 210 copies.

Starting from the other end, doing rather poorly, we find volumes of

---

[22] *Ady Endre összes prózai müvei* [The Complete Prose of Endre Ady], X (eds. Erzsébet Vezér and József Láng), Budapest: Akadémia, 1973: 111–12.

[23] For a valuable contemporary survey see Ildiko Erdélyi's articles, particularly "Hogyan és ki ismeri Adyt?" [Who knows Ady and how well?], *Népszabadság*, 19 February 1978.

[24] Hungarian State Archives, "Révai Testvérek," tétel Z 720.

[25] The Nyugat Company had published in the fiscal year 1910–11 fourteen volumes "by the most significant writers of the *Nyugat*, which were then sent onto the book market in 30,000 copies altogether." Memorandum found in the Archives of the Cégbiroság, Cg 628.

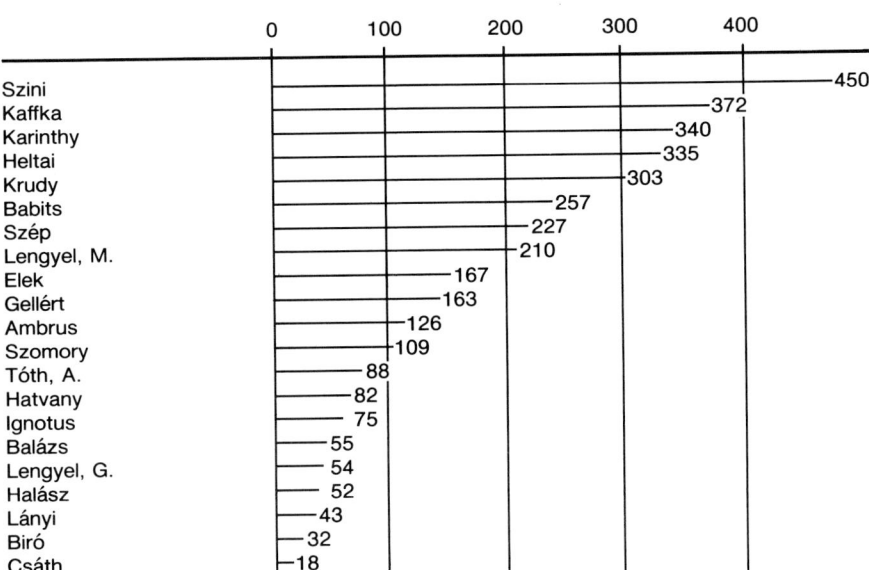

4. *Number of copies sold from December 1915 to May 1917 by the Nyugat publishing house.*

(When the stock included more than one work by a given author, I have taken an average.)

poetry by Wanda Tóth, with 11 copies, and by Anna Lesznai with 19 copies. A volume of short stories by Géza Csáth also sold 18 copies, a book by Lajos Biró sold 32 copies, a volume of poetry by Sarolta Lányi with 43 copies, a volume of essays by Lajos Hatvany with 38 copies, a volume of poetry by Balázs with 55 copies, and a historical survey by the veteran historian Halász with 52 copies.

What conclusions may we draw from these sales figures? With the possible exception of Szini, the best-selling books were by authors of high distinction. Modern critics would agree that Babits, Kaffka, Karinthy, and Krudy fully deserve such a rating, even if not necessarily with those particular works. It is curious, but perhaps not altogether unfair that, except for Kaffka, the women poets did rather poorly—Lesznai, Lányi, and Wanda Tóth are all toward the bottom of the list. Lesznai was to achieve stature and distinction with her autobiographical novel *Kezdetben volt a kert* (At the Beginning Was the Garden) published much later.

All these data, however, leave the basic issues moot; they certainly do not prove that progressive literature exercised a profound impression on the masses. Nor do they prove, on the other hand, that there was no connection between the literary revolution around 1908, and the political revolutions of 1918–19. The quantifiable data do not even prove, or disprove, that the Nyugat movement was increasingly a part of national and political awareness.

If I nevertheless must venture some kind of conclusion, it can only be that the statistical and quantitative approach does not allow final conclusions. Partly, of course, because the quantifiable data are sparse and incomplete—as, indeed, they are likely to be whenever the subject is literary influence some time in the past. I will also concede that our results may be inconclusive because of my limited knowledge of methods and techniques. The results are inconclusive, furthermore, because it is not possible to create the data most needed, the compiler or analyst must adapt his questions to the extant data, rather than the other way around; something along the order of administering an IQ test to Blaise Pascal! But, first and foremost, no final conclusions may be drawn simply because we are dealing with a social phenomenon that cannot be subjected to numerical reductionism.

VII. THE NYUGAT AND THE INTELLECTUALS

To proceed in my analysis, let me divide Hungarian society into classes or "consensus groups" and select a few of these for examination. Let us disregard, for the time being, the criteria used in this selection; the "groups" I have selected are the "intelligentsia," the "establishment," and the proletariat. We are concerned with the reception of the *Nyugat* by each of these groups.

This chapter will deal with the response of the intellectuals. Let us, by all means, avoid debates about definition. I have found my own, self-serving one: for purposes of this analysis intelligentsia is taken not in its usual East European sense—the professionals and certain categories of administrative or white-collar workers—but will be taken to refer to the progressive intellectuals. Hence, I will exclude those actively in the service of the regime, even though they may have had pretensions to intellectuality;[1] for they were seldom progressive and, in any case, they will be included in the following chapter, under the label "establishment." It must be conceded, however, that the relationship between progressive intellectuals and members of the establishment was not invariably one of conflict; in fact, there was some overlap.

To use a teleological approach, by progressive intellectuals I mean by and large those who could be identified with the revolution of October 1918. Hence it would be useless and redundant to ask: did these intellectuals eventually support or participate in the revolution? Even here distinctions are in order; while a handful of progressive intellectuals stood aloof from all revolutionary activity, the intellectual vanguard of the proletariat also backed Count Mihály Károlyi—i.e. the October revolution—in the first days of the new regime.

Perhaps a more productive and accurate method of identification would be to list the organizations and movements to which the progressive intellectuals belonged, in which they were active. These are, in approximate chronological order:

The review *Huszadik Század* and the Society of Social Scientists, founded in January 1900 and January 1901, respectively.

---

[1] "The man with a diploma, the government official, may remain content his entire life without ever purchasing a book, and without ever reading anything but a damned interesting novel, and even that only out of the most desperate boredom," wrote Babits, speaking through the mouth of his hero, Imrus. *Halálfiai*, 455–56.

The Free School organized by the above Society in 1902, but formally established only in 1906.

The Thália dramatic company, which lasted from 1904 to 1909.

The MIENK, the Circle of Hungarian Impressionists and Naturalists, organized in October 1907. Their first exhibit opened in January 1908. The Circle consisted of twenty-nine artist members in 1910.

The Martinovics Lodge of the Freemasons, established on 27 May 1908.

The Galilei Circle of the University of Budapest, founded on 22 November 1908.

The feminist organizations.

The Nagy Endre cabaret from 1909.

Another association of painters, the Eight, having their first exhibit in December 1909, but officially organized on 13 April 1911.

The daily *Világ*, which began publication in March 1910.

Various organizations promoting universal suffrage. The first of these was the League for Universal and Secret Suffrage supporting the program of József Kristoffy, founded on 27 August 1905. The National Association for the Right to Vote was established in April 1910, followed by the National Reform Club, an alliance of progressive forces primarily concerned with the extension of suffrage, formed on 9 November 1910. Another League for the Right to Vote was organized during the war in 1917; this League actually became the base of the National Council that was to seize power on 30 October 1918.

The UMZE—The Association for New Hungarian Music established in 1911.

The Bourgeois Radical Party founded on 29 May and 6 June 1914.

The Free Union of Teachers in Hungary, formed in November 1906 (officially recognized in 1910) and the Reform Party of the Teachers Union [Tanáregyesületi Reformpárt], a shortlived organization founded on 10 June 1914.

The "Sunday Circle" around György Lukács and Béla Balázs beginning in 1915.

The membership of these organizations came to some three thousand activists, bearing in mind that the members were wont to be active in more than one organization at a time. Thus Oszkár Jászi assumed a leading role at the review *Huszadik Század*, in the Society of Social Scientists, at the Free School of the Social Sciences, in the Martinovics Lodge, with the Bourgeois Radical Party, and with the daily *Világ*. Endre Ady was a member of the Martinovics Lodge, the Bourgeois Radical Party and, of course, was the star and even the editor of the *Nyugat*. To repeat, there were perhaps three thousand persons, and possibly a few thousand more, who gave them passive or moral support.

Let us take a closer look at some of these organizations or movements from the point of view of their ties to the Nyugat or to its individual writers.

a. The *Thália company* had its theater closed down for business reasons, rather than because it represented a "fire hazard,"[2] shortly after the *Nyugat* was launched. In the meantime, however, it had done good work. Its explicit objective was to introduce modern literature, in the guise of drama, to the Hungarian public. With a single exception, a full-length play by the would-be Nyugat writer Menyhért Lengyel, all the plays in its repertoire were by non-Hungarian authors: Ibsen, Gerhardt Hauptmann, Franz Wedekind, the greater and lesser stars of turn-of-the-century European literature. György Lukács was one of the founders of the company, at age nineteen, but then it should be remembered that he came from a prominent banking family, and could afford to indulge. He was to claim, in an article commemorating the fiftieth anniversary of the foundation of Thália, that it was the only one of the modern cultural "movements" that made a deliberate attempt to reach the working class.[3] This attempt took the form of special discount tickets for performances in "working-class districts" advertised as performances for the workers. The company gave sixty-one such performances, of which forty-six were in 1908–09, during its last season.[4]

b. The cabaret of *Endre Nagy,* opening around Christmas 1909 and lasting until 1913 was, in a sense, the successor of the Thália. It was a cabaret rather than a theater, that is it presented humorous skits rather than drama, but these were often sophisticated. The most regular contributor to the cabaret was the Socialist writer Béla Révész, but Ady, Lajos Nagy, and other Nyugat writers participated as well.[5] Even though the cabaret was a typically "bourgeois" institution, a deliberate effort was made to attract the working class.

c. The alliance with progressive art movements was openly sought by the Nyugat. In a letter to Lajos Hatvany, in 1909, Ignotus wrote:

We must tie ourselves to all so-called "modern" movements, whether in the theater, in music, in painting, or even in the social and political spheres. . . .[6]

Thus, it was no accident that the Nyugat publishing company undertook to print the memoirs of József Rippl-Rónai, the most distinguished "modern" artist of this period, rather than the memoirs of Gyula Benczur, or of some other more or less conventional disciple of the great nineteenth-century master Mihály Munkácsy.[7] Among the best-known works of Rippl-

---

[2] The fire hazard version is cited by Arato and Breines, op. cit., 11.
[3] "A Thália alapitásának 50. évfordulójára" [For the Fiftieth Anniversary of the Foundation of Thália], reprinted in *Magyar irodalom-magyar kultura,* 574 ff. Also, Ferenc Katona and Tibor Dénes, *A Thália története* [The History of Thália] (Budapest: Müvelt Nép, 1954).
[4] Katona and Dénes, op. cit., 155.
[5] Lajos Nagy to Zoltán Nagy, 19 August 1909, "Nagy Lajos levelei Nagy Zoltánhoz" [Letters of L. Nagy to Z. Nagy], *Kritika* (June 1977), 3.
[6] Letter of 28 October 1909, in *Levelek Hatvany Lajoshoz,* 78–79.
[7] Zoltán Horváth, who is the source of this observation, added that there developed, in-

Rónai we find pastel portraits of Zsigmond Móricz, Mihály Babits, Csinszka (Ady's wife), and a number of other Nyugat personalities. The most violent attack against István Tisza in the *Nyugat* came in response to the latter's incompetent criticism of the work of Rippl-Rónai: Tisza is too small, wrote Dezső Szabó in 1911, to diminish Rippl-Rónai's stature by even the breadth of a hair.[8]

d. Although Rippl-Rónai was not formally a member of a "school" (apart from the loosely organized MIENK—a group of "impressionist" and "naturalist" painters), the artists of Nagybánya, of the MIENK, and of the Eight were indebted to him. A noteworthy aspect of the development of modern art in Hungary was its parallels with literary trends (I do not mean that this is a peculiarly Hungarian phenomenon, but a readily observable one). For example, French styles and style-setters such as Impressionism or Cézanne were assimilated belatedly, as were contemporaneous literary styles. In France Impressionism had run its course by 1886, whereas "post-Impressionism" lasted until 1906. The paintings of the Nagybánya school, and even of Rippl-Rónai, or of the Eight, may seem anachronistic if viewed in the context of comparative art history.[9] After all, the Fauves had exhibited at the Salon d'Automne in 1905 and 1907, and a year later Picasso and Braque had already hit upon Cubism. Yet the Hungarians are not anachronistic if compared to the contemporaneous group of "the Eight" of Prague; is their similarity mere coincidence, or the product of a parallel evolution, a similar milieu?

Although the MIENK did not have a specific program beyond that of bringing together modern Hungarian artists (rather similar, in its lack of dogmatism, to the Nyugat), the art it sponsored turned out to be largely Impressionist, as witnessed by their exhibit of 17 January 1908. Even the future Nyugat poet Béla Balázs complained that "foreign influence" pervaded their work.[10] The group of the Eight, although still heterogeneous, went a step beyond the MIENK, of which it was an outcropping.[11] They sponsored something like an artistic revolution. Again, the network, "the alliance of revolutionary forces," becomes evident. It was György Lukács who delivered an address at the opening of the first exhibit of the Eight. The leader of the group of artists, Károly Kernstok, performed a function

---

tentionally or spontaneously, a united front. *Die Jahrhundertwende in Ungarn (1896–1914)* (Budapest: Lüchterhand, 1966), 409.

[8] This "Open letter to Tisza" was the first of Szabó's writings to appear in the *Nyugat*, 4 (1911), No. 1: 812; Tisza's attack had appeared in the *Magyar Figyelő*.

[9] Yet Rippl-Rónai did not "ape" Degas, Monet, Renoir, and Van Gogh, as Professor McCagg intimates, any more than the eminent Impressionists aped one another in general. *Jewish Nobles and Geniuses in Modern Hungary*, 45.

[10] Diary of Béla Balázs, Akadémiai Irattár, Ms 5023/16.

[11] The Eight were Róbert Berény, Dezső Czigány, Béla Czóbel, Károly Kernstok, Ödön Márffy (Ady's friend and Csinszka's second husband, after Ady's death), Dezső Orbán, Bertalan Pór, and Lajos Tihanyi (who painted several portraits of Ady). Anna Lesznai, writer and artist, has been mentioned as a ninth member of the group; among her works are cover

parallel to that of Ady who, incidentally, was his close friend.[12] Kernstok wrote for the *Nyugat*, was an active member of the bourgeois radicals, and was preoccupied by the issue of "proletarian art."[13] Reproductions of works by the Eight appeared at frequent intervals on the pages of the *Nyugat*.

  e. It is likewise no coincidence that *Béla Bartók's* name was so often mentioned in the periodical. He had cooperated on at least one Nyugat matinée. His concerts were regularly and favorably reviewed in the periodical. His genius was most fully recognized by Géza Csáth in a review published in the 16 January 1909 issue of the *Nyugat*.[14] In 1910 another music reviewer of the periodical compared the Bartók-Kodály team to Goethe and Schiller: "great artistic talents often come in pairs. . . ."[15] The *Nyugat* printed the entire score of "Allegro Barbaro" (of 1911), composed on a pentatonic scale, as a special insert to one of its 1913 issues. The authors of the libretti for Bartók's operas and ballets came from the ranks of the Nyugat: Béla Balázs wrote the libretti for "Bluebeard's Castle" and for the "Wooden Prince" (published in the 1912 volume of the journal), whereas Menyhért Lengyel wrote the erotic story of the "Miraculous Mandarin" (published in the 1917 volume of the journal).

  In December 1906 Kodály and Bartók published a selection of the folk music they had collected over the years in a volume titled "Hungarian Folksongs for Voice with Piano Accompaniment." In its preface they wrote: "The overwhelming majority of Hungarian society is not Hungarian enough, not cultured enough, and not naive enough to allow these songs to find room near their heart." Eventually, however, they overcame their apparent ethnocentrism to develop a deep concern for the musical expression of neighboring, and even of distant peoples. In 1919, during the Republic of Councils, Bartók, Kodály and Dohnányi were to form the "Music Directorate" of the revolutionary regime.

  f. Modern Hungarian music received some kind of an organizational base with the foundation of UMZE in 1911. While this club included conservative musicians, its guiding spirits were Bartók, Kodály and other innovative composers. In vain, however, did UMZE sponsor Bartók's concerts, and in vain did the music critic of the *Nyugat* wax enthusiastic; the audiences showed but scanty appreciation.[16]

  In fact, it is entirely appropriate to list Bartók and Rippl-Rónai, to mention only two artists in "related branches," as part of the Nyugat movement; and it would be almost incongruous to speak of "influence" or "interaction"

---

designer for the *Nyugat*. *Georg Lukács; Selected Correspondence, 1902-1920,* eds. Judith Marcus and Zoltán Tar (New York: Columbia U. Press, 1986), 126.

[12] Krisztina Passuth, *A Nyolcak festészete* [The Art of the Eight] (Budapest: Athenaum, 1967), 14.

[13] See *Nyugat*, 3 (1910): 99 ff.

[14] József Ujfalussy, *Bartók Béla,* (Budapest: Gondolat, 1976).

[15] *Nyugat*, 3 (1910), No. 1: 474.

[16] Paul Griffiths, op. cit., 66–67. See also *Magyarország története*, 50 and 57.

among new literature, new art, and new music; since it is a matter of one and the same movement, questions of precedence are irrelevant.

  g. Nor are questions of precedence much more significant when it comes to the literary revolution and the revolution in the social sciences. Did the social scientists "think progressively" before the creative artist or writer had begun to think progressively? Did the analysis presented by one social scientist or another open the eyes of some among the Nyugat, or was it, on the contrary, the spontaneous, perhaps instinctive revelations of some writer or poet that opened the eyes of the progressively inclined social scientist? Which type of innovative intellectual is closer to the "base," which is more liable to promote or hasten change by raising the consciousness of the masses, or of the bourgeoisie? Is it the social scientist, or the writer-artist?

  The *Huszadik század,* the journal of the sociologists, not only started eight years before the *Nyugat,* but achieved a larger circulation in spite of its scientific pretensions: at one time it sold as much as four thousand copies per issue, a circulation the *Nyugat* was able to achieve only in 1917–18.[17] Nevertheless, the role of the two reviews was not dissimilar; the *Huszadik század* was concerned with more than just social science, the *Nyugat* with more than simply literature: "the two together expressed more deeply than any political program the complete opposition to the Hungary of the ancien regime. . . ."[18] To be sure, it had been the *Huszadik század* that opened the siege against the ancien regime; certainly, the journal would deserve a treatment as extensive as this one and accessible to the Western reading public. But the task of making the abstract insights of the social scientists, to paraphrase Houghton Stuart Hughes, more concrete and more readily approachable devolved on literature; nor was literature merely borrowing from the social sciences: "it has fed its own discoveries back into the social theory in a dense interplay of mutual influences."[19]

  The two reviews shared a number of contributors. Ignotus was on the editorial board of the *Huszadik század* as well, whereas a number of social scientists wrote for the *Nyugat.* György Lukács, although sometimes identified with the *Huszadik század* in his pre-Marxist period, published at least as frequently in the *Nyugat.* The majority of the essays eventually collected in *The Soul and the Form* first appeared in the *Nyugat* between 1908 and 1910[20]—all the more remarkable as Lukács spent a great deal of time abroad, commuting between Heidelberg, Berlin, and Florence. Lukács achieved an unparalleled (and unintended) feat, by having two contributions published in the same issue of *Nyugat*—that of 1 Oct 1908. He may have complained

---

[17] Tibor Süle, op. cit., 170.
[18] *A szociológia elsö magyar mühelye,* 1: 7.
[19] Houghton Stuart Hughes, *Consciousness and Society* (The Reorientation of European Social Thought 1890–1930) (London: MacGibbon & Kee, 1959), 21.
[20] Andrew Arató and Paul Breines, *The Young Lukács and the Origins of Western Marxism* (New York: Seabury Press, 1979), 11. Some of Lukács's letters to Osvát are published in *Georg Lukács; Selected Correspondence 1902–1920,* eds. Judith Marcus and Zoltán Tar (New York: Columbia U. Press, 1986).

that the Nyugat was not radical enough, that Osvát had rejected those of his manuscripts which expressed his social views most clearly; but this complaint came as an afterthought, long after Osvát and the *Nyugat* were gone, after the Second World War.[21] It was not so much a love-hate relationship with the Nyugat, as Arnold Hauser claimed,[22] but perhaps a streak of dogmatism on the part of Lukács during the Stalin period. Yet, at the same time, Lukács confided to his friend Béla Balázs that the two of them—Balázs and Lukács—had stood to the right of the Nyugat in certain respects.

h. The *Society of Social Scientists* had 1,158 members in 1907, after the ouster of the conservative half in the summer of 1906. Those who remained, it may be presumed, were progressive or even radical intellectuals.[23] In Ady's words, pronounced in 1905, that is even before the split, the Society was "the oasis in the Hungarian Sahara."

In 1912 the Society devoted two months to a debate on the relationship between society and literature. The sessions were so well attended that the conference room of the Society proved exiguous most of the time. The introductory presentation was delivered by Ignotus; other speakers included Mihály Babits, Ernö Osvát, Aladár Schöpflin, Dezsö Szabó, Gyula Szini—to mention only those from the Nyugat.[24] The content of the debate was not particularly memorable. What is significant was the importance attached to this relationship by the Society, and the impetus it gave to the sociology of literature, a branch of sociology in which Hungarian-born thinkers have earned particular distinction.

i. Another significant undertaking sponsored by the Society was the *Free School of the Social Sciences*. The Society and the *Huszadik század* had sponsored courses for the benefit of workers as early as October 1902, with as many as 2,013 students attending regularly.[25] In the spring of 1906 the Free School became an independent and officially authorized institution. Almost free of tuition, it was also free in the sense that it was open to persons who held no diploma of any sort; the School made special efforts to reach the workers by means of publicity through labor unions and socialist papers. Among the occasional lecturers we find Ignotus, Béla Balázs, Lajos Biró, Miksa Fenyö, Lajos Hatvany, Ernö Osvát, Dezsö Szabó, Aladár Schöpflin—I have made no effort to compile a complete list.[26]

The question of motivation arises in connection with any worker-oriented

---

[21] Lukács's somewhat uncomplimentary remarks on Osvát are to be found in *Magyar irodalom-magyar kultura*.

[22] *Találkozásaim Lukács Györggyel* [My Meetings with György Lukács] (Budapest: Akadémiai, 1978), 46. According to Lukács himself, the "love-hate" relationship was with Osvát; in fact, it was "love-hate" at first sight. Lukács, *Record of a Life* (London: Vesco, 1983), 41.

[23] Tibor Süle, *Sozialdemokratie in Ungarn,* 170. Ferenc Fehér points out that few, if any, of the Society's members could be described as "Socialist" in any sense of the word. Op. cit., 323.

[24] *A szociológia elsö magyar mühelye,* 1: 529.

[25] Mucsi Ferenc, "A polgári radikalizmus Magyarországon, 1900–1914" [Bourgeois Radicalism in Hungary], *Történelmi Szemle,* 1977, No. 2: 301–302.

[26] For instance, see the program of the Free School in *Népmüvelés,* 12 (February-April 1911): 236–38.

movement or organization. Was the Free School devised and used to raise the consciousness of the workers? The choice of lecturers makes it clear that this could not have been its purpose; but neither do I have evidence to show that the Free School was deliberately coopted to mislead the working-class.

j. The political profile of the University of Budapest is proof enough that professionals, or persons with diplomas were not, for the most part, progressive—hence need not be discussed in this chapter. The University was a stronghold of academic conservatism. It was unusual for professors in the Hungarian Department even to refer to contemporary literature. A few, such as Dr. Gyula Pikler, albeit not a Socialist, caused scandal (rather than sensation), by expressing progressive notions in the course of lectures.

Eventually, however, the students manifested their impatience by founding a progressive organization, the *Galilei Circle*. This Circle was to expand rapidly, and its influence went even beyond its numbers. It had 256 members at its inception,[27] but was to comprise about 10 percent of the student body within two or three years.[28] It was founded by Ernö Seidler, who was to become one of the founding members of the Hungarian Communist Party as well in 1918; he was, incidentally, brother to Lukács's great love, Irma Seidler, who was to commit suicide in 1911. Like Seidler himself, the students came largely from the Jewish lower middle class or petite bourgeoisie, and they were needy, as students are wont to be; it is not likely, therefore, that a significant number of them could afford to subscribe to the *Nyugat* (even though the subscription rates were relatively low). Some members of the Galilei Circle may even have considered the *Nyugat* rather bourgeois, rather *dépassé*, more like a journal that belonged in their parents' drawing-room; after all, Young Budapest, writes Professor McCagg, evinces a cosmopolitan modernity which contrasts sharply with the social behavior of the Jewish capitalists, parochial and old-fashioned by most standards;[29] but such considerations certainly did not apply to Ady and, on the whole, the Circle can be included among the allies of the Nyugat movement.

Strong ties developed between Ady and the Galilei Circle, at least after 1910, when Ady was first requested to participate in its annual March celebration. Ady received the Circle's invitation while relaxing on the French

---

[27] Márta Tömöry, *Uj vizeken járok* [I walk on New Waters] (Budapest: Gondolat, 1960), 41–42. The title of this study about the Galilei Circle is actually the title of a poem by Ady.

[28] Pál Horváth, "Haladó ifjusági mozgalmak egyetemünkön a XX. században" [Progressive Youth Movements at our University in the Twentieth Century], *Felsőoktatási szemle*, 10 (1961), Nos. 1–2: 61. In 1910 there were 11,680 students enrolled at universities around the country, most of them at Budapest. *Magyar statisztikai évkönyv*, új folyam XVIII (1910), (Magyar Kir. Központi Statisztikai Hivatal, Budapest, 1911), 389. During the academic year 1911/12 there were 6,962 students enrolled at the University of Budapest, almost half of them at the Faculty of Law. *Magyarország története*, "kultur-történet," 25. The membership rolls of the Galilei Circle were found and published by János F. Varga, "A Galilei Kör névsora 1912-ból" [The Rolls of the Galilei Circle from 1912], *Történelmi szemle*, 19 (1974), No. 1–2: 211–33.

[29] *Jewish Nobles and Geniuses in Modern Hungary*, 44.

Riviera, and he seriously considered interrupting his holiday to honor the invitation.[30] He sent a poem instead, a gesture he was to repeat for five consecutive years.[31]

By way of example, in 1911 the program of the March celebration of the Circle included the following twelve items: three poems by Ady recited by different performers; speeches by Arthur Székely, the president of the Circle, by Lajos Biró, a writer from the Nyugat and a radical journalist, and by Oszkár Jászi; items pertaining to two progressive French writers, Anatole France and Edmond Rostand; one poem by Petőfi; a workers' song; and the Marseillaise[32]—in other words, an overwhelmingly literary program in which the poetry of Ady played a conspicuous part. Jolán Kelen, a militant member of the Circle, writes in her memoirs that "we were all enthusiastic about Ady. Not only because of the novelty and richness of his language, but especially because what he said seemed to blow from our own soul."[33]

The Circle was closed down by the police on 12 January 1918; there followed mass arrests of members active in the antiwar movement.

k. The daily *Világ* began publication in March 1910, with an average circulation of about twenty thousand, but "with an influence far beyond the publication figures"[34] (*nota bene,* this observation has been so often repeated, with reference to the Galilei Circle, to the *Nyugat*, and to other publications, that one is instinctively inclined to question its validity). The program of the *Világ*, as defined in its first issue on 30 March 1910, was "uncompromising free-thinking," a democratic, free Hungary, universal, secret, and equal suffrage, completely progressive taxation, and secularization. It was, in fact, the organ of the left wing of Freemasonry, as its political opponents seldom failed to point out. The *Világ* reviewed each issue of the *Nyugat*, and always approvingly. Ady, Kosztolányi, Karinthy, Kaffka—to mention only the most distinguished from the Nyugat—were among its regular contributors.

The *Világ* was the organ of the bourgeois radicals, not yet a political party, and Ady its most distinguished contributor. József Révai and Michael Löwy have both noted the dichotomy in Ady's politics: on one hand a revolutionary bourgeois democrat, on the other an artist who despised the bourgeoisie.[35] They might have added, however, that he was invariably a supporter of Socialist causes; the contradiction was merely on the surface.

---

[30] Ady to Fenyö, 16 March 1910. *Följegyzések és levelek a Nyugatról* [Notes and Letters Pertaining to the *Nyugat*], ed. Erzsébet Vezér (Budapest: Akadémia, 1975), 283.

[31] Zsigmond Kende, *A Galilei Kör megalakulása* [The Formation of the Galilei Circle] (Budapest: Akadémia, 1974), 123–24. Also Márta Tömöry, op. cit., 72.

[32] Márta Tömöry, op. cit., 179.

[33] Jolán Kelen, *Eliramlik az élet* [Life Speeds By] (Budapest: Kossuth, 1976), 38–39.

[34] Béla Dezsényi and György Nemes, *A magyar sajtó 250 éve* [250 Years of Hungarian Press], (Budapest: Müvelt Nép, 1954), 1: 235.

[35] Michael Löwy, *L'évolution politique de Lukács 1909–1929* (Lille: Université de Lille III, 1975), 120.

l. Ady gave full support to the Bourgeois Radical Party, and even ran for elections on the party ticket. In addition to Ady, a number of Nyugat writers were to be found among the organizers and activists of the party: Lajos Biró, Géza Lengyel, Károly Kernstok, Endre Nagy, the scholar in jurisprudence Rusztém Vámbéry, Aladár Kuncz and György Bölöni, both specialists in French literature. The party's program was rather similar to that of the *Világ:* general suffrage, democratization, a radical land reform, laws to control monopolies, radical tax reform, secularization of education, separation of church and state. With regard to the nationalities, implementation of the progressive law of 1868—use of the mother tongue in cultural and administrative matters—but federalism specifically rejected as a solution.[36] The closest equivalent of the Hungarian bourgeois radicals may have been the "National-sozialer Verein" of Friedrich Naumann in Germany, which included Thomas Mann and Friedrich Meinecke among its partisans; or the "Generación del 98" in Spain, which counted Miguel de Unamuno among its stars.[37]

m. Ady's interest in Freemasonry dates back to his Nagyvárad period. Having lost interest in the movement because of its conservative politics, he was to return to it in 1912 for the sake of Oszkár Jászi and the bourgeois radicals. He joined the Martinovics Lodge, named after a Hungarian revolutionary and "conspirator" of the period of the French Revolution. Indeed, the lodge was the most politicized and radical of all Freemason lodges. It was founded in June 1908 by Oszkár Jászi and seven other dissident members from another lodge.[38] The ubiquitous Jászi remained its guiding spirit, provoking clashes between his Lodge and the Grand Lodge. The Lodge was actually the nucleus of the Radical Bourgeois Party, and the activities and membership of the two organizations overlapped to a large extent. The records of the Lodge indicate that it gave financial support to a number of progressive organizations, including the Galilei Circle, the Free School of the Social Sciences, the League for the Right to Vote, the *Világ*, to which the members were obliged to subscribe, and even the *Népszava*, the daily of the Social-Democrats, which the Lodge undertook to mail to soldiers in the trenches during the war.[39]

The Lodge, which swelled from 74 members in 1912 to 342 by 1918, included a number of writers, all of whom belonged to the inner or outer circles of the Nyugat. Gyula Szini had already joined the Lodge in 1909; he was followed, in 1910, by Lajos Biró, who eventually became grandmaster of the Lodge; Géza Lengyel in 1910; also in 1910, Béla Reinitz, who set many of Ady's poems to music; György Bölöni, literary critic, friend, and biographer of Ady, in 1911; Ady himself in 1912; Endre Nagy in 1912;

---

[36] *Magyarország története,* 11: 80–81.
[37] Ibid., "Kulturtörténet," 111.
[38] *Kelet,* 20 (20 June 1908): 226.
[39] As per letter of 1 April 1916, from the Martinovics Lodge to the Grand Lodge, Országos Levéltár, Records of the Martinovics Lodge, P1123.

Aladár Schöpflin in 1915. Géza Csáth, the music critic of the *Nyugat*, was also an active member, although I was not able to discover the date he joined.[40] Miksa Fenyö must also have been a member, or else his name could not have been crossed off the rolls in 1918. Nor could I find the reason for the disciplinary action, but I surmise it was because of his record of poor attendance. Subsequently he repeatedly declared, contrary to evidence, that he had decided not to join the Freemasons, because the organization was childish and because—as he told those who urged him to join—"my wife allows me to stay out in the evening without having to use the Lodge as an excuse."[41]

Clearly, then, there were several points of contact between the Martinovics Lodge and the Nyugat; the accusation of Freemasonry leveled against the *Nyugat* as well as against the *Világ* was not without foundation. A separate research paper could be written about the role of Freemasonry in hastening or delaying the revolutionary process.

n. The Sunday Society was a small group of intellectuals which met regularly during the war, from 1915 on, usually in the flat of Béla Balázs; the Society was actually a salon of sorts in which the main subjects of conversation were philosophy and literature. "We never discussed politics," reminisced Arnold Hauser, one of the regulars of the Society.[42] The participants included, at one time or another, Frigyes Antal, Béla Fogarasi, Lajos Fülep, Tibor Gergely, Arnold Hauser, Edit Gyömröi, Juliska Láng, Anna Lesznai, György Káldor, Ernö Lörsi, György Lukács, Károly Mannheim, Mihály Polányi, László Radványi, Emma Ritóok, Ervin Sinkó, Vilmos Szilasi, Károly Tolnay, John Wilde, and the first and second wives of Balázs, Edit Hajos (later known in the West as Edith Bone, the author of *Seven Years in Jail*), and Anna Slamadinger.[43] There were writers, philosophers, economists, art historians, sociologists of art, about half of whom were to achieve international fame! At least four of them, namely Lukács, Balázs, Lesznai, and Ritóok, had published in the *Nyugat*. The memoir-writers all concur: Lukács set the tone for the Society and its participants.

The Free School of the Humanities was an offspring of the Sunday Society. It functioned for two semesters, in 1917 and 1918, in a school building in Budapest.[44] The audience averaged around seventy. Prime Minister István Tisza was among the audience, without an escort of bodyguards, on at least one occasion.[45] The keynote lecture of the series was delivered by

---

[40] Országos Levéltár, Martinovics Lodge, P1123.

[41] Fenyö, *Följegyzések* . . . , 33.

[42] Quoted in Eva Fekete, "Lukács György az elsö világháború éveiben" [Lukács in the Years of the First World War], *Valóság*, 1977, No. 2: 37.

[43] For an incomplete list see Michael Löwy, op. cit., 142–43. For a penetrating discussion of the Society see Mary Gluck, *Georg Lukács and His Generation 1900–1918* (Cambridge: Harvard U. Press, 1985), Ch. 1.

[44] Anna Wessely, "A Szellemi Tudományok Szabad Iskolája és a Vasárnapi Kör" [The Free School of Humanities and the Sunday Circle], *Világosság*, 16, No. 10 (October 1975): 613–20.

[45] Communication of Dr. Henry Lax to author.

Károly Mannheim, published later under the title *Lélek és kultura* [Soul and Culture].[46] Of all the lecturers who participated only Ervin Szabó and possibly Frigyes Antal could be considered to have had a Marxist approach at this early stage.

o. The Reform Party of the Teachers Union came into being in the summer of 1914, but the war disrupted its activities before it had a chance to achieve lasting results. A loose association of radical teachers (by radical I do not mean extreme left) had already developed in late 1906, and received official authorization in 1910, by which time it comprised several hundred members; among them were Aladár Kuncz, Marcell Benedek, Dezső Szabó, and Géza Lackó—Nyugat writers, and teachers by profession. When the association was banned some radical politicians organized a protest and collected twenty-one signatures on a petition, including that of Ady, Balázs, Lajos Biró, and Jászi.[47] In fact, even the more conservative and more inclusive Nation-Wide Union of State Teachers elected a Social Democratic president in 1912.

These were at least some of the organizations that took part in the struggle to bring about a modern Hungary. These "Young Hungarians" were not proletarians and, with few exceptions, were not in direct contact with the working class. They represented a network of progressive intellectuals.

In addition to the interdependence and interrelationships between the Nyugat and the above listed organizations, it is reasonable to assume that, by and large, the subscribers and readers of the periodical came from their ranks. As a further generalization, let us assume that a majority, if not an overwhelming majority of these progressive intellectuals were of Jewish extraction. If this second assumption is correct, the probability of the first increases, as we shall see below. The second assumption is supported by considerable circumstantial evidence, as well as evidence presented by witnesses. Fenyö, who knew his constituents well, claims that two-thirds of the readers of the review were Jewish.[48] Aladár Schöpflin, a contributor to the *Nyugat* from the start, also identified the readership of the review as mainly Jewish (in his history of modern Hungarian literature).[49] An examination of the rosters of the aforementioned organizations would show that their membership was likewise predominantly Jewish; over 90 percent of the members of the Galilei Circle, to take but one example, were Jewish or of Jewish extraction.[50] As pointed out in preceding chapters, a disproportionate number of Jews occupied certain professions: journalism, the

---

[46] Budapest: Sinkó Publishers, 1918.

[47] "Invitation of 10 December 1910," Országos Levéltár, Martinovics Páholy, P 1123.

[48] The remainder came from the Christian middle class. Miksa Fenyö, *Följegyzések* . . . , 63.

[49] Aladár Schöpflin, *A magyar irodalom története a XX. században* (Budapest: Grill Károly, 1937), 149.

[50] Ady was accused of being the "honorary goy" in the Galilei Circle. *Magyar Kultura*, 1913, No. 1: 463–64.

law, and medicine in particular. Hence it would be admissible to approach the problem of the reception of the Nyugat from an ethnic point of view.

Let me, however, proceed with my analysis: to determine the impact of the Nyugat on the category of progressive intellectuals. Take Oszkár Jászi, who played such a prominent role in the preparation of the October 1918 revolution and who was to become the Minister of Nationalities and Count Mihály Károlyi's right-hand man in the revolutionary government. Ady had given vent to his appreciation of Jászi's work on a number of occasions. He had referred to Jászi's review and Society, as oases in the Hungarian Sahara. He welcomed Jászi's book about nationalities and the formation of nation-states with enthusiasm: "in our nationalities problem, in this most visceral problem of ours, Jászi has found the Archimedal point of democracy," he wrote in the *Nyugat*.[51]

Jászi returned the compliment several times. He pointed out, back in 1914 that, just as Petöfi, rather than Kossuth or any other statesman, symbolizes the aspirations of the revolution of 1848, the future historian will have to deal with Ady to understand the crisis of Hungary at the beginning of the twentieth century.[52] Later, in his book on the revolutions of 1918–19, after enumerating "the heroes of the age," Jászi added:

> The last name in this review is that of one man who in himself counts for more than the work of whole organizations—the poet Andrew Ady, whom the proud Napoleonic dictum fits well: *L'empereur = cent mille hommes.* . . . His sublime visions, his flaming pictures, the lash of his prophecies and warnings were among the most powerful driving forces of the revolution. . . .[53]

And in his necrology of Ady, Jászi reiterated: without a doubt, future historians will see in the poet "the true prophet of the revolution and of a new Hungary"—at a time when it seemed the new Hungary was already under way.[54]

Mihály Károlyi was not particularly interested in literature, and perhaps does not fit into the category of "intellectual" as I have defined it. But he became Hungary's head of state as a result of the revolution of October 1918, the ultimate leader of the groups of individuals I described in the first part of this chapter, the foremost exponent of the political program they advocated. Lajos Hatvany testifies that he saw works by Ady, Babits, Kaffka, Karinthy, Szép, Kosztolányi, Móricz, Szomory, and Árpád Tóth on Károlyi's writing-desk. When queried about them Károlyi explained that both he and his wife read these works and had discovered a whole new world through them. For a long time these books had been the only man-

---

[51] *Ady Endre összes prózai müvei* [The Complete Prose Works of Ady], Vol. 10, eds. József Lang and Erzsébet Vezér (Budapest: Akadémia, 1973), 193.

[52] Lee Congdon, "Endre Ady's Summons to National Regeneration in Hungary, 1900–1919," *Slavic Review*, 33, No. 2 (June 1974): 305.

[53] *Revolution and Counter-Revolution in Hungary* (New York: Howard Fertig, 1969, 1st ed. 1924), 27.

[54] *Világ*, 29 January 1919. Reprinted in *Mindenki ujakra készül*, 2: 356.

ifestations of democracy, radicalism, progress: "I recognized that the literature of innovation had preceded innovating politics. . . . It was a pity that thought and action should have to walk apart."[55] Károlyi, the politician, recognized the particular significance of Ady no less than Jászi, the intellectual: "Our ideas," he wrote in his memoirs, "were also served with his whole genius by Andrew Ady, the immortal poet of the renascence of revolutionary Hungary."[56]

Once again Ady has been singled out; but at least one historian of literature remarked, without hesitation, without ambiguity, yet with some exaggeration, that the Nyugat in general had "prepared the Károlyi revolution insofar as literature was concerned"; it was, he claimed "the official review of the Károlyi regime."[57]

How did the writers view their own role? What political or social influence did they exert on one another? Did they take a stand with regard to "involved" literature? To what extent did they accept the political leadership of Ady (insofar as this leadership can be abstracted from his literary preeminence), and to what extent did they consciously reject it?

The results of a poll of eighty-seven writers and artists of note, taken by Béla Köhalmi towards the end of the First World War, may be considered relevant. Those polled were asked about their favorite authors, foreign or Hungarian. Ady was mentioned twenty-four times, *ex aequo* with the nineteenth-century poet Vörösmarty, ranked after Flaubert, but ahead of Heine and Ibsen. Among Hungarians only Arany, Mór Jókai, and Sándor Petöfi were mentioned more often. Móricz was mentioned eleven times and Mihály Babits ten times; no other Hungarian writer was mentioned more than ten times.[58]

György Lukács (not consulted for the poll) was among the first to acknowledge Ady's spiritual leadership:

Ady's decisive influence upon me reached its climax in that he never for a moment compromised with Hungarian reality. . . . I felt a yearning for such an ideology [Weltanschauung] already during my teens, but I was unable to conceptualize and generalize these feelings in my own way.[59]

In his recollections, *Record of a Life,* he states that his encounter with Ady's poetry, in 1906, was a turning point in life.[60] Presumably, Lukács found his feelings conceptualized in Ady's work. Although Lukács wrote this confession in 1969, it was not a matter of hindsight, for he described essentially the same feelings, in less analytical form, in 1909: "The whole

---

[55] Lajos Hatvany, *Emberek és korok* [Men and Periods] (Budapest: Szépirodalmi, 1964), 2: 241–42.
[56] *Fighting the World: the Struggle for Peace* (New York: Albert & Charles Boni, 1925), 266.
[57] Antal Szerb, *Magyar irodalomtörténet* [History of Hungarian Literature] (Budapest: Magvetö, 1972, 1st ed. 1935), 435.
[58] *Könyvek könyve* [The Book of Books] (Budapest: Lantos n.d., ca. 1918), passim.
[59] *Magyar irodalom-magyar kultura,* 3: 8 (Introduction).
[60] G. Lukács, *Record of a Life* (London: Verso, 1983), 39.

ageless poetry of Ady, the only one that matters in its social influence, is the most profoundly moving in its humanity, the most excitingly modern in current literature."[61] Two years later he noted that although Ady may have had no decisive artistic influence on the generation of contemporary poets, such vehemence and intensity must have had considerable, and even determining effect on something: "an effect that excites, that prompts action, or scares away from action."[62] This is all the more interesting because, in his later work, Lukács seldom broaches the problem area of the perception of a literary work's effect upon its public.

Many writers and critics have claimed credit, or have been given credit, for being the first, or "among the first," to recognize Ady's genius. If we immerse ourselves in "the spirit of the times," i.e. into the contemporary press, however, we come to the conclusion that very few had understood Ady before 1907, before the publication of *Vér és arany* [Blood and Gold]. Is it mere coincidence that the *Nyugat* started publication at the time when critics were beginning to respond to Ady's poetry? Even those who were to form the Nyugat movement had not always understood, had not necessarily responded positively before the movement itself. Certainly not Babits, certainly not Kosztolányi. Yet their college classmate and friend, Gyula Juhász, had responded with fervor from the beginning. As early as 1904, in his review of the year's literary production, Juhász singled out two rising poets: the Socialist Sándor Csizmadia (who was to consider Ady, a few years later, as a rival and a negative political factor), and Endre Ady.[63] In 1905, in connection with the publication of *Uj versek* [New Poems], he described Ady as the greatest Hungarian poet.[64] About the same time, or somewhat later, he wrote to Dezsö Szabó as follows:

I call your attention to our movement which will mean a new literature, a new art, and a *new history* [italics mine] for Hungary. Endre Ady has already broken in at the gates and we have already begun our conquest of the country. The Hungary of the *föispán* [lieutenant governors of the provinces] and of the *föszolgabirók* [chief magistrates of the provinces], the Hungary of Tisza is already dead. We are the reality: we Michelangelo, Balzac, Monet, Cézanne, Zola, Ady, Baudelaire, Gyula Juhász.[65]

And Juhász hailed the appearance of the *Nyugat* in 1908—as he had hailed the appearance of the *Figyelö* in 1905—as the coming of saviors. He reviewed each issue of the *Nyugat* in a daily at Szeged, where he taught high school, doing his utmost to boost the review's circulation.[66]

History itself, claimed Juhász, was undergoing renewal. Ady and com-

---

[61] Ibid., 52.
[62] From "A vándor énekel" [The Traveling Singer], 1911, ibid., 72.
[63] *Juhász Gyula összes müvei* [The Complete Works of Juhász] (Budapest: Akadémia, 1968), 5: 17.
[64] *Juhász Gyula összes müvei*, 5: 64.
[65] Quoted by Dezsö Szabó, *Életeim* [My Lives] (Budapest: Szépirodalmi, 1965), 2: 232.
[66] *Juhász Gyula összes müvei*, 5: 207–08, 231, 236.

pany were the persons destined to "blow up" the old regime; they were the brave young men who could not be restrained from exposing its abuses. Who were Ady's "company"? There was Lajos Biró, a "quiet and courteous revolutionary, a rebel with style. . . ."[67] There was Juhász himself who, next to Ady, was most sensitive to the relationship between politics and literature, and consistently attributed to literature an important social and national mission.[68] The revolution was around the corner, and it was up to the poet to announce its coming. The writer must act as a kind of seismograph, registering and predicting the tremors before anyone else, keeping "his people" on the alert, as Nikos Kazantzakis wrote.[69] And Juhász: "Some beasts can feel the earthquake coming, but there will be an earthquake, whether some beasts feel it coming or not."[70]

There may have been a dozen writers and critics who were aware of Ady's significance from the time of his second volume of poetry; and one of these was Béla Balázs who, despite his militarist posture in August and September of 1914, had shown sympathy to the socialist cause, insofar as he bothered with politics at all. He too had written a letter to Szabó calling attention to the *Nyugat,* around which a bunch of talented poets and writers had congregated, the "young Hungary!"[71]

Another critic to recognize Ady's genius early, although not without hesitation, was Lajos Hatvany. Hatvany recognized not merely Ady's literary genius, but his political significance as well. Drawing a parallel between the roles of Ady and of Sándor Petőfi, Hatvany wrote in 1910:

> Petőfi had as little to do with the revolution (of 1848) as Ady will have to do with the rebirth of our country. . . . Yet the appearance of Ady is still the only important, the only interesting occurrence in this land of drooping acacias. Because, although the poet can never be the cause of events, he is their infallible sign of warning. . . .[72]

that is, if he is a poet; and if he is infallible.

As mentioned, at one time Babits reacted in a negative and petty manner to Ady's verse, and to Ady's person. Did he stem from an old Magyar family? Babits had raised the question in a notorious letter to his classmate Kosztolányi (in whom he knew he would find the proper echo). "But even if he does, he should touch the topic [Hungary] only with reverence."[73]

---

[67] *Juhász Gyula összes művei,* 303.
[68] *Magyar irodalomtörténet,* 5: 304.
[69] Peter Bien, "Nikos Kazantzakis (1883–1957)," in *The Politics of Twentieth-Century Novelists,* ed. George A. Panichas (New York: Hawthorn Books, 1971), 141.
[70] Quoted in *Magyar irodalomtörténet,* 5: 303.
[71] Dezső Szabó, *Életeim,* 2: 221.
[72] Reprinted in Lajos Hatvany, *Emberek és könyvek* [Men and Books] (Budapest: Szépirodalmi, 1971), 209.
[73] Letter 21 February 1906. *Babits-Juhász-Kosztolányi levelezése* [The Correspondence between Babits, Kosztolányi, and Juhász], ed. György Bélia (Budapest: Akadémia, 1959), 114. It is perhaps ironic that while Babits could claim noble ancestry—and was proud of it—some thirty years later another distinguished Hungarian writer, László Németh, undertook to classify writers into two categories, the "deep-blooded" and the "superficial-blooded" Hungarians,

Thus Babits's initial response was the same as that of the conservative critics. Soon enough, however, Babits was to admit that Ady stood head and shoulders above everyone else; at the same time Babits would divest himself of his ethnic pride, of his nationalism, of his well-nigh reactionary stance with respect to contemporary literary currents. (Several times in his life Babits was to whitewash himself after having adopted a perilous course: after the publication of his first antiwar poems, and after his involvement with the Republic of Councils of 1919. One might accuse Babits of hypocrisy, were it not for the fact that I know, because it is obvious, that Babits was the most courageous, the most honest intellectual in those difficult times.)

In his lectures at the University of Budapest in 1919, under the Republic of Councils, Babits was to claim that a literary revolution may often become a cause of a political one; and that revolutionary change had appeared in Ady's poetry long before it had appeared in politics. When Ady wrote his visionary "Vizió a lápon" [Vision in the Marshland] in 1906, or earlier, nobody in Hungary could have guessed that a revolution was in the offing.[74] In 1930 Babits was to recall that what the young writers around the Nyugat had in fact intended, was to arouse the classes of the despised against their own—presumably the gentry, the bourgeoisie.[75] In the words of Christopher Caudwell (who paraphrases Marx), the bourgeois writer was acting in accordance with his future interests, rather than his present ones, in easing the path of the revolutionary process.[76]

It is hardly necessary to insist that Babits's analysis, or his memory, was at fault. For one thing, Babits's family background was not the rule: most Nyugat writers were not the scions of the gentry, nor were their parents well-to-do bourgeois, but rather petit-bourgeois and, not infrequently, "working-class."[77] Furthermore, class struggle was not what the Nyugat writers had in mind in 1908, or even in 1918.

---

possibly in order to deny Babits (whose surname is Serbian) the status of "deep-blooded" Hungarian writer. See also Zoltán Horváth, *Jahrhundertwende in Ungarn*, 391–92.

[74] Notes taken by a university student during the lectures, published in *Mindenki ujakra készül*, 4: 871 ff. Ady's poem reads, in part:

". . . Talán vulkán hegyekre lépel / Vérvörös büszke lobogóval / És torlaszok fölött süvöltök / Rombolni hivó bomba-szóval, / A büntengert szabaditom föl, / Hogy kiszakitson nádat, tölgyet, / Hogy végtöl-végig hömpölyögjön, / Hogy megtisztitsa jól a földet, / Hogy tobzodjék a rég veszteglö, / A gátra szomjas akarat . . ."

[75] Lajos Hatvany, *Emberek és könyvek*, 296–97.

[76] "In a bourgeois society most of the artists will be bourgeois artists . . . and faced with a revolutionary situation they can take the side of either the bourgeoisie or the proletariat—after a time they can no longer sit on the fence. Some of the bourgeois ideologists desert the bourgeoisie 'to defend their future interests,' and this is reflected in their poetry." Quoted in David N. Margolies, *The Function of Literature* (New York: International Publishers, 1969), 106.

[77] Out of fourteen writers taken at random, eight came from the petty-bourgeoisie or the working-class. In the same period only 8 percent of writers in France came from peasant or "working class" background, and another 8 percent from the "idle aristocracy." The respective figures for England were 8 and 18 percent. Robert Escarpit, *Sociologie de la littérature* (Paris: Presses Universitaires, 1959), 44.

At about the same time, in 1932, when Babits became editor-in-chief of the *Nyugat* (and was to remain its editor until his death and the death of the *Nyugat* itself in 1941), he reminisced about the early years in even more sanguine terms:

> We were leftists, that is to say, we were part of the opposition. . . . We were united in one thing: we were rebels and revolutionaries even when, especially when we clung most tenaciously to the roots of Hungarian traditions. . . .[78]

In the same vein, Aladár Schöpflin was to comment: "Nobody had more to do with the revolution of the Hungarians than Ady, not even those who made it."[79]

In her novel *Mária évei* [The Years of Mary] Margit Kaffka places the following words into the mouth of a young teacher of Hungarian literature, commenting on a sample of modern poetry:

> "Look, here is this poem . . . it seems nothing serious, does it? Who would take such a thing seriously? But we have never read anything like it, in such a style, so strange! Finally we accept it, and the rest of the stuff that goes along with it. . . ." And some time, in ten years, these belabored souls—adds the author—may become the breeding ground for a political, a social revolution.[80]

Such must have been Kaffka's notion of the function of modern poetry, of the poetry of Ady, or of her own.

I could go on for a hundred pages discussing, author by author, their concept of the function of literature; as for the reception of the work of Nyugat writers by other Nyugat writers, I could present another thousand pages of evidence. What I have actually done, however, is to present merely a sample; a sample of the writers' opinions about themselves, about their own or one another's political significance, about their own or one another's historical calling. To this sample we might add the editors' statements discussed in a previous chapter (although, to be sure, these statements were usually programmatic rather than analytic, projections for the future rather than interpretations of a process). They are a contribution to the interpretation of the role of the Nyugat, a contribution based on introspection. What is more, this introspective evidence originated with persons who, because of their sensitivity as writers, are or should be peculiarly qualified to understand themselves and see through others. Hence, despite their obvious bias, despite the natural tendency of any craftsman or professional to consider his craft or profession more important than it objectively is, I would nevertheless attach special weight to the testimony of writers when assessing the role of literature in general, and of the Nyugat in particular.

Where did all this lead? How did these writers react personally to the

---

[78] "A Nyugat régen és most" [The Nyugat Then and Now], *Nyugat*, 25 (1932): 70.

[79] Quoted in Lajos Hatvany, *Emberek és könyvek*, 312.

[80] Quoted by Aladár Komlos, *Vereckétöl Dévényig* [From Verecke to Dévény] (Budapest: Szépirodalmi, 1972), 286.

revolutions of 1918 and 1919? In what ways did the writers fulfill the role they had, on occasion, assigned to themselves?

On 29 October 1918, the Social Democrats reprinted a poem by Zseni Várnai titled "Katonafiamnak" [To My Soldier Son], originally published in 1913, during a strike. Várnai was not a member of the Nyugat, probably because her poetry seldom hit the mark, but she had collaborated with the "Holnap" and maintained friendly relations with a number of Nyugat writers. The poem, reprinted as a poster, elicited enthusiastic interest. Soldiers, workers, and others walked with leaflets on the streets, the whole city resounding with the poem's rousing refrain: "Don't shoot, my son, because I too will be there"—meaning at the anti-government demonstration![81] The demonstrators entered cafés and mounted a table or a chair to recite the poem; the guests would rise to their feet and join the demonstrators.

On the whole, the Nyugat writers regarded the regime following the October revolution as their own. Although identification with the Republic of Councils that followed seemed far less logical, only a few stayed aloof even then (Fenyö, Karinthy). Yet I have run across a number of contemporary complaints to the effect that "there was no new Petöfi on the scene, and the power of verse is small indeed" (excerpt from a poem that appeared in a daily on 3 November 1918, while Ady was still alive!).[82]

Proof of the activity of the Nyugat writers during the revolutions is contained in the four volumes and three thousand pages of *Mindenki ujakra készül* [Everyone Prepares for New Things], an anthology of contemporary literary production; however voluminous, it includes but a fraction of the literary works of value.[83]

The writers participated to different degrees, and with different degrees of conviction. Gyula Krudy, who had remained apolitical all along, accepted the editorship of a newspaper, and headed a committee to rename the streets of Budapest.[84] Nothing shows better that the Socialist and Communist leaders recognized the significance of the role of the Nyugat than the fact that they appointed Ernö Osvát, a non-writing critic, who had distinguished himself almost solely as the editor of the periodical, to the position of overseer of literature.

Mihály Babits had been a reluctant, hesitant "revolutionary" all along. Nevertheless, he was rewarded with an appointment to the chair of Hungarian literature at the University of Budapest under the October regime, and remained as sole editor of the *Nyugat* for a while. Babits actually occupied the chair only after the proclamation of the Republic of Councils. True, he was to publicly recant, during the White Terror that followed the

---

[81] Vilmos Böhm, *Két forradalom tüzében* [In the Crossfire of Two Revolutions] (Budapest: Népszava, n.d.), 44.
[82] *Mindenki ujakra készül*, ed. Farkas József (Budapest: Akadémia, 1959), 1: 43. A similar complaint was aired by Gyula Krudy a few days later. Ibid., 63 ff.
[83] See above.
[84] *Magyar irodalom története*, 5: 380.

revolutions, in an article likewise published in the *Nyugat,* under the title "A Hungarian Poet in Nineteen-Nineteen"; he nevertheless had to suffer demeaning forms of persecution.

Margit Kaffka died, a victim of the Spanish flu, barely a month after the October revolution. She had, however, made her profession of Socialist faith. Witness a letter in which she gave her estimate of Oszkár Jászi: "I am a Socialist, and he a bourgeois radical, which I feel is like squaring the circle, and he is not overly bright anyway. . . ."[85]

As for Zsigmond Móricz, he took part in the labors of the revolution with enthusiasm, gathering data about life in the country in preparation for the land reform that never came. He too was to pay dearly for his dedication to the revolutionary cause. He was interrogated, persecuted, excluded from literary societies during the early years of the counterrevolution.[86] No wonder he would argue later that writers should abstain from all political activity: if a writer takes a political initiative, that initiative is bound to fail, because writers have no sense of politics.

As readers of Lukács are wont to know, he was appointed Commissar of Public Education, even though he had joined the Communist Party as late as December 1918 (partly as a result of his failure to secure a post at Heidelberg).

The "Directoire of writers" functioning under the Commissariat of Public Education, headed by György Lukács, comprised the following members: Babits, Balázs, Lajos Barta, Lajos Biró, Lajos Kassák, Aladár Komját, Zsigmond Móricz, Ernö Osvát, Béla Révész, Gyula Szini, and Lukács *ex officio.* Only three (Barta, Komját, and Révész) were outside or to the left of the Nyugat movement, Kassák being an ex-Nyugat member.[87]

With what degree of conviction did the writers carry out the revolutionary function assigned to them? I will not even attempt an answer. It is not too significant, but still worth a mention, that in the book edited by Oszkár Gellért as a sort of memorial to the October revolution,[88] only one out of the seventy-five writers who contributed testimonials openly claimed to be a Socialist: Lajos Nagy. To be sure, there were a number of Socialists among the seventy-five, but they did not feel the need to emphasize the point, they did not feel any pressure to conform politically; hence it is not unreasonable to assume that their collaboration was by and large sincere. The memorial book, incidentally, included the photographic portraits of those writers who "participated in the preparation of the revolution": Ady, Babits, Móricz, Biró, and Gyula Pikler (Professor of Law and president of the Society of Social Sciences after its radicalization in 1906).[89]

---

[85] Quoted in *Magyar irodalomtörténet,* 5: 237.

[86] Ibid., 179.

[87] *Mindenki ujakra készül,* 4: 336.

[88] *A diadalmas forradalom könyve* [The Book of the Glorious Revolution], ed. Gellért Oszkár (Budapest: Légrády, 1919). For the role of Lajos Nagy, see Pál Kardos, *Nagy Lajos élete és müvei* [The Life and Works of Nagy] (Budapest: Bibliotheca, 1958).

[89] *A diadalmas forradalom könyve.*

VIII. THE NYUGAT AND THE WORKING CLASS

It should be clear from what precedes that the *Nyugat* was not designed for the "working-class," and that Socialism was not its political creed (insofar as it had one). In fact, the journal became the subject of attacks not only from the right but also, occasionally, by the *Népszava*, by Kassák and his avant-garde reviews, and from other leftist quarters. Nor did these attacks cease with the publication of the *Nyugat* itself; it took a while for the present Socialist regime of the Hungarian People's Republic to recognize its achievements, rather than dismiss it as a vehicle of bourgeois literature.[1]

The *Nyugat* was not intended for the working-class; yet, in the course of investigations bearing upon the readership of the journal, upon its reception in various quarters, I was able to collect quite a bit of information on the theme of the Nyugat and the working-class, more than enough to write a chapter. To make sense of the data collected, however, is another matter.

Did the workers read at all?

On the one hand, there are contemporary comments about the lack of literary culture among the proletariat; a lack, it is usually recognized, resulting from the miserable living conditions, from the exploitation of the workers, from their backwardness even in relation to the proletariats of Western European states. Their circumstances were similar to those of workers in nineteenth-century France: and how could they, "spending twelve to fourteen hours a day on the job, find time to read?" asks a French sociologist.[2]

On the other hand, I have found a number of comments claiming the opposite; comments to the effect that the Hungarian worker was thirsting for culture, that he grabbed the few opportunities offered him and made the best of them, that he exhibited a deep, albeit instinctive appreciation for the "higher things of life."

A good example of such positive evaluation is the following review of a performance by the Thália company—a special performance for workers. The author of the review was Gyula Szini, son of a Socialist, who was part of the Nyugat movement from its beginnings. The play under review is Ibsen's *Nora* [*A Doll's House*] as performed on an evening in December 1906:

---

[1] See the reprint of an essay dated 1952 which refutes the attacks against the *Nyugat:* Aladár Komlos, *Vereckétől Dévényig* (Budapest: Szépirodalmi, 1972), 279.

[2] Nicole Robine, in "Lettura," *Letteratura e societá*, ed. Robert Escarpit (Bologna: Mulino, 1972), 201.

If the intellectuals, the students, the aristocracy of money and of the mind have no use for Ibsen and Strindberg, how could I even think that the working class, which has no opportunity to prepare its mind for the reception of new intellectual currents, might become a grateful and understanding public for the productions of modern literature. Yes, if the play should have a direct bearing upon the issues of the workers' subsistence, if it should reveal the misery into which the worker has been thrust in his struggle against capital, if the poet should become a spokesman for the interests of the workers. . . . But *A Doll's House*? . . . I am delighted to confess that I very much underestimated the public of these "workers' performances." Because that public did understand Ibsen, clearly and instinctively. I took pleasure in the performance, and a thousand times greater pleasure in the public. . . .[3]

The emergence of the Nyugat coincided with the rise of the Social Democratic Party and of the labor unions in Hungary. Although far behind the West and even Austria, the proportion of industrial workers was on the increase, and so was their class consciousness. But we must be wary of overestimating their influence. Contemporary historians have emphasized class struggle in their analysis of twentieth-century Hungarian history; but in the decade 1908–18 the struggle was seldom primarily, and certainly not exclusively, a struggle between the proletariat and the ruling class. The recent multivolume history of Hungary published by the Academy of Science has recognized the complexity of the problem; it has recognized that the proletariat was often but an instrument, rather than a protagonist of this struggle, an instrument, that is, of the bourgeoisie in its struggle for a share of the power.

Furthermore, the role of the working class has sometimes been viewed in a false light because of a teleological interpretation of the Hungarian Republic of Councils, particularly the view that it had come about as a result of organic development, that the Social Democrats (hence Communists) were destined to become the protagonists of a nearly successful revolution, the Central European revolution that came closest to duplicating the achievement of the great October Socialist Revolution. In an attempt to explain this development historians have at times given undue importance to working-class consciousness and party organization in the period preceding the revolutions. If the proper distinctions are not made, one would have to assume that the Hungarian workers had achieved a deeper consciousness than, say, the proletarians of England, France, or Germany, since in those countries revolution in the aftermath of the war was even less successful, or not even attempted.

The Social Democrats and Communists eventually did become the "protagonists" of the revolution in Hungary. As the relatively progressive former Minister of the Interior, József Kristoffy, pointed out after the war, of all the great Social Democratic parties in Europe the Hungarian party, with a

---

[3] Quoted in Ferenc Katona and Tibor Dénes, *A Thália története, 1904–1908* [The History of Thalia] (Budapest: Müvelt Nép, 1954), 13–14.

membership of 152,332 at the apex of its popularity, was the weakest.⁴ It is true, he noted, that its membership increased by more than a hundred percent between April 1906 and April 1907, and it became for a while the "master of the streets" of Budapest. Yet we must conclude that party organization could have been but one factor, and probably not the most important, in the revolutionary process.

Nor must we overestimate the cultural aspirations of industrial workers. Ernö Bresztovszky, one of the Socialist intellectuals who wrote for the *Nyugat* in its first years,⁵ knew well that the great masses of proletarians, no matter how rapidly their consciousness may have been rising, were far from counting as "consumers on the art market." On the other hand, added Bresztovszky, the "proletarian ideology" was making rapid conquests among the artists: "I could mention, right off the bat, eighteen Hungarian artists and writers who came from the workshops."⁶ True, this is not evidence that they sympathized with those who remained in the workshops; though Schöpflin testified, some twenty-five years later, that the young writers around the *Nyugat* "with hardly an exception, were poor; and knowing the curse of poverty they were prone to side with the poor."⁷

Others disagreed; as mentioned, Socialist intellectuals often attributed an instinctive appreciation of the "higher things of life" to workers. According to one Socialist the working class had grown gradually strong and self-confident, and among its most important needs was the *book*.⁸ Another Socialist intellectual, Pál Kéri, in analyzing the relationship between Ady and the proletariat, wrote that the poet could be considered the embodiment of the proletarian, witness his "tremendous hungers," his "unlimited yearning for culture."⁹

If indeed the worker developed a need for books and culture, what kind of books, what kind of culture did he require? We have no quantitative data to rely on; but we have already seen that there is some correlation between the availability of literary works by progressive writers and labor union libraries, or libraries located in "working-class districts." The pattern in Budapest does not seem to resemble the pattern in England where, according to Queenie D. Leavis, the "lowbrow" public ignores the "highbrow" writers.¹⁰ In 1913 the weekly journal *Everyman*, launched to "foster a taste for books among the proletariat," had to cease publication after eighteen months (on the other hand, it had been launched with an initial

---

⁴ *Magyarország kálváriája* [The Calvary of Hungary] (Budapest: Wodianer, 1927), 489.
⁵ Bresztovszky also attacked the *Nyugat* on occasions; for instance, in *Népszava*, issues of 1 and 5 October 1911.
⁶ "Uj hedonizmus" [New Hedonism], *Nyugat*, 2 (1909), No. 1: 486 ff.
⁷ *Magyar irodalom a XX században*, 144.
⁸ Ferencz Kende, "A könyvek uj fogyasztói" [The New Consumers of Books], *Corvina*, 33 (1910), No. 18: 114.
⁹ "Ady Endre szociális gyökerei" [The Social Roots of Ady], *Nyugat*, 2 (1909), No. 1: 528.
¹⁰ *Fiction and the Reading Public* (London: Chatto and Windus, 1965, 1st ed. 1932), 35.

circulation of over one hundred thousand copies!).[11] In Hungary, either the working class was not lowbrow, or this lowbrow public nevertheless had some appreciation for sophisticated realistic literature. At any rate, I have found nothing to support the contention that dime novels were more popular with the industrial workers than with other classes or strata.

Let the workers speak for themselves. As we know, the printers were often the most articulate and most radical element among the unionized workers. Witness the enthusiastic reception accorded Ady, and other "hypermodern" writers, "mocked, despised, but triumphant," on the pages of the journal of the printers' union.[12] A year later, another printers' journal hailed the Nyugat Library series for selling first-rate literary works at an unparalleled low price of thirty fillérs a copy. It mentions among the "excellent" or "widely respected authors," Ady, Ambrus, Biró, Hatvany, Ignotus, Móricz, and Szomory[13]—a list which indicates, among other things, that depth of political commitment on the part of the author was not necessarily the most important criterion in these workers' appreciation of literature. The availability of cheap editions, however, may well have been a major factor affecting the rate of sale of a literary work (we have evidence that such was indeed the case in the United States).[14]

The memoirs of Kassák are a mine of information regarding the relationship between the Nyugat and industrial workers—beginning with himself, one of the few writers of that generation with an authentically proletarian background and experience. "We read and listen to Ady's poems," he wrote, "we dissect them in order to reconstitute them anew in triumph. And so it goes almost until dawn. We eat poems and we regurgitate politics. . . ."[15] Kassák belonged to a social club of workers called the Home (*Otthon*). At their gatherings, there was less and less dancing, and more and more recitation of poetry. Occasionally the workers themselves recited poems by Ady, Kosztolányi, or foreign poets, and the audience waxed enthusiastic.[16] The Home, incidentally, subscribed to the *Nyugat*.[17]

Or witness the young Ferenc Münnich, also from a working-class background, who was to achieve political prominence in the early years of the Hungarian People's Republic; he acknowledges the influence of Petőfi, Ady, Vörösmarty, and Arany on the poetry he wrote as a teenager in the early 1900s.[18] If, however, we take such testimonials literally, it would

---

[11] John Gross, *The Rise and Fall of the Man of Letters* (London: Macmillan, 1969), 210.

[12] József Noti, "Az uj magyar lirikusok" [The New Hungarian Poets], *Csak szorosan*, 9 (1909), No. 10: 2.

[13] "A Nyugat könyvtár" [The Nyugat Library], *Typographia*, 42, No. 49 (December 9, 1910).

[14] According to F. L. Mott authors become more popular, more widely read, if their works are available in cheap editions. *Golden Multitudes* (New York: R. R. Bowker, 1947), 106, 291–97.

[15] *Egy ember élete* [One Man's Life] (Budapest: Magvető, 1957), 2: 260.

[16] Lajos Kassák, op. cit., 341.

[17] Ibid., 260.

[18] Ferenc Münnich, *Viharos út* [Stormy Road] (Budapest: Szépirodalmi, 1966), 9.

mean that the young Münnich had been among the very first to be impressed by Ady.

In answer to critics, Ignotus wrote in the midst of the war that the *Nyugat* had never fared better; and that its subscribers came from all ranks, from corporal to general, including a good many who could by no means be classified as "intellectual."[19] Again, however, the evidence must be taken with a grain of salt; it is vague, and Ignotus has a record of not being particularly accurate in such matters.

The written confessions of young workers may not be completely satisfactory evidence either. Ignotus wrote at one time that the workers have been short-changed everywhere, even in literature, because by the time they will have learned to think, observe, and write, the bourgeois writers will have "written away part of their themes."[20] In any case, the worker who writes is altogether exceptional in a capitalist, class society; having written and published—as had, for instance, Kassák—the manual worker will no longer be considered a manual worker or, at least, not simply a manual worker, but will be ascribed to a different stratum of the proletariat, or of the petite bourgeoisie. His consciousness, too, will have undergone change, inasmuch as he no longer is subject to the general predicament of the masses of workers. The works of certain writers of proletarian background present not only a picture of life among the workers or the peasants, but often include normative evaluations we are bound to recognize as "middle-class." But what of the worker or peasant who does not possess intellectual predispositions, who has never felt the urge to express himself in writing? Can she or he be a reader? If he is, where does one find evidence regarding his reading and regarding the impact it may have had on him? Is it at all possible to expect answers to such questions?

The wise peasant did not read, according to Zsigmond Móricz. In one of his novels, a peasant lad argues:

Where we live we send the children to school only because, if we didn't, we are likely to get in trouble with the law.... Justice, in my village, means to behave properly, to greet the gentlemen first, not to get into fights, not to steal, not to make too many mistakes, to be careful with the girls. That is the way to stay out of trouble. We live under religious justice, and we cannot need any other kind. Our priest delivers us a sermon every Sunday, we don't attend union meetings, we do not read the newspapers. In our village we must live so that nobody will find fault with our behavior....[21]

---

[19] "A Nyugat körül" [Around the Nyugat], *Nyugat*, 9 (1916): 246–48.

[20] *Ignotus válogatott írásai*, 220.

[21] *A boldog ember* [The Happy Man] (Budapest: Szépirodalmi, 1968, 1st ed. 1935), 253–55. Móricz refers to this novel as a "document" and, indeed, it was an outstanding example of the literary production of the so-called "village investigators" active in revealing the conditions and social injustices prevalent in the countryside during the thirties and early forties. Apart from the fact that Móricz's characters are almost always real, one of his favorite devices as a writer was to record conversations he overheard in public places verbatim, in shorthand.

The cautious, submissive peasant does not read or write, or prefers not to admit it, even if he should know how. Thus, there can be no first-hand record of his intellectual curiosity.

What can we infer about the literary taste of the working class from countries where such research has been conducted more systematically? The curiosity of the British industrial worker, we are told, was by and large limited to dime novels, low in price but also devoid of literary value.[22] (*Nota bene*, Richard Hoggart's work on the culture of the working class—to which I am mainly referring—has a scientific, particularly sociological pretension, but upon closer examination it becomes evident that the arguments are often based on the author's personal and subjective experiences, on the logic of "I must know, since I come from this milieu," the force of which most of us have no alternative but to concede.) According to Werner Sombart, the taste of the German working-class must have been rather similar.[23] The French worker's orientation, on the other hand, is quite different if we are to believe Michel Zéraffa; the French workers yearn to read books about "their concrete existence"—a yearning which is, according to Zéraffa, a manifestation of extreme alienation, since the worker's day to day reality is already alienating enough in itself.[24]

To find evidence regarding the literary tastes of the Hungarian worker we are better off looking at the Social Democratic press. If I were to write about the cultural policy of the daily *Népszava*, or of the monthly *Szocializmus* (printed in about five hundred copies per issue), Ady and the *Nyugat* would occupy a prominent place. Besides Ady, Gyula Juhász, Oszkár Gellért, Lajos Biró, Géza Csáth, Lajos Nagy, and Géza Lengyel, to mention only writers from the Nyugat, contributed to the literary supplement of the *Népszava* published during part of the years 1907 and 1908.[25] The contact with Ady dates back to November 1906 when the *Népszava* printed one of his short stories. Beginning in January 1907 it was to publish some of his poetry,[26] a practice that would continue even after Ady had agreed to the request of the editors of the *Nyugat* to submit all his poetry to that journal first (and it was technically these "exclusive" or "first rights" that the *Nyugat* remunerated with a monthly stipend of six hundred crowns). Further evidence of cooperation between Ady and the Social Democratic

---

[22] See the thesis of Richard Hoggart, and Q. D. Leavis, op. cit., and Tibor Szobotka, *Közönség és irodalom* [Literature and the Public] (Budapest: Gondolat, 1964), 209.

[23] Ervin Szabó, "Mit olvasnak és mit olvassanak" [What They Do Read, and What They Should Read], 63.

[24] *Roman et société* (Paris: Presses Universitaires, 1971), 174–75. Daniel Mornet writes that the famous work of Necker, the *Compte rendu*, which had a direct bearing on the "aristocratic phase" of the French revolution, sold one hundred thousand copies, and even fishwives read it. *Les origines intellectuelles de la Révolution Française*, 363.

[25] Ernö Kabos, "A Népszava olvasótára 1907–08-ban" [The Readers of the Népszava in 1907–08] *Tanulmányok a magyar szocialista irodalom történetéből* [Studies in the History of Socialist Literature in Hungary] (Budapest: Akadémia, 1962), 31.

[26] Zoltán Horváth, *Die Jahrhundertwende in Ungarn* (Budapest: Lüchterhand, 1966), 275.

press was his signature added to a petition published in the *Népszava* in early 1913, protesting against the contemplated arrest of the paper's editors on account of the general strike they advocated (but later timidly called off); it is true that those who signed the petition identified themselves as "not members of the Social Democratic Party."[27]

Of course, the *Népszava* also published "working-class" poetry written by genuine "proletarian" poets. One consequence was occasional conflict resulting from divergent interpretations of the function of literature, the most notable example being the Ady-Csizmadia controversy. Sándor Csizmadia was both an author of "working-class verse" (sometimes poetry) and a party activist who had attained a leadership position. Csizmadia's direct opponents were the partisans of Ady in the ranks of the Party, Socialists who felt that Ady was a truly great poet as well as a militant progressive; and that the *Népszava* should make room, or make more room, for his poetry. Csizmadia initiated the polemic in a review of a volume of poetry by another "card-carrying" poet, in the 26 January 1909 issue of the Socialist daily. The author of the volume was highly praised and contrasted to poets who wrote abstruse symbolic poetry—clearly a reference to Ady. The editors of the *Népszava*, however, saw fit to add a note to Csizmadia's review, warning the readers that it represented only the personal opinion of its author, and that they, the editors, reserved the right to have their say in the matter. In fact, Ernö Bresztovszky, one of the editors, came to the defence of Ady in the next day's issue.[28] The matter did not rest there. Another editor took Csizmadia's side and attacked Ady for being too difficult to interpret; his poetry was not meant for the worker, hence the *Népszava* need not make room for it.[29]

The debate continued on the pages of the theoretical journal *Szocializmus*. One participant in the debate argued that the works of authors such as Ambrus, Sándor Brody, Ignotus, and Ady, would certainly do the workers no harm. The writings of Dickens, Tolstoy, Gogol or Strindberg had not harmed them, although the latter were not party members either, yet were read by members of the party in Hungary (and elsewhere).[30] The argument was repeated, incidentally, by Ervin Szabó in his analysis of "proletarian poetry": Dickens and Zola had written most movingly about the poor without being on the roster of any Socialist party, whereas good Socialists might

---

[27] Zoltán Horváth, op. cit., 332–33.
[28] *Népszava*, 26 and 27 January 1909. Gyula Juhász, whose political views were sometimes close to those of the Social Democrats, also came to Ady's defense in the daily at Szeged to which he was a regular contributor. *Juhász Gyula összes művei* [The Complete Works of Juhász], 5: 256–57. Jakab Weltner, another editor of the *Népszava*, testified in a book published much later that Csizmadia was simply jealous of Ady and expected greater royalties from the daily. *'Milliók egy miatt!'* [Millions for One] (Budapest, 1927), 227 ff.
[29] Article by Béla Somogyi in *Népszava*, 30 January 1909.
[30] Sándor Antal, "A Népszava és a szépirodalom" [The Népszava and Belles-Lettres], *Szocializmus*, 3 (1908–09): 236. The Socialist periodical *A tudás*, appearing in 1918, would also bring items by Ady, Karinthy, and other Nyugat writers.

well write about themes other than the predicament of the working-class.[31] But even on the pages of *Szocializmus* there were some who argued that Ady was too difficult for a worker to understand. Nevertheless, it was the positive tone that prevailed: having defended Ady in the *Népszava* Bresztovszky came to the defense of the entire Nyugat in the pages of *Szocializmus*. He hailed the recently initiated Nyugat Library series as "twenty books, full of value." This publishing venture, he added, was the "fortunate manifestation of a trend, but at the same time promotes that trend,"[32] meaning, presumably, a growing interest in good literature. But his praise was not unqualified; he chided the Nyugat writers for their ivory-tower attitude,[33] an attack he was to repeat a year or two later specifically against Babits.[34]

Szocializmus also welcomed the opening of the Endre Nagy cabaret which, like the Thália drama society a few years earlier, made an effort to provide entertainment of value at a price accessible to workers. In fact, the original intent had been to call the cabaret the "Workers' Theater."[35] It counted Ady and a number of Nyugat writers among its contributors; Ady's poems were often presented to the public as set to music by Béla Reinitz (other composers had set his poetry to music, but with less success).[36]

To what extent did the Nyugat writers deserve praise from the Social Democrats? Did they reciprocate the compliments received from the working class?

Let us consider a specific instance: the protest demonstrations on 23 May 1912—"Bloody Thursday." Ady was deeply affected by the event; it seems to have determined the content and mood of much of his poetry for years to come, the clearest example being the poem "Rohanunk a forradalomba" [We are Running Headlong into Revolution]. The rapport between Babits and the *Népszava* was not always felicitous. The editors of the Socialist daily had solicited a poem from Babits, which he duly submitted to them under a pen-name (!), but it was not printed, and may have led to resentment on the part of Babits. Yet his celebrated poem "Május huszonhárom Rákospalotán" [At Rákospalota on 23 May], was reprinted in the *Népszava*

---

[31] Review of Zseni Várnai's poems in *Nyugat*, 7 (1914), No. 2: 643–45.

[32] "A Nyugat és kiadványai" [The Nyugat and its Publications], *Szocializmus*, 4 (1909–10): 187.

[33] Ibid. For a response see *Nyugat*, 4 (1911): 683 ff.

[34] In 1912 Bresztovszky claimed that while modern literature had been a fighting literature at its beginnings, it had lost faith; he accused Babits of having crossed out the adjective "red" from all his poetry, past and present. "Vissza az őserdőbe" [Back to the Jungle], *Szocializmus*, 7 (1912–13), No. 9: 474–77. Babits responded: "I am not a coward, and if to desire change means revolution, I am a revolutionary. But I have nothing to do with political parties. And especially not with the party which, after encouraging the poor and infinitely excited people to do battle, does not dare take responsibility for the action. . . ." The reference was to the hesitations of the Social Democrats. *Nyugat*, 5 (1912), No. 1: 1074. See also Oszkár Gellért's polemical writing in *Nyugat*, 4 (1911), No. 20: 686.

[35] "Nagy Lajos levelei Nagy Zoltánhoz" [Letters of Lajos Nagy to Zoltán Nagy], *Kritika* (June 1977): 3.

[36] József Pogány, in *Szocializmus*, 5 (1911): 47–48.

of 2 June 1912, a day after its publication in the *Nyugat*.[37] Babits was to read to an audience of young people in 1919, adding that he had been a "revolutionary before the revolution."[38] Although the poem expresses sympathy for the victims of the demonstration, that is the workers, both those who died and those who did not, it is by no means a revolutionary war song; the poem evinces mixed sentiments.

A stronger statement, a more belligerent poem is the one by Margit Kaffka, "Hajnali ritmusok: 1912 május 23" [Sunrise Rhythms: 23 May 1912], also published in the *Nyugat*:

"Men," I said quietly, and looked into their handsome bright eyes
"If anything should happen, don't forget to send for us too!"
. . .
If only for a short while, you might untie the chains binding us
(It is better for us to charge with the charge than to cry, to wait, to give birth, to tremble)
And, as in previous revolutions, thrust us onto your barricades again.[39]

The lines remind me of some of the beautiful feminist verse of the Puerto Rican poetess Julia de Burgos.

Lest we attach too much significance to such expressions of sympathy for the strike and for the workers, two factors should be borne in mind:

1) Expressions of sympathy came from many sides. I have found, in the provincial press, poems expressing similar or stronger sentiments by poets long since forgotten.[40] On the other hand, most Nyugat writers did not feel an urge to record the event. Béla Balázs, whose diary from the period has been preserved (and remains partly unpublished), does not even make mention of the event in his entry for 23 May, or subsequently; the space is devoted to "woman problems" [Asszony historiák],[41] intimating, most probably, his own problems with the ladies.

2) The journal *Szocializmus* was largely justified in berating "progressive" Hungarian writers for their apathy. Belgian writers, wrote one of its editors, had declared their solidarity with striking workers: witness the outspoken support by Maurice Maeterlinck, Emile Verhaeren, and others. Hungarian writers had done next to nothing. In any case most of them, being servants

---

[37] *Nyugat*, 5 (1912), No. 1: 913–14.
[38] Notes for a speech, Babits Papers, III/1810, Országos Széchenyi Irattár. Also, Zoltán Éder, *Babits a katedrán* [Babits on the Podium] (Budapest: Szépirodalmi, 1966), 135.
[39] *Nyugat*, 5 (1912), No. 2: 36–37.
[40] For instance, Sándor Hangay, "Véres csütörtök" [Bloody Thursday], *Erdélyi lapok*, 5 (1912): 549.
[41] Balázs Papers, Ms 5023/17, Akadémia Irattár. Elsewhere in his diary Balázs writes "it seems that at the root of my personality there is the simple and indivisible desire that *every* woman I notice, even barely, should love me. . . . I wonder if all men feel the same way?" Ibid. Oszkár Gellért claims to have written a poem on this occasion, but "kept it for his desk." *Egy iró élete*, 1: 273.

of capitalism, could not be expected to support the workers.[42] "Yet there are some comforting signs," noted the critic:

> There is, of course, Endre Ady, who supports our cause with tremendous lyrical power. Endre Nagy is also encouraging us loudly and openly, he is sympathetic to Socialist goals, he exerts his talent on our behalf, but he can afford to do it, because he is financially independent. It is certain that the wonderful and excellent Ignotus is also on our side in thought and feeling, but unfortunately his situation does not allow him to take a stand where he would prefer to take a stand, and where he could make valuable contributions to our cause. Sándor Brody, Gyula Krudy—both brilliant talents—probably sympathize with us, but they feel too comfortable and somnolent to speak out loud. . . .[43]

Endre Nagy, Ignotus, Bródy, Krudy—a rather short list from among the stars of the Nyugat constellation, and how lukewarm their support! At least, according to the author of the above article.

The author describes Herczeg, Jenö Rákosi, and other conservative writers as servants of capitalism. The Nyugat movement on the whole was exempt from such a charge. Yet among the regular targets of the *Népszava*, as already noted, there was the GyOSz, the organization of Hungarian industrialists, which financed not the conservative papers of Herczeg or Rákosi (*Magyar Figyelö, Budapesti Hirlap*), but rather the *Nyugat!*

The *Nyugat* offered discount tickets to unionized workers (and students) at matinées, in Budapest and elsewhere.[44] With what results, it is difficult to say. In a review of the matinée on 29 January 1911, at a theater in Budapest, the *Népszava* reviewer remarked that the best seats were occupied by the burghers from Lipotváros (the Jewish nouveau-riche district), and there were many teenage girls, but few boys. In the cheaper sections "the serious and enthusiastic interest of the workers" was manifest.[45] The details regarding the composition of the audience lend the statement plausibility.

Or let us look at the evidence presented by workers' libraries. In 1910 the "people's libraries" in Budapest contained about sixty-five thousand volumes altogether (considerably less than similar libraries in Vienna).[46] Labor unions and other workingmen's associations owned another forty

---

[42] In this connection I have found an interesting document in the State Archives: a request for subvention on the part of a projected pro-government daily. The petition explains that its policy would be to cater to the provincial reader and to attack the opposition parties. "It would appear on eight pages, with a good serialized novel, for which purpose I would acquire the best and most popular writers and journalists." Petition dated 15 September 1912, ME 6166 (1912). Hence it seemed natural, to some, that popular and good novelists should serve the interests of official policy.

[43] Ferenc Göndör, "Az irók és a tömegsztrájk" [Writers and the Mass Strike], *Szocializmus*, 7 (1912–13), No. 6: 330–31.

[44] *Népszava*, 31 January 1911.

[45] See advertisement in *Népszava*, 25 January 1911, or the Arad paper *Függetlenség* for 11 November 1909, "Entrance, standing room, 1 crown. Workers and students, 50 fillérs. . . ."

[46] Ervin Szabó, "Községi nyilvános könyvtár Budapesten" [Community Public Library in Budapest], *Városi szemle*, 3 (1910): 453.

thousand volumes.[47] With the help of data provided by German libraries Ervin Szabó (who, in addition to being the most creative Socialist thinker in Hungary, was a librarian by profession) argued, against Werner Sombart, that proletarians do read good books and do have good taste in literature.[48] Szabó had only one reservation: since proletarians do not read critical reviews (such as the *Nyugat*), they may have some difficulty deciding which books to check out from the library.[49] Szabó's optimistic assessment of the culture of poverty was shared by József Pogány, a Social Democratic leader: it was the proletariat, he asserted somewhat romantically but not too convincingly, that had understood and appreciated Ady's poetry first.[50] Jolán Kelen also testified that she used to recite the great "inflammatory poems" of Ady to working class audiences, and these were always received with enthusiastic applause.[51] Or witness the fact that large numbers of workers took advantage of the scanty educational opportunities offered them. In its first year of operation the Free School of the Social Sciences made room for 241 workers; and their numbers increased year by year.[52] Among the visiting lecturers at the Free School we find the names of a number of Nyugat personalities.

The kind of audience Szabó, Pogány, and Kelen had in mind was blue collar; they themselves, and practically the entire leadership of the Social Democratic Party, and of the future Communist Party no less, came from a petit bourgeois background. Many of them had been journalists at one time, on the staff of the *Népszava* or elsewhere. Their praxis consisted precisely in writing (and public speaking). They were the people about whom Lenin had said, we must do the revolution with them, we must rely on them, for what else is there?

In one instance, Szabó was proven wrong: he had argued (somewhat in contradiction to his optimistic assessment of the culture of the working class) that the cultural underdevelopment of the Hungarian worker would render the collaboration of intellectuals unbearable to them.[53] Not so; for the fact is that a group of petit bourgeois intellectuals was to constitute the leadership of the Hungarian Republic of Councils. As I have already noted, the main reservoir of Hungarian radical intelligentsia was the Jews. "Frustrated by their marginality, repudiated by both the gentry and the bourgeois value systems, they were to form the bulk of the Socialist and Communist elites in the coming revolutions," according to two Western

---

[47] Ervin Szabó, "Községi nyilvános könyvtár Budapesten," 455.
[48] Ervin Szabó, "Mit olvasnak és mit olvassanak?" 63.
[49] Ibid.
[50] *Szocializmus*, 5 (1911): 48.
[51] *Eliramlik az élet*, 53.
[52] Márta Tömöry, *Uj vizeken járok*, 11.
[53] Letter from Szabó to Kunfi dated 1908, quoted in Tibor Süle, *Sozialdemokratie in Ungarn* (Köln: Bohlau, 1967), 187.

historians.[54] To be sure, this factor, that the bulk of these "elites"—i.e. the vanguard—was Jewish, does not explain the revolutions; but neither can it be dismissed as irrelevant.

Elements of this vanguard had not only taken cognizance of the Nyugat movement in the Socialist press; many of them had actually contributed to the journal: Ervin Szabó (who, however, died just before the revolutions), Ernö Bresztovszky, Béla Révész, Zsigmond Kunfi, Pál Kéri, not to mention future militants of the party such as Lukács, Balázs, or Tibor Déry.

The leadership of the Hungarian Republic of Councils publicly recognized Ady and, to a lesser extent, the Nyugat, as its cultural mentor; so had the leaders of the previous revolutionary regime, the bourgeois radicals who had held power for a few months following October 1918. After all, to paraphrase Lenin, there was no Chinese wall separating the bourgeois-democratic revolution from the Socialist revolution. Otto Korvin, the chief of the political police of the Republic, was to pay his homage to literature in prison; having acquired a sanguinary reputation while in office, he became one of the victims and martyrs of the counterrevolution. During his days on death-row he found comfort in keeping a diary. This diary is filled with literary references, and includes an exalted litany to nature and to books, somewhat in the style of St. Francis of Assisi. Along with the names of Baudelaire, Tolstoy, Zola, Flaubert, Romain Rolland, Reiner [sic] Maria Rilke, and some others less familiar to the modern reader, Korvin itemizes:

> I thank Endre Ady for every line he wrote: he was the first to find an echo in me. I thank Dezsö Szomory for his *Isteni kert* [Divine Garden], Kosztolányi for his *Szegény kisgyermek panaszai* [Lamentations of a Poor Child] and especially for his "Öszi koncert" [Autumn Concert], I thank Ignotus for his *Tavaszi rügyek* [Vernal Buds] . . . I thank Karinthy for his "Martinovics" poem. . . .[55]

All these writers were part of the Nyugat; Korvin did not mention any who were not.

Similar evidence can be found in Jakab Weltner's *Milliók egy miatt* [Millions on Behalf of One]. Weltner, a Social Democrat and editor of the *Népszava*, writes in these recollections about the passionate confrontations among workers at the time of the polemics between Csizmadia and Ady, but adds that Ady's poetry was recited more and more often at the "social evenings" organized by workers. He cites the example of a party official named Sándor Vincze who had belonged to the camp of Ady's enemies, but came about and eventually learned every one of Ady's poems by heart.[56]

---

[54] Andrew Janos and William B. Slottman, *Revolution in Perspective* (Berkeley: University of California Press, 1971), 59.

[55] "Korvin Ottó börtönnaplója" [The Prison Diary of Korvin], *Kritika*, 1975, No. 3, 5: and passim. The same diary and other documents pertaining to Korvin are reprinted in Otto Korvin ". . . *a gondolat él* . . ." [. . . the Idea Lives . . .], ed. András Simor (Budapest: Magvetö, 1976).

[56] Budapest: author's edition, 1927, 227 ff., 239.

Ady is mentioned a number of times in the contemporary articles of Tibor Szamuely, a journalist who became the commissar in charge of education (along with Lukács) during the Republic of Councils; but he also writes about Menyhért Lengyel, one of whose plays about life in the provinces, *Falusi idill* [Idyll in the Village], aroused the ire of the chauvinists: "It is great treason to write such a play," they claimed, and it must not be performed abroad.[57] Yet that was precisely what happened to a number of Lengyel's plays; this was a period when Hungarian drama enjoyed something close to international vogue. Socialist politicians, such as Vilmos Böhm and Manó Buchinger, who likewise could not resist the urge to publish memoirs, also quote Ady occasionally.[58]

I have already mentioned Béla Kun, who happened to be a private pupil of Ady, a few years his senior at the secondary school in the county of Zilah. Mrs. Kun recalls that her husband referred to Ady as the greatest poet of the twentieth century: "History will prove Ady right," he declared around 1912 or 1913. In their Kolozsvár apartment, the young Kun couple hung only one picture on the wall: a photograph of Ady.[59]

Of course, the name of György Lukács cannot be omitted here; was he not the cultural commissar of the Republic of Councils, and a loyal member of the Communist Party (despite occasional hesitations) for the remainder of his life? His attitude is summed up in a statement from 1969: although he had written frequently for the *Nyugat*, he "never felt a deeper solidarity with this movement, except for Ady."[60] The choice of words was deliberate; for Lukács had not felt "deeper" solidarity with any movement, especially not a political movement, until near the end of the war—and in this he was not particularly different from other members of the Nyugat, again "except for Ady." Of course, he would have objected to being described as a member of the Nyugat; yet he eventually recognized (and how could he have failed to recognize it, given his unqualified admiration for Ady), that the Nyugat was the breeze announcing the storm.[61] As for Ady, he was already the storm. Lukács considered Ady the greatest poet of the era, and not simply on the Hungarian scale. "I am not worried," he would declare later, "that I might be accused of chauvinism on account of this assessment."[62]

---

[57] *Szamuely Tibor: összegyüjtött irások és beszédek* [The Collected Writings and Speeches of Szamuely], ed. Simor András (Budapest: Magvetö, 1975), 75, 212, etc.

[58] Vilmos Böhm, *Két forradalom tüzében* [In the Cross-Fire of Two Revolutions] (Budapest: Népszava, no date); and Manó Buchinger, *Küzdelem a szocializmusért* [Struggle for Socialism], (Népszava, no date), 17.

[59] Mrs. Béla Kun, *Kun Béla* (Budapest: Magvetö: 1966), 44–45.

[60] *Magyar irodalom—magyar kultura*, 12.

[61] Ibid., 444.

[62] Ibid., 606.

IX. THE NYUGAT VERSUS THE ESTABLISHMENT

In 1908 and 1909 most academicians found it beneath their dignity to take cognizance of modern literature.[1] The contemporary writers upon whom they bestowed praise and prizes were simply not modern. Yet the silence of the academicians did not achieve its presumed end; since it was so evidently deliberate, it alerted the reading public. Inevitably, the attention of the public and of the critics led, in turn, to explicit condemnation by the regime and its conservative supporters, i.e., the establishment. The conspiracy of silence had failed; after 1909 the establishment fought Ady and *Nyugat* along several fronts, tooth and nail.

The attacks against Ady, however, had begun earlier; a separate essay would be needed to analyze the reception of Ady and his poetry from his years as a small-town journalist in Nagyvárad to his appearance in the first issue of *Nyugat*. Suffice it to say that the antagonisms aroused by Ady necessarily rubbed off on the review with which he identified from the start. The degree of this identification between the poet and the review varied according to the critic, from season to season, or even according to the moods of Ady himself. As for the moods of Ady, subsequent criticism, especially in the period between 1945 and 1956, sought to exploit the so-called "contradiction" between the radical or "nearly" Socialist Ady, and the bourgeois *Nyugat*. But the contradiction was mostly, if not entirely, in the minds of the critics. It would, however, serve no purpose to elaborate on the strange workings of literary Stalinism within the framework of this essay.

Contemporary critics did not perceive contradictions but, on the contrary, gradually identified Ady with *Nyugat,* and *Nyugat* with Ady. As I have suggested, there were variations as to the degree of this identification. One variation consisted in condemning *Nyugat* for a variety of sins, including that of mediocrity, while sparing Ady. A curious example of this variation can be found in a comment by the Tharaud brothers, who acquired some fame as novelists in France and notoriety because of their anti-Semitism. Jérôme Tharaud had had occasion to familiarize himself with Hungarian conditions during his years as instructor of French at the University of Budapest, from 1899 to 1903. In a post-World War I issue of the *Revue des Deux Mondes*—ironically, the literary review the editors of *Nyugat* had held in such high esteem—the Tharaud brothers referred to *Nyugat* and to

---

[1] Lujza Farkas, *A Nyugat és a századeleji irodalomforduló* (Budapest: Gyarmati, 1935), 61, 65.

Huszadik Század as forums which, deplorably enough, had prepared the ground for the revolutions of 1918 and 1919; they added that *Nyugat* "was worthless except for the great poet Ady."[2]

Other variations consisted in describing *Nyugat* as "Ady and company," or the *Nyugat* poets as "the Adys." The friendlier critics recognized differences in style, or at least certain nuances, whereas others recognized only differences in degree of degeneracy. They were soon joined by the chorus of academicians.

What were the most common accusations leveled against the new literature? Dezsö Szabó, one of the most outspoken of the young writers, summarized the charges as follows:

1) The new literature is not Hungarian, but cosmopolitan. It is based on Western models rather than on traditions set by the great nineteenth-century poets Petöfi and Arany.

2) The new literature brings to the Hungarian public the decadent morals of the West.

3) The new literature is a "front" for the destructive or subversive activities of the Jews.

4) The new literature is too free in form and language; it denies pure and healthy Hungarian traditions in these respects.[3]

Let us examine each of these charges in some detail. The new literature was not Hungarian, but cosmopolitan, that is eminently urban and urbane (a synonym for polite—from *polis*—and cosmopolitan); in other words it was the literature of Budapest. There was, indeed, no end to the derogatory epithets heaped upon the capital city of Hungary; it was a cosmopolis, an inferior copy of decadent Paris, a center of degeneracy, of softness, of immorality. "Remain the East! Remain the East!" apostrophized Aladár Bodor as he passed through the capital on his way from Transylvania to Paris, where he was to become Ady's companion. "Remain beautiful in an eastern way!" he exhorted the city of Budapest.[4] The exhortation must have been in vain. Hungarian nationalists and conservative politicians reminded their audience time and again that Budapest was Western rather than Eastern, out of touch with the real (rural) Hungary. The conservatives and puritans insisted that "all people do there is hold meetings to discuss free love," or that it was a nest swarming with Jews.[5] Cosmopolitanism, when used by the critics of modern Hungarian literature, was often equated with French influence. The grounds for that charge were Ady's repeated and extended visits to Paris, and the appreciation he evinced, in his poetry

---

[2] "Bolchévistes de Hongrie," *Revue des Deux Mondes* (1921): 764. Similar treatment of the issue occurs in Jérôme and Jean Tharaud's *Quand Israël est roi* (Paris: Plon-Nourrit, 1921).

[3] Dezsö Szabó, *Életeim* (Budapest: Szépirodalmi Kiadó, 1965), 2: 244.

[4] *Keletiek Nyugaton* (Losoncz: Károly Nyomda, 1909), 7–9.

[5] Margit Kaffka's review of Anna Szederkényi's novel *Lángok, tüzek*, reprinted in *Az élet utján* (Budapest: Szépirodalmi, 1972), 250.

and his journalism, for French literature and its political context. Had he not translated (however freely) three sonnets of Baudelaire? The charge, often reiterated, was that Ady had been unable "to free himself from the influence of Baudelaire and Verlaine."[6] Undeniably, Ady wore francophilism on his sleeve; he expressed irritation when the *Figyelő* or the *Nyugat* occasionally devoted more space to German than to French works.[7]

It was but one step from the charge of French influence to accusations of lack of patriotism. Objectively, Ady was a patriot of the truest sort. Unlike many Hungarians, he felt no contempt for the national "minorities" who lived on Hungarian territory, and his vision of the nation was unobstructed by personal or class considerations; but his critics noted or pretended to note only his attacks on his country and on his compatriots: "I flee from my country in a train concealed/for my country is the home of hounds today, not mine/and should a single one of my disciples remain, the holy fellow/I will have even my corpse removed from there!"[8] The critics could not forgive Ady for what they might have forgiven Ignotus or some other "cosmopolitan" writer: his attacks on Hungary or, to be precise, on the prevailing regime. They could not forgive his attacks and denunciations, because Ady was ethnically Magyar, and gentry at that! *A la rigueur* Ignotus could be forgiven, for what could one expect from a Jew! But there was no denying that Ady was ethnically a "pure" Hungarian and that he could have easily reaped kudos from the prevailing system, he could have been one of them, one of the establishment; and if he was not, it was because he chose not to be. Ady had opted to reject the Hungary of the *ancien régime*, and forfeited all tangible benefits.

If Ady's blows were heavy, so were the counterblows; witness the attack by a priest in an organ of the Roman Catholic Church: "A windbag of a Hungarian such as [Ady] not only does not deserve that God's sun should shine upon him, but it were better if he had not been born." Or: "It is certain that Petőfi's lowest thought is worth more than the visions of the highest order produced by Ady's sick fantasy."[9]

Perhaps special mention should be made of the series of attacks launched by Jenő Rákosi in the daily *Budapesti Hirlap* during the fall and winter of 1915–16. Rákosi's attacks were broad in scope and directed at more than one target: Ady, Babits, and Móricz, the most distinguished triumvirate of *Nyugat*. Rákosi was the spokesman for the policy of Magyar supremacy;

---

[6] See, for instance, a review of Ady's volume of poetry, *Illés szekerén* by one Gyula Csefko in *Uránia* (a magazine of popular science), 10, No. 11 (1909): 482–84. Aladár Bodor remarked: "Some assert that Ady had learned from the French. Nonsense. A poet can no more learn poetry, than to be born. . . ." *Keletiek Nyugaton,* 112. Miksa Fenyö and Gyula Illyés also denied that Ady was influenced by French poetry. *A magyar irodalom története*, 5, ed. Miklós Szabolcsi (Budapest: Akadémiai Kiadó, 1965): 94.

[7] Miksa Fenyö, *Följegyzések a Nyugat folyoiratról és környékéről* (Toronto: Pátria, 1960), 86.

[8] First published in *Nyugat*, 6 (1913): 648.

[9] Vince Kocsis, "Ady Endre 'hazafias' költészete," *Kalazantium* (a monthly journal published by the Piarist Order in Kolozsvár), 16 (1910): 232.

he felt no compunctions about reiterating the charges already repeated *ad nauseam*. He accused Ady of having become inebriated with the spirit of the decadent literatures of France and Germany.[10] He charged Ady, Babits, and "*tutti quanti*" with "disturbing the notions of good taste and morality in the heads of a hundred young men and a hundred young women."[11] He lumped together, in his attacks, Manó Buchinger, Zsigmond Kunfi (two Socialist politicians) with Babits, Ignotus, and Fenyö (mostly writers).[12] Above all, he accused *tutti quanti* of a lack of patriotism.

Rákosi was not the only chauvinist; many other defenders of Magyar supremacy discovered their natural enemy in *Nyugat:* "the unnational character of today's pseudo-modern writers becomes obvious enough by throwing a glance [!] at Ady's most recent poetry, or at Menyhért Lengyel's most recent play," wrote a critic in the Christmas 1915 issue of a provincial paper,[13] oblivious to the fact that friend and foe alike found Ady's poetry difficult, even after careful scrutiny. The charges were repeated right up to 1918: Ignotus (as well as Oszkár Jászi) was an internationalist, a cosmopolitan, who expected to attain power with the support of ethnic minority political groupings, claimed Count István Bethlen, who was to become Hungary's prime minister during the first decade of the counterrevolutionary Horthy regime.[14]

The new literature introduced the decadent morals of a tired West. The same clergyman who attacked Ady for his "lack of patriotism" identified him as the victim of the "enthralling, bewitching" bondage of Paris, the metropolis notorious for its "lascivious excesses, and its worship of matter. . . ."[15] The charge was repeated by other "critics" in terms no less crude. Immediately after the first appearance of *Nyugat*, one of the members of the conservative Kisfaludy literary society charged that the modern writers were attempting to "inject the poison" of an alien spirit into Hungarian literature.[16] The emphasis lay on "poison."

Among the letters received by the writer and patron of the arts, Lajos Hatvany (about half of which have been published), there are a number

---

[10] *Budapesti Hirlap,* 12 Nov. 1915, 4–6.

[11] Ibid., 23 Nov. 1915, 7–8.

[12] Ibid. The reply to these attacks was written by Fenyö, "Irodalmi vita," *Nyugat,* 8, No. 2 (1915): 1302–03 and 1313–17. In all fairness to Rákosi, it should be noted that he came out in defense of Gustav Mahler when the great composer was dismissed from his position as director of the Budapest Opera in 1891. "This German Jew was the only man capable of transforming the hitherto polyglot Hungarian opera into a unified national institution." Egon Gartenberg, *Mahler* (N.Y.: Schimmer, 1978), 34–35.

[13] Tiszántul (pseudonym), "A marsolyázok. Az Adyak," *Tiszántul* 25 Dec. 1915: 5. The play by Lengyel must have been *Charlotte kisasszony.* [Miss Charlotte].

[14] *Ignotus válogatott irásai,* ed. Aladár Komlos (Budapest: Szépirodalmi Könyvkiadó, 1969), 686.

[15] Vince Kocsis, 186.

[16] Quoted in Ady Endre, *összes prózai müvei* 9, ed. József Láng and Erzsébet Vezér (Budapest: Akadémiai Kiadó, 1973): 524. The same person, Gyula Vargha, was to repeat the same accusation twenty years later: Ady's poetry, he would declare, "is poison to the Hungarian youth." Lóránt Hegedüs, *Ady és Tisza* (Budapest: Nyugat, n.d. [1940]), 22.

from persons who declined his invitation to subscribe to *Nyugat* or who, having subscribed in response to his entreaties, changed their mind. One lady from a distinguished family complained that the journal contained too much eroticism.[17] The member of parliament, Géza Szüllö, who had gone so far as to accept membership on the board of directors of the *Nyugat* company, resigned from that board because the journal had carried items "in bad taste," presumably of an erotic nature.[18]

The *Magyar Figyelö* came about as a sort of counter-*Huszadik Század* as well as counter-*Nyugat*, beginning 1 January 1911. It too made an explicit bid to appeal to the "Hungarian intellectuals" although it approached that stratum by a path altogether different from the one taken by *Nyugat*. In its first issues the playwright, novelist, and editor-in-chief, Ferenc Herczeg, commented on Western decadence, on cultural over-refinement, on "internationalism, atheism, and pornography."[19] The attack was directed primarily against the bourgeois-radical daily *Világ* and its editor Oszkár Jászi; *Nyugat* remained unnamed for several issues, but the nature of the alliance of progressive forces was such that it could justifiably feel included in the attack. The first explicit mention of it occurred in response to the 6 April 1911 issue of *Nyugat*, which contained the text of a circular sent out to some high-school teachers regarding low wages and political repression in public schools (written by Aladár Kuncz, himself a high-school teacher); apart from its misleading contents, according to the *Magyar Figyelö*, the circular was merely a device to entice teachers to subscribe to *Nyugat*.[20]

The charge of pornography or "excessive eroticism" was not always coupled with that of French influence; at times it was raised on its own, as somehow indigenous to *Nyugat*. The accusation was reiterated endlessly in the right-wing and anti-Semitic *Magyar Kultura*, another Catholic periodical. Few *Nyugat* writers were spared: Sándor Brody was described as a professional pornographer,[21] the short stories of Lajos Nagy as unadulterated pornography,[22] and even the poetry of Sarolta Lányi in late 1914, although it had a suitably war-mongering tone (eventually she was to change her attitude about the war), used improperly erotic language for the purpose.[23] The same epithet was applied to a novel by Gyula Szini, *Profán szerelem* [Profane Love] which almost became a best-seller;[24] and, of course, to Zsigmond Móricz who wrote "pornography pure and simple."[25] I say "of course" for even his friends occasionally accused Móricz

---

[17] Mrs. Emil Desewffy to Hatvany, Jan., 1911, *Levelek Hatvany Lajoshoz* (Budapest: Szépirodalmi Könyvkiadó, 1976), 106–07.
[18] Szüllö to Hatvany, 25 March 1911, ibid., 122.
[19] *Magyar Figyelö*, No. 1: 5.
[20] Ibid., No. 2: 260–61.
[21] *Magyar Kultura*, 2 (1914): 32.
[22] Ibid., 130.
[23] Ibid., 2, No. 2 (1914): 53 ff.
[24] Ibid., 3 (1915): 519–20.
[25] Ibid., 10 (1917): 995.

of indulging too much in eroticism. Thus the *Magyar Kultura* was not above referring to the whole of *Nyugat* as pornographic and denouncing it as "titillating the Jewish disposition to lascivity,"[26] thus seizing the opportunity to make an ethnic slur and accusing the editors of *Nyugat* of venality all at one blow.

The new literature was a "front" for the subversive activities of the Jews. János Horváth, the mildest of the conservative critics to attack *Nyugat*, later wrote that Ady had been used as a "battering-ram often against his own nation, against his Hungarian race. . . ."[27] Horváth declared contritely that "while we had difficulty understanding Ady at the time, the entire cultivated Jewish community would sleep and rise with the volumes of Ady's poetry."[28] Thus, Horváth claimed, *Nyugat* was the organ of the educated Jews. Although the real talents of the movement were not Jewish, all of them were "actively and provocatively philosemitic."[29] This charge, if it be a charge, had been answered a few years earlier by one of the non-Jewish writers, Margit Kaffka. Of the eleven names on the cover of *Nyugat*, she wrote in 1915, seven were not Jewish but "arch-Aryans" and pure Hungarians and, of the remaining four, only two wrote regularly for *Nyugat*.[30] To be sure, Horváth was far off the mark; *Nyugat* was the periodical of the Jews who aspired to complete assimilation and acceptance, made easier by the presence and participation of eminent non-Jewish writers. Kaffka herself was an example of active philosemitism.

Commenting upon a matinée organized by the journal and featuring Ady, Babits, and Móricz—three "Aryans"—Béla Balázs, a Jewish contributor to *Nyugat*, recorded in his diary:

> I have known for a long time that they hate the Semitic literature tied around the neck of Budapest, and that they are suspicious of every writer who is Jewish. . . . Within ten years there will be an outbreak of considerable anti-Semitism in Hungarian literature.[31]

The entry dates from 1912, and the prediction was to prove uncannily accurate. The anti-Semitism that emerged in the wake of the counterrevolution in 1919 was quantitatively and qualitatively distinct from the anti-Semitism of earlier years. At the time Balázs made his prediction, anti-Semitism, when expressed at all, was expressed in veiled terms or euphemisms. The anti-Semites usually felt a compulsion to protest their innocence of any racist slur; hence the occasional racist attacks against *Nyugat* stand

---

[26] Ibid., 9 (1917): 286.
[27] János Horváth, *Aranytól Adyig* (Budapest: Pallas, n.d.), 38.
[28] Ibid., 44.
[29] Ibid., 45–56.
[30] Margit Kaffka, *Az élet utján*, anthology edited by György Bodnár (Budapest: Szépirodalmi, 1972), 31. Ignotus presented the same defense when the *Nyugat* was accused of being essentially in the hands of Jews, but ceased to be convincing when he asserted that the readership of the journal was not predominantly Jewish. "Nyilt levél Dr. Concha Győző egyetemi tanár úrhoz," *Nyugat*, 10, No. 2 (1917): 254.
[31] Diary of Béla Balázs, ca. December 1911 or January 1912, Ms 5023/17, MTA Irattár.

out in their crudeness. *Magyar Kultura,* for instance, reminded its readers that *Nyugat* "maintains a strong blood and race relationship" with the periodical *A Hét,*[32] the editors and contributors of which were almost exclusively Jewish or of Jewish extraction. The same journal attacked Count Gyula Andrássy because, although "the distinguished bearer of a name full of beautiful historical connotations, he has so far forgotten himself as to wallow in the company of Ignotus and Fenyö."[33] The journal did not feel the need to specify that Ignotus and Fenyö were of Jewish extraction, since it could reasonably assume that its readers knew. Similarly, it was the practice of this journal, and of other anti-Semitic organs, to refer to the person under attack by two names: the legal Hungarian name of the individual in question, and his family name before he had it "magyarized," added in parenthesis or connected by a hyphen, thus—Ignotus = Veigelsberg (a practice seldom applied to persons of German or Slavic ethnic descent who had likewise adopted Magyar-sounding names).[34] *Magyar Kultura* would also publish statistics to the effect that 40 percent of the high school students in Budapest were Jewish;[35] or that the number of Jewish physicians was almost twice that of Christian physicians.[36] Even the more subtle critics of *Nyugat,* such as László Németh, who became the outstanding novelist of the next generation, drew a distinction between Jews and non-Jews, accusing the latter of having distorted the message, or betrayed the spirit of the great writers of the nineteenth century.[37]

The new literature was too free in form and language. This accusation was formulated by János Horváth in 1911, and with some authority, for Horváth was a respected professor and critic who abstained from insults and even conceded some virtues to the *Nyugat* movement, and genius to Ady in particular.

Horváth insisted, however, that the *Nyugat* writers were either unable or unwilling to write proper Hungarian prose. Unable in the case of György Lukács and of the "inimitable" Dezsö Szomory (who, indeed, had developed a particularly idiosyncratic style); unwilling in the case of Ignotus or Margit Kaffka who were capable of writing properly when so inclined.[38] Horváth admitted that in this respect, as in others, there were exceptions among the *Nyugat* writers: Móricz and Babits wrote well consistently.[39]

Ignotus was not grateful for the half-compliment. In a reply to Horváth he argued that what really worried the professor was not bad syntax, but that members of other ethnic groups (i.e., Jews) might take over Hungarian

---

[32] *Magyar Kultura,* 1, No. 2 (1913): 74.
[33] Ibid., 9 (1917): 286–87.
[34] A list of magyarized writers' names and their former aliases was published in *Magyar Kultura,* 9 (1917): 430–33.
[35] Ibid., 1 (1913): 62.
[36] Ibid., 158 ff.
[37] György Litván, "*Magyar gondolat-szabad gondolat*" (Budapest: Magvetö, 1978), 25.
[38] János Horváth, *A 'Nyugat' magyartalanságairól* (Budapest: n.p., 1911), 7.
[39] Ibid., 15.

literature.⁴⁰ Thus objections to freedom of form and language merged into and became identical with anti-Semitism.

More often than not the charges indicated above did not appear separately, but in combination. An example of such a combination is provided by one of the characters in Mihály Babits's novel *Halálfiai* (Sons of Death):

. . . nowadays the poets are different; they are alien, their principles are bastard principles. They are the flag-bearers of decadent Parisian confusions, and our youth is already rotten!

Another character in the novel, a village doctor, echoes the outburst: "They are not even Hungarian! They are Jews!"⁴¹

Szabó's categories do not exhaust the range of accusations leveled at *Nyugat*; another widely accepted view, especially in clerical circles, was that there existed a declared or undeclared alliance between *Nyugat* and the Socialists; or even that the *Nyugat* writers were themselves crypto-Socialists. "These modern writers are all Socialists, yet they have a total disregard for those whom the Socialists intend to help, namely the people . . . ," wrote a Protestant clergyman of Debrecen at the time of the first *Nyugat* "matinée" held in that city.⁴² A prominent right-radical journalist who was to contribute, later, to the rise of native fascism spoke of "the community of interest of the capitalists and radicals" which had guided and encouraged *Nyugat*, while *Nyugat* supported them in turn.⁴³ There was scarcely a conservative critic who did not make an association between Socialism and the new literature.⁴⁴ Often the point of departure for these "charges" was Ady's provocations of the Tisza regime and his genuine support of the Social Democrats, sufficient for the entire literary movement to become the target of "political fire."⁴⁵ Even Frigyes Karinthy, the most brilliant wit in the *Nyugat* constellation, but one who deliberately abstained from any political involvement beyond pacifism, and who was among the very few to stay aloof from the Republic of Councils of 1919, was referred to as a "poor, idiotic Socialist" in the reactionary clerical press.⁴⁶

Perhaps it was the poet Gyula Juhász who was best able to account for the real motives behind the general fear those in power exhibited in the presence of Ady's poetry and prose: "They hate the Adys in our country, because Ady and his friends explode the myths, because they are not afraid to say that something stinks in Denmark." The critics, continued Juhász,

---

⁴⁰ "A Nyugat magyartalanságairól," *Nyugat*, 4, No. 2 (1911): 1028–40, reprinted in *Ignotus válogatott írásai*, 651–54.

⁴¹ Mihály Babits, *Halálfiai* (Budapest: Szépirodalmi Könyvkiadó, 1972), 626.

⁴² Quoted by Pál Kardos, "A 'Nyugat' debreceni kapcsolatai," in *Acta Universitatis Debreceniensis de Ludovico Kossuth Nominate* (1955), 99.

⁴³ Cited in György Litván, 57.

⁴⁴ *A magyar irodalom története*, 5: 34.

⁴⁵ Aladár Schöpflin, *A magyar irodalom története a XX. században* (Budapest: Grill Károly, 1973), 131.

⁴⁶ Review of *Nyugat* as periodical by Péter Nagy in *Magyar Kultúra*, 3 (1915): 134.

believe that to denounce abuses is to offend national dignity.[47] Indeed, perhaps the critics were not unaware of the abuses (nor were they innocent of their perpetration), but opted to live with them or disregard them, if only because these were part of a system in which they had a stake. They feared the explosion, but were not sufficiently intelligent to foresee and forestall it. It seemed to them that the bombs were planted by Ady and his companions, while they took no notice of the explosions underground. They resented Ady in particular, because he had all the makings of a member of the ruling class; yet he chose to ignore or look down on them.

Though he was the prime target, by and large Ady got away with being a renegade, a "traitor to his class." In spite of the numbers of his opponents and the coalition of reactionary forces, Ady seems to have attained a status of immunity. This immunity, of course, was a corollary of his fame. Ignotus remarked somewhere that famous artists, writers, and "other such do not get hanged once they become involved in revolutionary activity. And revolutions, or the wresting of justice as in the case of the Dreyfus affair, require the contribution of individuals who are immune, who dare to undertake measures for which others would get hanged."[48] Consider, for example, the personal confrontation between Ady, the leading poet, and Tisza, the political leader—the man most directly responsible for Hungary's fortunes before and during the war. The confrontation, it is true, was too personal to fit into any pattern of rebellion and repression. It was a particular case, sufficiently significant to form the subject of a monograph by Loránt Hegedüs, an industrialist and executive of the national association of manufacturers, who was both a supporter of Tisza and a friend of Ady; his pamphlet titled "Ady and Tisza" was more than a hundred pages long.[49]

In 1903 Ady had called upon Tisza to request a state grant to travel to Paris; much later, in 1916, the poet again turned to Tisza for help when he ran into difficulties with the father of his fiancée, who was most reluctant to allow his teenage daughter to marry the "dissolute" and by then fatally-ill poet.[50]

In between, however, the two men feuded. Tisza's general attitude is summarized in a statement to Hegedüs in November, 1910: "Ady and *Nyugat* are parasites on the palm-tree of Hungarian culture." At a time when he was not prime minister, and hence could afford the time to worry about cultural issues, Tisza—using the pen-name Rusticus—attacked modern literature, modern music, and modern art (the paintings of Rippl-Rónai in particular) in his own review, the *Magyar Figyelő*.[51] Another of

---

[47] *Juhász Gyula összes művei*, 5 (Budapest: Akadémiai Kiadó, 1968–72): 249–50.
[48] Reprinted from a collection of aphorisms titled "Olvasás közben"—[While Reading]—in *Ignotus válogatott irásai*, 470–71.
[49] *Ady és Tisza* (Budapest: Nyugat, n.d.).
[50] Ibid., 56–61.
[51] Letter from Rusticus, *Magyar Figyelő*, 2 (1911), 423. Also November, 1912, issue of the same periodical, and the pertinent comments in *Ady és Tisza*, 98–100.

Tisza's papers, the *Budapesti Napló,* regularly published attacks on the *Nyugat.* The pen-name Rusticus was appropriate. Indeed, Tisza was an unrefined aristocrat from the provinces; and since he was not interested in poetry, he could not support his attacks on aesthetic grounds. Nevertheless, wrote Aladár Schöpflin, Tisza expressed opinions characteristic of the great majority of the Hungarian gentry.[52] Since these opinions had no genuine artistic or aesthetic foundations, one is justified in regarding them as politically motivated.

Ady did not turn the other cheek. Prompted by Tisza's ruthless repression of the workers' demonstration of 23 May 1912, and of strikers in general, and perhaps also by Tisza's above-quoted comment on *Nyugat,* he wrote and published the poem "Enyhe, ujévi átok" [A Mild New Year's Curse]: "And let him be afflicted by all the plagues/let paralysis numb him to the bone."[53] While this "mild" curse does not mention Tisza by name, he *is* named in a number of poems from the same period,[54] and Ady actually dedicated an almost equally unflattering poem to him in 1913: "Rengj csak, föld!" [Quake, Earth!].

It should be noted, however, that Ady did not express universal contempt for the aristocracy, let alone the bourgeoisie. For instance, he publicly praised Count Albert Apponyi, who had helped his brother secure employment, and with whom he had had occasion to converse on literary subjects.[55]

Nor did aristocrats invariably attack or despise *Nyugat.* Count Gyula Andrássy, for one, established a link with the journal through its editor-in-chief Ignotus, who had placed his talents at the service of the count's political program. Thus Andrássy was led to take an interest in modern art and literature, and brought the journal a number of subscribers from the ranks of the aristocratic National Casino.[56] (The library of the Casino, however, did not subscribe to *Nyugat,* as far as I could tell from the catalogue of that library.)

The outbreak of World War I had the effect of hardening the position of the establishment, but not that of the opposition; censorship became institutionalized. True, there had always been censorship of sorts. Fenyö, and others, argued then and later that the "old regime" was liberal, at least in matters of culture, that practically everything was permitted, since the establishment did not feel seriously threatened.[57] The "old regime" was

---

[52] *A magyar irodalom története a XX. században,* 133–35.
[53] "Hogy fussanak rá minden nyavalyák
   Hogy a törés jókedvvel törje,
   Akarásunkat durván az, aki
   Bánatokig és átkokig gyötörte:
   Ez a gazember még lakolni fog."
Népszava, 1 Jan. 1913.
[54] "Két kuruc beszélget"; "Ülj törvényt Werböczi"; "Nem nagy dolog."
[55] *Ady Endre összes prózai művei,* 10: 390.
[56] Miksa Fenyö, 63.
[57] Ibid.

liberal, relatively speaking; but this liberalism had its limits. Publications had been confiscated or prohibited on a number of occasions. The *Népszava*—the newspaper of the Social Democrats—had been confiscated on 21 May 1912, a couple of days before the general strike it had advocated; and again on 9 March 1913, because it published a certain poem by a young Communist.[58] The anarchist periodical, *Társadalmi forradalom* (Social Revolution), was confiscated repeatedly even though it had a very limited circulation and could not have posed a serious threat no matter what it advocated.

Long before the war, and long before the famous "Fortissimo" case, Hungarian writers had been prosecuted for certain types of "misdemeanors": Frigyes Karinthy, for instance, was charged with "antireligious agitation and blasphemy" (reminiscent of the type of charges leveled at the *philosophes* of the Enlightenment), as he revealed in a protest letter published in *Nyugat* (April 1909):

> The censorship before the revolution would be more clement towards me if it understood that my satire is directed against anti-social tendencies. . . . It is incredible that I should have to bear the police in mind while writing, here, in a civilized country. . . .[59]

Nota bene, Karinthy did not bother to explain the source of his revolutionary vision; what could he have meant by "before the revolution" in 1909, ten years before the political revolution broke out?

There was, moreover, the implicit, preventive autocensorship alluded to by Ervin Szabó, the most distinguished and original socialist thinker in Hungary:

> The Hungarian bourgeois—yes, bourgeois—journalists do not know that freedom of the press never existed in this country, neither before 1867 nor thereafter. What does exist, is that it is possible to write as much as does not jeopardize the rule of the ruling class in its essence, or else to write that which they are incapable of preventing from being written, for lack of power.[60]

Indirect censorship was of various kinds. In addition to the kinds already mentioned, there was the policy of subsidies. Thus the editors of *Nyugat* were elated when the Ministry of War, apparently unaware of the tendency of the review, agreed to advertise in it; there was no question of rejecting the offer on ethical or ideological grounds.[61] But if government advertising could be a substantial financial contribution, the deprivation or withdrawal of such advertising could cause substantial damage. I found correspondence

---

[58] The young Communist was Aladár Komját: see István Király, "Az elsö kommunista magyar költö . . .," in *Forradalmi magyar irodalom*, ed. Miklós Szabolcsi and László Illés (Budapest: Akadémiai Kiadó, 1963), 60.

[59] *Nyugat*, 1 (1909): 448.

[60] Ervin Szabó, "Disputa," *Nyugat*, 7 (1914): 152.

[61] The advertisement would have represented an income of one to two thousand crowns a year, according to Fenyö's communication to Hatvany, 15 May 1908, *Levelek Hatvany Lajoshoz*, 35.

between the Prime Minister's office and the Ministry of Cults regarding the advisability of withdrawing government advertising from certain opposition papers such as *Világ*.[62] The copies of *Nyugat* that I have seen in an unbound state, with all the pages of advertisements included, did not contain any sponsored by the government (except for train schedules but, to my knowledge, their publication was compulsory and not remunerated); hence, this source of revenue seems not to have materialized.

Another type of control was the one exercised by publishing houses. At a time when Babits boasted in *Világ* (25 December 1912) that his writings were appreciated even by the conservatives,[63] he received the jolt of indirect censorship. The editors of the journal *Élet*, a Roman Catholic periodical founded in order to reach the masses and to counteract the influence of progressive journals such as *Nyugat*, had decided to issue a series of volumes in collaboration with the well-known publishing house of Révai Brothers. As part of the series, they had accepted for publication a volume of critical essays by Babits and a collection of short stories by Dezsö Kosztolányi. In fact, this decision of the editors of *Élet* may have been the very cause of Babits's above-mentioned optimism. But later, during a meeting of the board in charge of the series, objections were raised against the publication of the two volumes on the grounds that both Babits and Kosztolányi had published items in *Nyugat* that "a good Catholic could not approve of. . . ."[64] *Élet* canceled the two volumes. Babits continued to negotiate with Révai Brothers regarding the publication of his volume of essays, without success.

The matinées organized by *Nyugat* did not always have clear sailing either; witness the request for a matinée to be held at the National Theater in 1913, with the participation of Ignotus, Ady, Babits, and Móricz. Fenyö had requested police authorization for 23 February; it was not granted, however, until 20 April. The series of delays was partly the fault of the organizers, but police also delayed the authorization on the grounds that the theater would be used twice the same day, which would "overtax" the energies of firemen and of theater personnel! It is more likely, however, that given the reputation of *Nyugat*, the authorities were worried that the matinée might contribute to the atmosphere of tension occasioned by a projected general strike; once the Social Democratic Party decided to call off the general strike, the *Nyugat* matinée appeared harmless, and permission was finally granted, by way of "exception."[65]

---

[62] Memorandum of 30 September 1911, ME 465/1912; and letter of 4 February 1913, ME 803/1913, Országos Levéltár.

[63] *Ady Endre összes prózai müvei*, 10: 571.

[64] Jegyzökönyv 30 April 1915, and subsequent correspondence, Elet Z 720 (137), Z section, Országos Levéltár. A letter from an official of the Révai Brothers to Babits, dated 22 March 1916, states that "shortly after we had reached agreement about the publication of the essays you published a novel in *Nyugat*, which caused a great deal of displeasure in certain Catholic quarters, especially since the open discussion of certain erotic matters is practically diametrically opposed to the Catholic concept of morality." The novel referred to was the *Gólyakalifa*, published in English under the title *Nightmare*.

[65] See the records in the Mayor's Office, III 512/1913 in the Municipal Archives of Budapest.

Under the circumstances it may be surprising that the government felt a need to tighten censorship, which took the form of the press law of 1912; presumably it was prompted by increased agitation among the nationalities. According to this law any periodical publication had to apply for permission to distribute from the local administration. Furthermore, the responsibility for an item published rested not only with the author, but with all those who assisted him or her in its preparation, including the editors. Most important in view of the coming conflagration, the government acquired the right of censorship prior to publication in times of war—a right to be exercised by an agency with the unsightly name of "Hadfelügyeleti bizottság sajtóbizottsága" [The Press Committee of the Armed Forces Inspection Committee].[66]

The first evidence of censorship as applied to *Nyugat* can be found in an issue from early 1916. About half of an installment of Menyhért Lengyel's series "Simple Thoughts" was left blank.[67] A year later an article by Fenyö entitled "The War Objectives of the Monarchy" had to be left entirely blank except for the title;[68] in vain had *Nyugat* obtained official authorization, shortly before, to deal with political matters. Blank pages were frequent in the issues from 1916 and 1917. In the course of 1917, however, the blank pages ceased, because the censorship office prohibited the practice; henceforth, the censored parts had to be deleted so as to leave no trace.

It was in 1917 that the *cas* or *cause célèbre* of the confiscation of *Nyugat* took place, the motive being the inclusion of Babits's antiwar poem "Fortissimo." It was not the first time that the poet had had a run-in with the authorities because of his antiwar poems. The first such "scandal" had been occasioned by "Játszottam a kezével" [I Played with Her Hand] published in the 16 August 1915 issue of *Nyugat*; there he resorted to a not altogether novel poetic conceit, namely that he would rather shed blood for the sake of his beloved than for the sake of a hundred kings or flags. Babits then became the target of angry attacks by Austro-Hungarian nationalists, notably Jenö Rákosi,[69] and lost his position as teacher in a public high school. His poem "Husvét elött" (Before Easter), recited to a cheering crowd at a matinée in Budapest and published in *Nyugat,* also provoked a series of attacks. But "Fortissimo" is certainly one of the most powerful antiwar poems in world literature. The March 1917 issue of *Nyugat* was confiscated by the authorities (see p. 72).[70]

Nyugat was on the stands again a few days later, without the poem; and the charges against Babits and the editors were dropped, thanks to the

---

[66] Béla Dezsényi and György Nemes, *A magyar sajtó 250 éve* (Budapest: Művelt Nép Könyvkiadó, 1954), 1: 271. See also *Magyarország története,* 7 (Budapest: Akadémiai Kiadó, 1978). György Lukács had the misfortune of working for this committee for awhile.
[67] 9, No. 1 (1916): 241–43.
[68] 10, No. 1 (1917): 128–32.
[69] *Budapesti Hirlap* (9 Nov. 1915), 1–3.
[70] Babits papers, 111/1591, Országos Széchenyi Irattár.

intervention of friends and benefactors. Babits, however, was seriously hampered in his work; he seems to have spent considerable time preparing his defense, culling examples of "blasphemy" from the poetry of Petőfi, Dante, and others. The affair cost him at least 150 crowns in lawyer's fees, and his high-school position, for the second time.[71]

To be sure, wartime censorship was by no means peculiar to Hungary. Censorship by the Hungarian state could have been far more heavy-handed; only on few occasions did the censor, the police, or the judge intervene, even for political reasons, to defend the establishment. As I have already mentioned, at least one of the *Nyugat* editors argued that there was considerable literary leeway in the eras of Deák, or Tisza, and even of Horthy, perhaps because these regimes were wise enough not to overestimate the impact of literature on the citizenry, and *minima non curat praetor.*[72]

Yet I remain unconvinced by this thesis: if literature was indeed a small matter, the establishment had nothing to fear from it. The thesis is based on incomplete or incorrectly interpreted data; for the establishment did react. I am tempted to say "overreacted," if this were not an epistemological contradiction; for the significance of the *Nyugat* movement was accorded to it, at least in part, by the establishment itself. It became "dangerous," that is effective, to the extent that its enemies reacted. The danger was all the greater as the progressive writers were not partisans (party-men) and did not set out deliberately to destroy the ruling class. One thing, however, was clear, then as now: the *Nyugat* writers did not write in the interest or for the benefit of the establishment. As Ady put it in 1908: "It is beautiful, after what has been said, that those who own all of Hungary, cannot reconcile themselves to the fact that they do not own its literature. . . . Does it not mean something that nowadays, in Hungary, literature excites even those who have no use for it?"[73] And let us recall, once again, the remark of the Tharaud brothers, who were to "blame" the Republic of Councils, *Huszadik Század*, and *Nyugat* on the Jews; or Jenő Rákosi, the spokesman for Hungarian chauvinism, Ady's arch-enemy, who was to claim during the counterrevolutionary regime, that "Endre Ady, Lajos Hatvany, and a bunch of smaller fry" were the ones who had made the revolution along with the politicians Mihály Károlyi, Zsigmond Kunfi, and Oszkár Jászi.[74]

But the effectiveness of the *Nyugat* movement was not simply a function of lesser or greater repression. There had been progress in the reception of *Nyugat* and of Ady. The growing circulation figures of the periodical are the most tangible evidence of this trend. The tendency had not escaped contemporary witnesses, critics, and reviewers, however impressionistic their analysis may have been: "The fact that even from the conservative

---

[71] Lawyer's bill of 10 Aug. 1917, Babits papers, III/1581, Országos Széchenyi Irattár.
[72] Miksa Fenyö, *Följegyzések*, 99.
[73] "Irodalmi háborgás és szocializmus," *Szocializmus*, 3, No. 3 (1908–09): 112–14.
[74] Quoted in Géza Lengyel, *Magyar ujságmágnások* (Budapest: Akadémiai Kiadó, 1963), 120.

side the critics seem to have surrendered to Ady is sufficient proof of considerable progress in Hungarian literary matters in the past ten years . . . ," wrote a critic in the radical review *Ma*.[75] In 1918 the conservative literary society which had usurped, so to speak, the name "Petőfi" to designate itself, felt the time had come to expand its membership by inviting some prominent *Nyugat* writers to join; the latter, however, preferred to form their own body, the Vörösmarty Academy, named after another progressive poet of the previous century.[76]

I would suggest that it was not so much a matter of "conservative surrender" as the critic asserted, but rather a widening of the ranks of the opposition, an ever more open and outspoken opposition to the regime. The revolutions in Russia made revolution seem possible in Hungary. The widening circles who accepted Ady and *Nyugat* also accepted this possibility. *Their* revolution, that of October, 1918, corresponded, by and large, to the "bourgeois" phase; but even the "proletarian" revolution of March, 1919, found considerable support among progressive intellectuals.

---

[75] László F. Boross, *Ma* (15 Oct. 1918), 111. Boross adds, by way of criticism, that Ady is subjective and self-centered, not objective in a revolutionary way.

[76] Oszkár Gellért, *Egy író élete* (Budapest: Bibliotheca, 1958), 1: 328.

X. THE MIRROR OR THE HAMMER

As Perry Anderson has already pointed out,[1] Marxist thought in this century, but particularly after Lenin, has been especially concerned, perhaps even obsessed, with the domain of esthetics, the work of art, the literary work. Suffice to refer to the bulk of the essays of György Lukács and Lucien Goldmann, Walter Benjamin, Theodor Adorno, Ernst Fischer, Christopher Caudwell, Ralph Fox; and to a substantial portion, if not the bulk, of the works of Antonio Gramsci, Jean-Paul Sartre, or Leon Trotsky.

Looking at the evolution of ideas from a different angle, that of the proliferation of disciplines and increasing specialization, we note that sociology of literature has come into its own as a branch of the social sciences. Witness the research centers, or the professorial chairs devoted to that field of endeavor; and witness also the number of anthologies and collections of essays by a single author, or by diverse authors, dealing with, and often bearing the very title "Literature and Society."[2] Despite the fact that the writings of Lukács, and of many others among those mentioned above, tend to be difficult of access, particularly to the working class, because of their abstruse language and arguments, they have been reprinted in paperback editions (I have even found copies of Lukács sold at airport bookstalls). Thus we may assume that this new discipline, this new approach to literature, is just as much a response to certain societal needs as are changes in literary style or literary fashion, as is the transformation of literary forms; perhaps it is time for someone to broach the subject of the sociology of the sociology of literature.

Yet the authors cited are not particularly concerned with the functions of literature. They tend to regard literature, and the domain of esthetics in general, simply as part of the superstructure; that is, as something that is immediately perceptible to the senses, and that allows us to draw inferences regarding the deeper, more fundamental social or economic changes. Since, more often than not, they are concerned with literary works or movements which had appeared before their own time, their analysis bears upon his-

---

[1] *Considerations on Western Marxism* (London: Schocken, 1976).

[2] Among such anthologies we may cite, in chronological order, L. Bacandall, ed., *Marxism and Aesthetics* (New York: Humanities Press, 1968), and the same editor's *Radical Perspectives in the Arts* (Baltimore: Penguin Books, 1972). Berel Lang and Forrest Williams, eds., *Marxism and Art* (New York: David McKay, 1972). Elizabeth and Tom Burns, eds., *Marxists on Literature—An Anthology* (London: Penguin, 1975). Similar anthologies have appeared in other languages: for instance, Roger Garaudy, Jean-Paul Sartre, Ernst Fischer, Eduard Goldstücker, *Estética y Marxismo* (Barcelona: Martinez Roca, 1969).

torical change; in other words, it is aided by hindsight. Thus, these authors, whether or not they write in a post-capitalist society, deal with literature in a capitalist, or pre-Socialist society.

For instance, Lenin underlines the key role played by the bourgeois intellectuals, or by certain bourgeois intellectuals, in the preparation of the working class for the revolutionary struggle; but the intellectual activists he had in mind were not usually authors of novels, they were seldom engaged in the production of belles-lettres, even as a side-line—they had urgent and direct tasks to perform. As for the author of novels—he cannot be a free agent, argued Lenin, because he is dependent upon the bourgeois publisher and a bourgeois reading public.[3]

Still, Lenin thought of Leo Tolstoy much in the same terms as Marx and Engels (and Lukács) could appreciate the work of Balzac. The latter admired the work of Balzac in spite of its author's explicit political views, which were royalist, hence rather reactionary. Nevertheless, Balzac's work "shatters the optimism of the bourgeois, instils doubt as to the eternal character of the existing order, although the author does not offer any definite solution or does not even line up openly on any particular side."[4] Jorge Luis Borges, incidentally, had the same perception of the work of Rudyard Kipling (which may indicate that you do not have to be a Marxist to advocate Marxist views or to agree with Marx): Kipling's intentions and plans hardly matter; he "dedicated his life to writing in terms of certain political ideals, he tried to make his work an instrument of propaganda and yet, at the end of his life, he was obliged to confess that the true essence of a writer's work is usually unknown to him . . ."[5]

The works of Tolstoy, like those of Balzac, have a progressive function, quite independent of the author's political preference or intent.[6] But at this point Lenin hesitates in his evaluation of Tolstoy's impact. Must there be a successful revolution in order for Tolstoy's work to enjoy popularity, to be popularized? Or, on the contrary, should his work be popularized and widely distributed first in order to facilitate or hasten the coming of the revolution? "If his great works are really to be made the possession of all," wrote Lenin, "a socialist revolution must be accomplished."[7] On the other hand, by studying the works of Tolstoy, the working class will get to know its enemies better.[8] Therefore, Lenin added, Tolstoy's works must be re-

---

[3] "Are you free in relation to your bourgeois publisher, Mr. Writer, in relation to your bourgeois public, which demands that you provide it with pornography . . .?" Lenin, "Party Organization and Party Literature," in *On Literature and Art* (Moscow: Progress Publishers, 1970), 26.

[4] Quoted in Diana T. Laurenson and Alan Swingewood, *The Sociology of Literature* (New York: Schocken Books, 1972), 48.

[5] *Labyrinths* (Penguin: London, 1970), 219.

[6] For a thorough analysis of Marx's and Engels's attitude towards Balzac, see György Lukács, *Balzac et le réalisme français* (Paris: François Maspéro, 1969).

[7] "L. N. Tolstoy," in *On Literature and Art*, 48.

[8] "Tolstoy and the Proletarian Struggle," in *On Literature and Art*, 56. In a travel book by the British "sportsman" and author John G. Millais I came across the following observation:

printed in hundreds of thousands of copies for the benefit of peasants and workers (clearly a populist approach); for, indeed, a great writer, or a great artist, is nothing less than a scientific observer, "a ruthless observer."[9] Had Lenin paid more systematic attention to the issue of the political function of literature, instead of scattering remarks in diverse pamphlets, the contradiction would have become readily apparent. Whether the contradiction needs to be resolved, is another matter; after all, it intimates the dialectical process.

Lenin implicitly recognized, and probably exaggerated, the power of the man of letters, as a potential enemy of the revolution. In a letter to a friend, dated 5 August 1921, he argued against freedom of the press. In a beleaguered Soviet Union freedom of the press would amount to freedom of political organization for the bourgeoisie which is "still very much stronger than we are." This kind of freedom, he added, might simply mean that the "international bourgeoisie" would buy up hundreds and thousands of writers; it would mean suicide for the Socialist Revolution![10]

The question comes to mind: did freedom of the press under the preceding bourgeois regime mean suicide for that regime? Or was it that freedom of the press had not existed even then? Or again, were the "thousands of writers" faithful allies of that regime, were they faithful members of their own bourgeois class?

It might be possible to write a monograph on Lenin's concept or concepts of the intellectual; but as for his concept of the writer, there is not much to go by. Part of the problem in interpreting Lenin's notions of the function of literature is that he does not define literature, and often uses the word to mean "party literature," the writing of political pamphlets. Hence the collection of Lenin's writings published in Moscow under the title *On Literature and Art* contains only a few items that deal directly with either one of those subjects.

Not so with Plekhanov or Trotsky; their works are among the first dealing specifically with the relationship between literature and society. Plekhanov's *Art and Society* appeared in 1912. It contains no intimation, however, that art, or literature, is anything but a mirror, a reflection of socioeconomic change. Their function is passive.

Trotsky's analysis tends to be more positive. Like Marx and Engels, who had, like true romantics, or like true idealists of any age, not been above writing poetry in their youth, Trotsky too was a man of letters, and remained

---

Tolstoy's "pernicious doctrines, veiled in language all could understand [sic!], made him the real author of the Russian Revolution." *Far Away Up the Nile* (London: Longmans, Green, and Co., 1924), 4.

[9] Pierre Macherey, *Pour une théorie de la production littéraire* (Paris: François Maspéro, 1966), 140, 146. At times Lenin seemed to lack critical acumen in literary matters: witness his ambivalence to the works of Mayakovsky. See Jürgen Rühle, *Literatur und Revolution: die Schriftsteller und der Kommunismus* (Köln: Kiepenheuer & Witsch, 1960), 25.

[10] Lenin, *On Literature and Art*, 216.

so throughout his life.[11] His often sarcastic reviews of the works of individual writers in *Literature and Revolution* were written shortly after 1917, at a time when—one has the right to surmise—Trotsky could or should have been too busy to read or write or worry about literature. Clearly, he attached much importance to the function of literature. Yet he is wary of any romantic, Shelleyan notion about the mission of the poet:

> The traditional identification of poet and prophet is acceptable only in the sense that the poet is about as slow in reflecting his epoch as the prophet. If there are poets and prophets who can be said to be "ahead of their time" it is because they have expressed certain demands of social evolution not quite as slowly as the rest of their kind.
>
> Before even a tremor of revolutionary presentiment could pass through Russian literature at the end of the last century and the beginning of this, history had to produce the deepest changes in the basis of economics, in land tenure, in social relations, and in the feelings of the masses.[12]

In other words, the theory of literature propounded by Trotsky was strictly orthodox. If we are to take this theory at face value, we may well wonder why Lenin feared the bourgeois press, or why literature commands so much respect in certain "socialist" countries, first of all in the Soviet Union.[13] Why is it that those writers who support the Soviet regime, and especially those by whom the regime wishes to be supported, receive signal honors? And why is it that those who dare to be openly critical (although distinctions are usually made between "friendly" and "unfriendly" criticism) may be considered as public enemies and are, at times, dealt with as harshly as the most unsocial criminal?[14] Indeed, the attitude of the socialist regimes in Eastern Europe and the Soviet Union gives the lie to Trotsky's assessment of the role of the poet.

But then, so did Trotsky himself. In the same work in which he banished all poets to irrelevance, and the Russian writer in particular, for not having felt the coming of the October Revolution, he wrote:

> Works of art are the embodiments of presentiments; therefore, pre-revolutionary art is the real art of the Revolution . . . It is absolutely unquestionable that the war and the Revolution were prepared in the material conditions and in the consciousness of the classes. It is also unquestionable that the preparation was reflected in different ways in art.[15]

---

[11] Edmund Wilson, *The Triple Thinkers* (London: John Lehmann, 1952), 191.

[12] Leon Trotsky, *Literature and Revolution* (Ann Arbor: University of Michigan Press, 1960), 20.

[13] Trotsky likewise feared the bourgeois press. "We are destroying the press of the counterrevolution . . ." he boasted in *Terrorism and Communism* (reprinted by University of Michigan Press, 1961), 61.

[14] George Steiner, "Marxism and the Literary Critic," *Sociology of Literature and Drama*, eds. Elizabeth and Tom Burns (London: Penguin, 1973), 177.

[15] Trotsky, op. cit., 110.

As for literature, Trotsky added, it is not a mirror, but a hammer, and it is a hammer that shapes and educates the individual, the social group, the class, the nation.[16]

The contradictions were not resolved by the next generation of Marxist thinkers, such as György Lukács and his "disciple," Lucien Goldmann, even though their major works centered on esthetics and literature. While both admitted the legitimacy of an analysis of the impact of literature upon its recipients, as one of the three or four major concerns of the sociology of literature,[17] this type of analysis was intentionally bypassed by both. At a certain juncture Lukács seemed to agree with Trotsky (although Trotsky is not given credit for the idea) that literature leaves the reader in the lurch (*im Stich*) when it comes to taking important decisions, because writers are not cleverer than their times.[18] Elsewhere Lukács observes: "Every writer is the son of his age . . . Thus it is very difficult for the writer really to free himself from the currents and fluctuations of his time and, within them, from those of his class."[19] But only a few pages further Lukács seems to have already changed his mind. During the rise of Hitler, he wrote, the change in political outlook of the exiled German writers anticipated a turning point in the destiny of the German people.[20] Nor was it merely a matter of anticipation: the writers may even contribute to radical change. The German writers who wrote historical novels based on the lives of Henri IV of France, of Cervantes, of Erasmus, and of Flavius Josephus, had a "political and social aim: knowledge of the great struggles of the past, familiarity with the great forefighters of progress will inspire man in the present with aims and ideals, courage and consolation amid the brutal terrors of Fascism."[21]

At times Lukács was quite emphatic about the political impact of literature. "It is obvious," he wrote, still in 1936, "that precisely the historical novel can and surely will play an enormous part in this anti-Fascist struggle."[22] It is a pity that no one, not even Lukács, had bothered to write an assessment in retrospect of the actual role historical novels, or literature in general, may have played in bringing about the downfall of Fascism and of its National Socialist variety. There was nothing obvious about it. Those of us who prefer to believe (along with Lukács) that literature matters historically, have instinctively felt that it may be best not to investigate that issue; or else one might well come to the conclusion that literature inside Germany, or beyond its borders, had precious little to do with the

---

[16] Ibid., 137, 168.
[17] See Newald, introduction to György Lukács, *Sociología da la literatura* (Barcelona: Ediciones Peninsula, 1968), 20–23.
[18] Quoted in Jürgen Ruhle, op. cit., 245.
[19] György Lukács, *The Historical Novel* (London: Merton Press, 1962, 1st ed. Moscow, 1937), 254.
[20] Ibid., 266.
[21] Lukács, *The Historical Novel*, 271.
[22] Ibid., 277.

defeat of Fascism. Indeed, the skillfully manipulated worship of the German classics on the one hand, and the silence of certain eminent contemporary German writers on the other, may have even retarded that process. But if the presence of literature has a meaning, so does its absence. In any case, how could the German writer defy an all-pervasive censorship during the *Gleichschaltung*?[23] How different the type of censorship imposed on the writers of the French Enlightenment from the one instituted by totalitarian regimes in Hitler's Germany or elsewhere!

Goldmann, no more than Lukács, was particularly concerned with the literary work's impact on the reader. In his work on the novel he favored a "structuralist" approach. He described the function of the novel, within the context of structuralism, not as a mirror of collective awareness, but rather as one of its most important components, since it is the one that allows members of "the group" to become conscious of what they think, feel, and do, without previous knowledge of its objective meaning.[24] But perhaps Goldmann is merely begging the questions. Are feeling and thinking distinct from consciousness? And what, exactly, is the meaning of objective meaning? More important, for our purposes, is the significance Goldmann attaches to the novel as a component of collective awareness: "The literary work itself is an historical fact of the highest importance by virtue of the influence which it had at a certain moment and which it still has on the modes of thought and feeling of men who constitute certain social groups," he wrote, with reference to Racine and Kierkegaard.[25] Indeed, at one point he calls for "particularly urgent" empirical research on the nature of the act of reading, as well as on the relationship between the "creators"—meaning, presumably, writers and artists—and the elite groups who are responsible for economic, social, and political decisions.[26] ILTAM, the institute directed by Robert Escarpit at Bordeaux, is one place which has already undertaken some of this type of empirical research.[27]

Jean-Paul Sartre, and the two young British Marxist critics active in the thirties, Ralph Fox and Christopher Caudwell, have skirted the problem area of the political function of literature. Sartre does not hesitate to ascribe

---

[23] Bertolt Brecht, who did not see eye to eye with Lukács on certain basic issues, wrote in 1935: "Anyone who wishes to combat lies and ignorance and to write the truth . . . must have the *courage* to write the truth when the truth is everywhere opposed; the *keenness* to recognize it, although it is everywhere concealed . . . These are formidable problems for a writer living under Fascism, but they also exist for those writers who have fled or been exiled; they exist for writers working in countries where civil liberty prevails." Quoted by Meredith Tax, *Marxism and Alienation*, 17.

[24] Lucien Goldmann, *Pour une sociologie du roman* (Paris: Gallimard, 1964), 346–47.

[25] Lucien Goldmann, *The Human Sciences and Philosophy* (London: Jonathan Cape, 1969), 31. More recently, Goldmann observed, off the cuff: "Any important work, any philosophical or artistic current, has a scope and exercises an influence on the behavior of members of the group . . ." In "Dialectical Materialism and Literary History," *New Left Review*, 92 (July–August 1975): 44.

[26] *Pour une sociologie du roman*, 371–72.

[27] Regarding the psychology or psychoanalysis of the reader, see Simon O. Lesser, *Fiction and the Unconscious* (London: Peter Owen, 1960).

power to literature, presumably including his own. "Words are loaded pistols," he proclaims.[28] The writer must become involved, *engagé*, if only to feel alive, if only as an existential task. And involvement is praxis. Hence Sartre's call to arms to writers and all intellectuals: ". . . I don't think you can have an intellectual without his being 'left-wing.' "[29] To be sure, Sartre's opinion sounds more like an injunction or exhortation than an uncommitted observation. Should any writer follow this injunction it would become clear that involvement is no mere existential self-satisfaction, that the written word, like the spoken word, can become action (*la parole est action*). Then Sartre's own written word will have made a convert. The point that words are loaded pistols will have been demonstrated.[30]

Involvement requires courage, of course, and there may be a direct correlation between the depth of commitment and the degree of courage. For it is the ruling class which oversees the distribution of jobs and the appointment of intellectuals.[31] Thus Molière, his genius notwithstanding, hardly deserves praise for depicting the bourgeois as an object of ridicule, particularly as someone aping the aristocrat; for Molière was appointed by the court, whereas the bourgeoisie was still a century and a half away from becoming the ruling class. Nevertheless, functionally, the intellectual tends to move in opposition to the interests of those who keep him alive, according to Sartre.[32] Thus, in the eighteenth century, some writers, whether deliberately or unconsciously, incited their bourgeois, or not so bourgeois public to revolt.[33]

Eric Williams tells us, in his history of the Caribbean, how Toussaint L'Ouverture used to "read and re-read" the following passage in the writings of the Abbé Raynal: "Where is that great man whom nature owes to her afflicted, oppressed and tormented children? Where is he? He will undoubtedly appear, he will lift up the sacred standard of liberty." And that was how L'Ouverture changed from coachman to his master to coachman of the Haitian war of liberation.[34]

When it comes to the twentieth century Sartre is no longer so sanguine about the political role of the artist or the intellectual. "The 'Massacre of Guernica'—does anyone think it won over a single heart to the Spanish

---

[28] *What is Literature?* (New York: Harper & Row, 1965), 18.
[29] *Politics and Literature* (London: Calder & Boyars, 1973), 13.
[30] Sartre himself claimed that the reading of Freud, Kafka, and Joyce, often described by Marxist criticism as "decadent," was among the factors that led him towards Marxism. Roger Garaudy, et al., *Estética y Marxismo*, 58.
[31] *Politics and Literature*, 15.
[32] Many would disagree. Leszek Kolakowski, for instance, writes: "It is obvious, for example, that in capitalist countries civil servants, for whom the maintenance of government represents a guarantee of a lifetime job, must be more conservative than artists." The question is, at what point does a creative artist become a civil servant? *Marxism and Beyond* (London: Pall Mall Press, 1968), 178. Marx's famous remark about the ideology of the ruling class is also relevant.
[33] *What is Literature?* 101, 260.
[34] *From Columbus to Castro* (London: André Deutsch, 1970), 216.

cause?" he writes.³⁵ (With a bit of malice, one might paraphrase the question to read: "The Massacre of Guernica, as opposed to *Le mur*, does anyone think . . .") It is not only the relevance of the contributions of the painter, the composer, or the poet (actually, he has summarily dismissed all of poetry, along with Picasso, as politically irrelevant) that Sartre now questions. He questions himself; his own self-confidence seems to come and go. Writers of all kinds may prove to be useless individuals. In times of crisis, "an author shot is one mouth less to feed. The least important producer would be a greater loss to the nation."³⁶ In times of crisis, literature becomes a luxury commodity.

Although Sartre's credentials as a Marxist are open to question (and he himself has accepted and rejected Marx at various times, and on various levels)³⁷ there can be little doubt about the credentials of either Fox or Caudwell. They lived far from the Soviet Union, and died too young and too soon to become embroiled in controversies about Stalinism. Yet they had no fear of exploring virgin territory. Fox was a Marxist humanist, long before the young Marx had been severed from the old (and joined together again). The emphasis, in Fox's critique, is on the human being and the writer: "The really great writer, regardless of his own political views, must always engage in a terrible and revolutionary battle with reality, revolutionary because he must seek to change reality."³⁸ As with Sartre's remark about intellectuals being of the left, the statement may be understood as an exhortation; but it is also an implicit recognition of the writer's function and power. Unfortunately, the novel, "the most important gift of the bourgeois, or capitalist civilization to the world's imaginative culture," has fallen on bad days, particularly in England.³⁹ The novels written "nowadays" lack heroes, hardly deserve to be called novels. Then Fox proceeds to outline a novel of socialist realism, the kind that would revitalize the genre. This novel would have as its hero the Bulgarian Communist leader, Georgi Dimitrov, at the time of his trial in connection with the Reichstag fire. Fox, however, never wrote that novel; and there is no cause for us to deplore that omission.

Caudwell's essays in literary criticism and Marxist esthetics also deal with the decline of bourgeois culture. Quite independently he reaches conclusions similar to those reached by Lukács, whose work on the historical novel was first published in 1937, the year Caudwell died in Spain, virtually

---

³⁵ *Politics and Literature*, 5.
³⁶ *What is Literature?* 228. Elsewhere, however, Sartre argues that the writer, fortunately for himself and the public, enjoys a status of immunity, that is, does not get shot even when he resorts to outspoken criticism of the actions or policies of the dictatorial regime under which he lives.
³⁷ The second half of *What is Literature?* is hardly more than a diatribe against the French Communist Party, written years before 1956, when Sartre again attacked the French CP, along with the Soviet Union, because of the Hungarian question.
³⁸ Ralph Fox, *The Novel and the People* (London: Cobbett, 1944, 1st ed. 1937), 38.
³⁹ Ibid., 53 ff.

unknown. Heroes from the age of humanism, Lukács wrote, create "*models which accelerate the consciousness and resoluteness of the longing for liberation.*"[40] Caudwell, on his part, asserts that the mission of art is the widening of consciousness: to change the reader's or viewer's attitude towards reality. Art will "in proportion to the amount of conscious poignancy accompanying the experience and nature of the experience, modify the subject's general attitude towards life itself."[41] The dialectical process is described in somewhat oversimplified terms: "Literature and Society exist in a dialectical unity and thus not only does social existence determine literature, but literature also influences society."[42] Compare this statement with Engels:

> The economic situation is the basis, but the various elements of the superstructure—political forms of the class struggle . . . and then even the reflexes of these actual struggles in the brains of the combatants . . . also exercise their influence upon the course of the historical struggles and in many cases preponderate upon determining their *form*.

Among these reflexes in the "brains of the combatants" Engels includes philosophical ideas, and presumably, the notions and attitudes of heroes in literature.[43]

His careless literary expression notwithstanding Caudwell went a step further than any of the critics I have mentioned or left unmentioned. He broaches the subject of the impact of the literary work upon the individual reader or recipient, and upon society. It is a pity that the analysis remains at the level of intuition.

All in all, the political impact of literature has been but dimly perceived on the theoretical level. The thinkers mentioned in this brief survey have not investigated the issue, even though they devoted much of their creative efforts to the subject of esthetics or the field of sociology of literature. They agree with one another, however, that literature is useless and useful, passive and active, the by-product of societal change and a cause of it!

The confusion may be more apparent than real; it stems from the nature of dialectics itself. It stems from the confusion prevailing with regard to definitions of "superstructure," and from the confusion affecting the relationship of the constituent elements of the superstructure. Thus our thinkers have not seriously attempted to answer the theoretical questions regarding the political function of literature, or even the basic one, that is, whether literature does or does not have a political function. Yet there is an implicit, instinctive recognition of such a function; could it be simply because intellectuals, like other craft- or tradesmen, prefer to believe that

---

[40] *The Historical Novel*, 340.
[41] *Studies in a Dying Culture* (New York: Dodd Mead, 1948), 50.
[42] Quoted in David Margolies, *The Function of Literature* (New York: International Publishers, 1969), 11.
[43] Quoted by Raymond Williams, *Culture and Society 1780–1950* (Doubleday: Garden City, 1960), 285–86.

they are indeed important? There is only one way to find the answer: to heed the advice of Lucien Goldmann and undertake empirical research, multiply case studies, and compare results.

* * *

It seems, nevertheless, that the more recent Marxist critics have managed to remain aloof from political turmoil, that they have, by and large, been content with "interpreting" the world, that they are doubly removed from action. Twice removed, for the case I have studied tends to indicate that novels and poetry are already once removed from practice, that they do not have as direct a bearing on political events as political pamphlets and daily newspapers often do. Marxist critics no longer resort to journalism and pamphlet-writing in the tradition of Marx, Engels, Lenin, or Trotsky. On the other hand, they write about, and sometimes for the benefit of, novelists and poets: hence they remain twice removed from the general reading public, and perhaps even further removed from the working class.

The assertion that literature seldom has a direct bearing on political events does not mean that it cannot have a political impact at all; and it would be altogether a misinterpretation to deny the political significance of the Nyugat on the basis of the evidence presented in the preceding nine chapters. Whether or not anyone has denied it is mostly a matter of semantics. György Bölöni, Ady's friend and biographer, argued that the Nyugat made literature; and it was "to the Nyugat that Hungarians owe the renaissance of their literature, but it had nothing to do with the fermentation of Hungarian political life. What's more, it even kept aloof from the revolutions the sources of which it had actually fed . . ." As proof of its abstention from all revolutionary manifestations, Bölöni cites the fact that the *Nyugat* did not publish revolutionary poems.[44] The Nyugat had no political significance, claims Bölöni, but in the same breath he argues that it had actually fed the sources of revolution! Similarly, Miksa Fenyö wrote in his reminiscences about the Nyugat that he was planning to write an essay on the "overestimation of the social significance of literature," yet he was guilty of precisely that when he claimed, in the same book of reminiscences, that the political revolution derived, of "iron necessity," from the literary one. The same paradox can be found in the by now classic essay of Zoltán Horváth titled "The Turn of the Century in Hungary." On the one hand he dismisses the *Nyugat* as a review without a public, in which a select or elite group of intellectuals "wrote for one another"; on the other hand, about a third of his lengthy essay is devoted to Ady and the *Nyugat* which he describes as the most significant "event" in early twentieth century Hungary.

---

[44] György Bölöni, *Nemzedékről nemzedékre* [From Generation to Generation] (Budapest: Szépirodalmi, 1966), 362–64. Reprinted in *Magyarsag—emberség* [Hungarians and Humanity] (Budapest: Magvető, 1959), 523–27.

I tend to agree with the second of Horváth's propositions. My study provides specific and concrete evidence to show that the Nyugat achieved at least three objectives it pursued more or less consciously. (1) It attacked the dominating ideology of conservative nationalism; there would be no point in specifying that it attacked this ideology on the literary or "cultural" level, for ideologies do not have levels that can be differentiated and dealt with in isolation. (2) The Nyugat either introduced to segments of the Hungarian public or helped spread certain notions of democracy and civil liberty prevailing in the West. (3) It accepted without reservation and, what's more, took up the cudgels for Ady the radical, even if or even when it did not identify completely with his political views and expectations.

No elaborate analysis is needed to show that the influence of the Nyugat on political events in general, and those events which culminated in the revolutions in particular, was indirect rather than direct. Of course, to a limited extent it also played a direct role inasmuch as members of the Nyugat had been, as we have seen, journalists at one time or another; and inasmuch as several of them, in addition to Ady, had assumed an active, albeit not necessarily radical, political role before or during the revolutions. Nevertheless, the most important political act of the Nyugat consisted in turning away from politics in the name of the inviolability of art and literature, under the "banner" (or was it camouflage?) of art for art's sake, thus freeing writers from the dominant ideology, freeing them from the pressures of a nationalist pose, freeing them from the restraint of traditions of all kinds.

Periodicals, in any case, have a more direct relationship to their readers than literature in book form. As Malcolm Bradbury states:

The periodical is one of the most immediate contexts for literature, in that it normally provides a fairly close communicating medium between the writers who contribute to it and the readers who take it . . . Unlike books, they appear serially, and therefore adapt to situations fed back into them; they mediate writers to readers and readers to writers; they also often maintain a running discussion of their aesthetic aims and priorities.[45]

But is it possible to draw a clear line between direct and indirect influence? I think not. Lukács writes somewhere, with reference to Attila József, the great poet of the generation after Ady, that even his landscapes instigate to revolt.[46] Babits argued that a book was an antiwar demonstration; as he put it, "every true book was basically antiwar if only because it existed and it was a book—that is, spirit and liberty."[47] But the emphasis should lie on the word "true."

I am conscious, however, that I have resolved little or nothing. I have not answered, at least not to my own satisfaction, the question regarding the political function of the Nyugat, let alone the general theme I set out

---

[45] *The Social Context of Modern English Literature*, 180.
[46] *Magyar irodalom—magyar kultúra*, 548.
[47] Babits Papers, Széchenyi Irattár, III/1596.

to examine, what is the political function of literature? I have, however, raised several theoretical or practical issues; and this, I feel, is a worthwhile accomplishment in itself.

Before it is possible to proceed with the elucidation of the relationship between literature and social or political change, or to raise more issues, further studies of this nature should be undertaken. Was the case of Hungary, and of the Nyugat, an exceptional, an unclassifiable phenomenon? Or was it, on the contrary, typical of certain nation-states or societies at a certain stage of evolution?

I feel justified, from a scientific, "objective" point of view, in having chosen Hungary as the first area in a series of projected monographs dealing with literature and politics. Among those mentioned in the introduction, those contemporaries of the Nyugat writers who have made a name for themselves abroad, several achieved fame precisely because of their exploration of the connections between social dynamics and the creative activities of man: Arnold Hauser and Antal Friedrich in sociology of art, Béla Balázs in the sociology of the film, Károly Mannheim in the sociology of the intellectual ("the sociology of knowledge"), and Lukács in the sociology of literature. Was it mere accident that all were born and raised in Hungary within the same decade or two?

Nevertheless, the close interaction between literature and social change, or literature and politics, and the explicit scholarly exploration of this interaction, are not purely or peculiarly Hungarian phenomena. On the basis of whatever slim evidence I have gleaned so far in my readings and research I would venture the hypothesis that this close interaction is common to a number of East European cultures. The "political function of literature" which may strike the Anglo-American reader, and particularly the American reader, as a rather unfamiliar notion would, in fact, strike a familiar chord among Poles, Russians, Czechs, Slovaks, Romanians, and perhaps other peoples of the Balkans as well. The function of literature in most cultures in Eastern Europe seems rather different from its function in the West. Yet it would make no sense to argue that this function is geographically determined; anyone with some familiarity with the history of the peoples of Eastern Europe would know that these similarities cannot always be ascribed to cultural "diffusion." It would make more sense to argue that this function is historically and economically determined. Perhaps by seeking elsewhere on the peripheries of Europe, in Ireland or Spain, for instance, where historical and economic conditions are not unlike those in Eastern Europe, we may find the answer to some of our questions. But this sort of research, as I had mentioned at the beginning, could only be carried out collectively and cooperatively.

BIBLIOGRAPHY

Listed below are those items I actually consulted in the preparation of this book; otherwise the list of pertinent works would be endless. I have included only those literary works which have direct (rather than indirect) documentary relevance.

UNPUBLISHED RECORDS AND MANUSCRIPTS

Akadémiai Irattár, Ms 380/j, 381/ny, 383/b, 385/f, 387/k, 5023/16,17,18.
Babits Papers, Széchenyi Irattár.
Fövárosi cégbiroság, Cg 628.
Fövárosi levéltár, The Mayor's Office: I 7875/907, III 5112/1913, IV 1407/B.
Országos levéltár: Office of the Prime Minister, Martinovics Lodge, Révai Publishers, etc.
Petöfi Irodalmi Muzeum, V 3736/1.
Schöpflin Papers, Széchenyi Irattár.

PERIODICALS

Aurora
Budapesti hirlap
Budapesti napló
Budapesti szemle
Corvina
Csak szorosan
Élet
Esztendök
Figyelö
Hét
Huszadik század
Ifjumunkás
Ma
Magyar gyáripar
Magyar kultura
Magyar Minerva
Május
Népszava
Nyugat, 1908–1919
Pesti napló
Renaissance
Szerda
Szocializmus
Társadalmi forradalom
Tipográfia
A tett
Uj idök
Vasárnapi ujság
Világ

BOOKS

Ady, Endre, *The Explosive Country; a selection of articles and studies,* Budapest: Corvina, 1977.
Ady Endre összes prózai müvei, 11 volumes, Budapest: Akadémia, 1955–.
Ady's Generation and Cosmopolitanism in Hungary, eds. Enikö Basa and Dalma H. Brunauer, Chicago: MLA Special Sessions, 1977.
Althusser, Louis, *For Marx,* London: Penguin, 1971.
Arató, A. and Paul Breines, *The Young Lukács and the Origins of Western Marxism,* New York: Seabury Press, 1979.
Babits, Mihály, *Halálfiai,* Budapest: Szépirodalmi, 1959.
Babits-Juhász-Kosztolányi levelezése, ed. György Bélia, Budapest: Akadémia, 1959.
Baxandall, Lee, ed., *Marxism and Aesthetics,* New York: Humanities Press, 1968.
———, ed., *Radical Perspectives in Art,* Baltimore: Penguin, 1972.
Béla Bartók's Letters, ed. Janos Demeny, London: Faber and Faber, 1971.
Berger, John, *Art and Revolution,* New York: Pantheon, 1969.
Bethge, Hans, *Lyrik des Auslandes in neuere Zeit,* Leipzig: Max Hesse, 1907.
Bibó, István, *Harmadik út,* London, 1960.
Bodor, Aladár, *Keletiek Nyugaton,* Losoncz: Károly, 1909.
Böhm, Vilmos, *Két forradalom tüzében,* Budapest: Népszava, n. d.
Bölöni, György, *Magyarság, emberiség,* Budapest: Magvetö, 1959.
———, *Nemzedékröl nemzedékre,* Budapest: Szépirodalmi, 1966.
Bon, Frédéric, *Les nouveaux intellectuels,* Paris: Cujas, 1966.
Bradbury, Malcolm, *The Social Context of Modern English Literature,* Oxford: Basil Blackwell, 1971.

Broch, Hermann, *Hugo von Hofmannsthal and his Time,* Chicago: University of Chicago Press, 1984.
Brod, Max, *Der Prager Kreis,* Stuttgart: W. Kohlhammer, 1966.
Buchinger, Manó, *Küzdelem a szocializmusért,* Budapest: Népszava, n. d.
Budapesti ujságirók egyesülete: 1909 évi almanachja, Budapest, 1909.
Burns, Elizabeth and Tom, *Sociology of Literature and Drama,* London: Penguin, 1973.
Canetti, Elias, *Auto da Fé,* New York: Seabury Press, 1979 (1st ed. 1935).
Caudwell, Christopher, *Studies in a Dying Culture,* New York: Dodd Mead, 1948.
Daiches, David, *Literature and Society,* New York: Haskell, 1970 (1st ed. 1938).
Demetz, P., *Marx, Engels, and the Poets,* Chicago: University of Chicago Press, 1967.
Dezsényi, Béla and György Nemes, *A magyar sajtó 250 éve,* Budapest: Müvelt Nép, 2 vols., 1954.
Dobossy, László, *Hašek világa,* Budapest: Europa, 1970.
Domokos, József, *Achim L. András,* Budapest: Kossuth, 1971.
Domokos, Sámuel, *A román irodalom magyar bibliográfiája, 1831–1960,* Budapest: Irodalmi Könyvkiadó, 1966.
Éder, Zoltán, *Babits a katedrán,* Budapest: Szépirodalmi, 1966.
Eisenmann, Louis, *Le compromis austro-hongrois de 1867,* Paris: Société nouvelle de librairie et d'édition, 1904.
Eliot, T. S., *The Use of Poetry and the Use of Criticism,* London: Faber & Faber, 1964.
Escarpit, Robert, *The Book Revolution,* London: Harrap, 1966.
———, *Sociologie de la littérature,* Paris: Presses Universitaires, 1958.
———, ed., *Letteratura e società,* Bologna: Mulino, 1972.
Farkas, József, *A magyar sajtótörténet irodalmának válogatott bibliográfiája,* Budapest: MUOSz, 1972.
Farkas, Julius, *Der Freiheitskampf des ungarischen Geistes, 1867–1914,* Berlin: Walter de Gruyter, 1940.
Farkas, Lujza, *A Nyugat és a szazadeleji irodalomforduló,* Budapest: Gyarmati, 1935.
Fenyö, Miksa, *Följegyzések a 'Nyugat' folyoiratról és környékéről,* Niagara Falls: Patria, 1960.
Forradalmi magyar irodalom, eds., Miklós Szabolcsi, László Illés, Budapest: Akadémia, 1963.
Fox, Ralph, *The Novel and the People,* London: Cobbett, 1944 (1st ed. 1937).
Franyó, Zoltán, *A pokol tornácán,* Bucharest: Irodalmi Könyvkiadó, 1969.
Fügen, Hans Norbert, *Hauptrichtungen der Literatursoziologie,* Bonn: H. Bouvier, 1964.
Fukász, György, *A magyarországi polgári radikalizmus története,* Budapest: 1968.
Garaudy, Roger, J.-P. Sartre, Ernst Fischer, Eduard Goldstücker, *Estética y marxismo,* Barcelona: Martinez Roca, 1969.
Gartenberg, Egon, *Mahler,* New York: Schimmer, 1978.
Gellért, Oszkár, *Egy iró élete,* 2 vols., Budapest: Bibliotheca, 1958, 1962.
———, *Kortársaim,* Budapest: Müvelt Nép, 1954.
———, ed., *A diadalmas forradalom könyve,* Budapest: Légrády, 1919.
Gesellschaft, Literatur, Lesen, by Manfred Naumann, et al., Berlin: Aufbau, 1973.
Gluck, Mary, *Georg Lukács and his Generation, 1900–1918,* Cambridge: Harvard University Press, 1985.
Goldmann, Lucien, *Pour une sociologie du roman,* Paris: Gallimard, 1964.
———, *The Human Sciences and Philosophy,* London: Jonathan Cape, 1969.
Gonnard, René, *La Hongrie au XXe siècle,* Paris: Armand Colin, 1908.
Gramsci, Antonio, *Letteratura e vita nazionale,* Milano: Einaudi, 1954.
Grátz, Gusztáv, *A dualizmus kora, 1867–1918,* Budapest: n.p., 1930.
———, *A liberalizmus,* Budapest: n.p., 1904.
Griffiths, Paul, *Bartok,* London: J. M. Dent & Sons, 1984.
Gross, John, *The Rise and Fall of the Man of Letters,* London: Macmillan, 1969.
Gsell, Paul, *Les matinées de la villa Saïd,* Paris: Bernard Grasset, 1921.
Gyergyai, Albert, *A Nyugat árnyékában,* Budapest: Szépirodalmi, 1968.
Györi, Judit, *Thomas Mann Magyarországon,* Budapest: Akadémia, 1968.
Hanák, Péter and István Király, *Ady és a századforduló,* Budapest: Tudományos Ismeretterjesztö Társulat Központja, 1977.
Harsányi, Zoltán, *A 'franciás' Nyugat,* Debrecen, 1942.
Hatvany, Lajos, *Emberek és könyvek,* Budapest: Szépirodalmi, 1971.
———, *Emberek és korok,* Budapest: Szépirodalmi, 1964.
Hauser, Arnold, *Találkozásaim Lukács Györggyel,* Budapest: Akadémia, 1978.
Hegedüs, Loránt, *Ady és Tisza,* Budapest: Nyugat, n.d.

Heller, Agnes, ed., *Lukács Revalued,* Oxford: Basil Blackwell, 1983.
Hoggart, Richard, *The Uses of Literacy,* Fairlawn, N.J.: Essential Books, 1957.
Horvat, Heinrich, *Neue ungarische Lyrik in Nachdichtungen,* München: Georg Müller, 1918.
Horváth, János, *Aranytól Adyig,* Budapest: Pallas, n.d.
———, *A Nyugat magyartalanságairól,* Budapest, 1911.
Horváth, Zoltán, *Die Jahrhundertwende in Ungarn,* Budapest: Lüchterhand, 1966.
Ignotus válogatott irásai, ed. Aladár Komlós, Budapest: Szépirodalmi, 1969.
Janik, Allan, and Stephen Toulmin, *Wittgenstein's Vienna,* New York: Simon & Schuster, 1973.
Janos, Andrew C., and William B. Slottman, eds., *Revolution in Perspective: Essays on the Hungarian Soviet Republic of 1919,* Berkeley: University of California, 1972.
Jászi, Oszkár, *A nemzetiségi kérdés és Magyarország jövöje,* Budapest: Galilei Kör, No. 5, n.d.
———, *Revolution and Counter-Revolution in Hungary,* New York: Howard Fertig, 1969.
Johnston, William M., *The Austrian Mind,* Berkeley: University of California, 1972.
Juhász Gyula összes müvei, Budapest: Akadémia, 1968.
Kaffka, Margit, *Szinek és évek,* Budapest: Szépirodalmi, 1961.
———, *Az élet utján,* Budapest: Szépirodalmi, 1972.
Karátson, André, *Le symbolisme en Hongrie,* Paris: Presses Universitaires, 1971.
Kardos, Pál, *Nagy Lajos élete és müvei,* Budapest: Bibliotheca, 1958.
Károlyi, Mihály, *Faith without Illusions,* New York: Dutton, 1957.
———, *Az új Magyarországért; válogatott irások és beszédek, 1908-1919,* ed. György Litván, Budapest: Magvetö, 1968.
———, *Fighting the World; the Struggle for Peace,* New York: Albert & Charles Boni, 1924.
Kassák, Lajos, *Egy ember élete,* 2 vols., Budapest: Magvetö, 1957.
Katona, Ferenc, and Dénes Tibor, *A Thália története, 1904-1908,* Budapest: Müvelt Nép, 1954.
Kelen, Jolán, *Eliramlik az élet,* Budapest: Kossuth, 1976.
Kende, Zsigmond, *Galilei Kör megalakulása,* Budapest: Akadémia, 1974.
Király, István, *Ady,* 2 vols., Budapest: Magvetö, 1970.
Kiss, Ferenc, *A beérkezés küszöbén,* Budapest: Akadémia, 1962.
Köhalmi, Béla, *Könyvek könyve,* Budapest: Lantos, 1918.
———, *A magyar tanácsköztársaság könyvtárügye,* Budapest: Gondolat, 1959.
Kolakowski, Leszek, *Marxism and Beyond,* London: Pall Mall, 1968.
Komlos, Aladár, *Vereckétöl Dévényig,* Budapest: Szépirodalmi, 1972.
Kont, Ignace, *La littérature hongroise d'aujourd'hui,* Paris: E. Sansot, 1908.
Korek, Valéria, *Hangulat és valóság,* Munich: Aurora, 1976.
Kovács, Máté, *A könyv és a könyvtár a magyar társadalom életében,* 2 vols., Budapest: Gondolat, 1970.
Kristoffy, József, *Magyarország kálváriája,* Budapest: Wodianer, 1927.
Krudy, Gyula, *A tegnapok ködlovagjai,* Budapest: Tevan, 1925.
Kun Memoirs, ed. Irén Kun, Budapest: Magvetö, 1966.
Kunszery, Gyula, *Magyar irók és bünperei,* Budapest: Aurora, 1942.
Lakatos, Ernö, *A magyar politikai vezetöréteg 1848-1918,* Budapest: Egyetemi Nyomda, 1942.
Lang, Berel, and Forrest Williams, eds., *Marxism and Art,* New York: David McKay, 1971.
Latin American Revolutionary Poetry, ed. R. Marquez, New York: Monthly Review, 1974.
Laurenson, Diana T., and Alan Swingewood, *The Sociology of Literature,* New York: Schocken, 1972.
Leavis, Queenie D., *Fiction and the Reading Public,* London: Chatto and Windus, 1965 (1st ed. 1932).
Lengyel, Géza, *Magyar ujságmágnások,* Budapest: Akadémia, 1963.
Lenin, V. U., *On Literature and Art,* Moscow: Progress Publishers, 1970.
Lesser, Simon O., *Fiction and the Unconscious,* London: Peter Owen, 1960.
Lesznai, Anna, *Kezdetben volt a kert,* 2 vols., Budapest: Szépirodalmi, 1966.
Levelek Hatvany Lajoshoz, Budapest: Szépirodalmi, 1967.
Lindner, Heinz, *Revolution and Konterrevolution in Ungarn in der Jahren 1918/19,* Berlin: Dietz, 1958.
Littérature et société, Bruxelles: Université Libre, 1967.
Littérature et société canadiennes-françaises, ed. F. Dumont, 1964.
Litván, György, "*Magyar gondolat—szabad gondolat,*" Budapest: Magvetö, 1978.
———, ed., *A szociológia elsö magyar mühelye,* 2 vols. Budapest: Gondolat, 1973.
Löwenthal, Leo, *Literature, Popular Culture and Society,* Englewood Cliffs, N.J.: Prentice Hall, 1961.
———, *Literature and the Image of Man,* New York: Books for Libraries Press, 1970.

Löwy, Michael, *Pour une sociologie des intellectuels révolutionnaires; l'évolution politique de Lukács 1909–1929*, Paris: Presses Universitaires, 1976.
Lucien Goldmann et la sociologie de la littérature, Bruxelles: Univ. of Bruxelles, 1975.
Lukács, György, *Balzac et le réalisme français*, Paris: François Maspéro, 1969.
——, *The Historical Novel*, London: Merlin, 1962.
——, *Magyar irodalom—magyar kultura*, Budapest: Gondolat, 1970.
——, *Record of a Life*, London: Vesco, 1983.
——, *Selected Correspondence 1902–1920*, New York: Columbia U. Press, 1986.
Lunacharski, A. V., *Müvészet és forradalom*, Budapest: Kriterion, 1975.
Macherey, Pierre, *Pour une théorie de la production littéraire*, Paris: François Maspéro, 1966.
A magyar irodalom története, Vol. 5, ed. Miklós Szabolcsi, Budapest: Akadémia, 1965.
A magyar szociólogiai irodalom bibliográfiája, 2 vols. Budapest: 1980.
Magyar statisztikai évkönyv, 18 (1910), Budapest: Statisztikai Hivatal, 1911.
Magyarország története, Vol. 7, Budapest: Akadémia, 1978.
Major, Máté, *Egy gyerekkor és egy kisváros emléke*, Budapest: Magvetö, 1973.
Mannheim, Károly, *Lélek és kultura*, Budapest: Sinkó, 1918.
Mann, Thomas, *Diaries 1918–1939*, New York: Harry N. Abrams, 1982.
Margolies, David, *The Function of Literature*, New York: International Publishers, 1969.
Martin, Henri-Jean, *Livre, pouvoir et société à Paris au XVIIe siècle*, 2 vols., Genève: Droz, 1969.
May, Arthur J., *The Habsburg Monarchy 1867–1914*, New York: W. W. Norton, 1968 (1st ed. 1951).
McCagg, William O., *Jewish Nobles and Geniuses in Modern History*, Boulder: East European Quarterly, 1972.
Mérei, Gyula, *A polgári radikalizmus története Magyarországon*, Budapest, 1947.
Mindenki ujakra készül, ed. Farkas József, 4 vols., Budapest: Akadémia, 1959.
Moore, J. Barrington, *Social Origins of Dictatorship and Democracy*, Boston, 1966.
Móricz, Virág, *Apám regénye*, Budapest: Szépirodalmi, 1953.
Móricz, Zsigmond, *A boldog ember*, Budapest: Szépirodalmi, 1968.
Móricz Zsigmond levelei, ed. Dora Csanák, Budapest: Akadémia, 1968.
Mornet, Daniel, *Les origines intellectuelles de la Révolution Française, 1715–1787*, Paris: Armand Colin, 1967.
Mott, F. L., *Golden Multitudes: The Story of Best-Sellers*, New York: R. R. Bowker, 1947.
Muir, E., *Essays on Literature and Society*, London: Hogarth Press, 1949.
Münnich, Ferenc, *Viharos út*, Budapest: Szépirodalmi, 1966.
Nagy, Péter, *Szabó Dezsö*, Budapest: Akadémia, 1964.
Nyilas, Márta, *A budapesti nyomdászkönyvtár*, Budapest, 1955.
Nyugat almanachja, Budapest: Nyugat, 1912.
Nyugat repertorium, ed. Ferenc Galambos, Budapest: Akadémia, 1959.
Osvát Ernö összes irásai, ed. Kálmán Osvát, Budapest: Nyugat, 1945.
Passuth, Krisztina, *A Nyolcak festészete*, Budapest: Athenaeum, 1967.
The Politics of Twentieth-Century Novelists, ed. George Panichas, New York: Hawthorn Books, 1971.
Pomogáts, Béla, *Kuncz Aladár*, Budapest: Akadémia, 1968.
Pörtner, Paul, *Literatur Revolution 1910–1925*, Darmstadt: Leuchterwand, 1960.
Ragon, M., *Histoire de la littérature ouvrière*, Paris: Editions ouvrières, 1953.
Ránki, György, and Iván Berend, *Magyarország gyáripara az imperializmus elsö világháboru elötti idö-szakában*, Budapest: Szikra, 1955.
Read, Herbert, *Art and Society*, London: Faber and Faber, 1967.
Rieff, Philip, ed., *On Intellectuals*, Garden City, New York: Doubleday, 1970.
Ritoók, Emma, *A szellem kalandorai*, Budapest: Göncöl, 1922.
Ronay, György, *A nagy nemzedék*, Budapest: Szépirodalmi, 1971.
Rosengren, Karl Erik, *Sociological Aspects of Literary Systems*, Stockholm: Natur och Kultur, 1968.
Rühle, Jürgen, *Literatur und Revolution*, Köln: Kiepenheuer and Witsch, 1960.
Sartre, Jean-Paul, *Politics and Literature*, London: Calder and Boyars, 1973.
——, *What is Literature?* New York: Harper and Row, 1965.
Schöpflin, Aladár, *A magyar irodalom története a XX században*, Budapest: Grill, 1937.
Schuecking, Levin L., *The Sociology of Taste*, London: Kegan Paul, Trench, Trubner, 1944.
Sik, Sándor, *Gárdonyi, Ady, Prohászka*, Budapest, 1928.
Simor, András, *Korvin Otto: a gondolat él*, Budapest: Magvetö, 1976.

——, ed., *Szamuely Tibor: összegyüjtött írások és beszédek*, Budapest: Magvetö, 1975.
Sötér, István and Otto Süpek, eds., *Littérature hongroise, littérature européenne*, Budapest: Akadémia, 1973.
Spearman, Diana, *The Novel and Society*, London: Routledge and Kegan Paul, 1966.
Stark, Werner, *The Sociology of Knowledge*, Glencoe: Free Press, 1958.
Süle, Tibor, *Sozialdemokratie in Ungarn: Zur Rolle der Intelligenz in der Arbeiterbewegung, 1899–1910*, Köln: Bohlau, 1967.
Szabó, Dezsö, *Eleteim*, Budapest: Szépirodalmi, 1965.
Szalay, Károly, *Karinthy Frigyes*, Budapest: Gondolat, 1961.
Szekfü, Gyula, *Három nemzedék és ami utána következik*, Budapest: Egyetem, 1930.
——, *Magyar történet*, 5 vols., Budapest: Egyetem, 1936.
Szerb, Antal, *Magyar irodalomtörténet*, Budapest: Magvetö, 1972 (1st ed. 1935).
Szobotka, T., *Közönség és irodalom*, Budapest: Gondolat, 1964.
Tezla, Albert, *Hungarian Authors; A Bibliographical Handbook*, Cambridge: Harvard U. Press, 1970.
Thomas Mann und Ungarn, eds. Judit Györi and Antal Mádl, Budapest: Akadémia, 1977.
Tömöry, Márta, *Uj vizeken járok*, Budapest: Gondolat, 1960.
Trotsky, Leon, *Literature and Revolution*, Ann Arbor: Univ. of Michigan Press, 1960.
Ujfalussy, József, *Bartók Béla*, Budapest: Gondolat, 1976.
Vallomások a Nyugatról, ed. László Rónay, 1971.
Vezér, Erzsébet, *Ady Endre élete és pályája*, Budapest: Gondolat, 1977.
——, *Lesznai Anna élete*, Budapest: Kossuth, 1979.
Weltner, Jakab, *Milliók egy miatt*, Budapest, 1927.
Wiesner, Emil, *Der ungarische Buchhandel*, Budapest, n.d.
Williams, Raymond, *Culture and Society, 1780–1950*, Garden City, N.Y.: Doubleday, 1960.
——, *The Long Revolution*, Westport, Conn: Greenwood Press, 1975.
Wilson, Edmund, *The Triple Thinkers*, London: John Lehmann, 1952.
Zéraffa, Michel, *Roman et société*, Paris: Presses Universitaires, 1971.

Articles

I have listed only those articles which did not appear in the periodicals already listed.
Babits, Mihály, "A Nyugat régen és most," *Nyugat* 25 (1932): 69–70.
Bélia, György and Anna Sándor, "Schöpflin Aladár hagyatékából," *Irodalomtörténeti közlemények* (1953): 324–38.
Congdon, Lee, "Endre Ady's Summons to National Regeneration in Hungary, 1900–1919," *Slavic Review* 33: 302–32.
——, "The Making of a Hungarian Revolutionary," *Journal of Contemporary History* 8: 57–74.
——, "Polányi and the Treason of the Intellectuals," *Canadian-American Review of Hungarian Studies* 2: 79–90.
Dersi, Tamás, "Kun Béla és az irodalom," *Könyvtáros* (1960) 11: 635–46.
Elekes, Dezsö, "A magyar könyvtermelés statisztikája," *Magyar statisztikai szemle* (1930): 629–44.
Erdélyi, Ildiko, Márta Nagy, "Ady-kép '77," *Tömegkommunikációs kutatóközpont* 10 (1978): 3–11.
Fehér, Ferenc, "Balázs Béla és Lukács György szövetsége a forradalomig," *Irodalomtörténet*, 51 (1969): 317–46, 530–60.
Fehér, Pál, "A Gyosz és a Nyugat," *Élet és irodalom* (1965, No. 39).
Fenyo, Mario D., "Rebels and Revolutionaries," *Arion* 10 (1977).
——, "A viharmadarak: a haladó magyar irodalom és olvasóközönsége 1908-tól a forradalmakig," *Könyvtári figyelö* (1977): 340–49.
——, "Writers in Politics: the Role of the *Nyugat* in Hungary, 1908–19," *Journal of Contemporary History* 11 (1976): 185–98.
Fenyö, Miksa, "Két jóbarátot vesztettem el," *Irodalmi Ujság* (1969, October 23, November 1).
——, "Közéleti emlekezések," *Irodalmi Ujság* (1970, January 15).
——, "Önéletrajz," *Uj látohatár* (Munich, 1963–1968).
——, "Az olvasás gyönyörüsége," *Irodalmi Ujság* (1967, September 15).
——, "Uj magyar irodalomtörténet," *Irodalmi Ujság* (1966, January 15).
Ferenczi, Béla, "Irók olvasók nélkül," *Erdélyi lapok* (1912): 536–38.
Ficzay, Dénes, "Ady, a 'Holnap,' és a 'Nyugat' Aradon," *Nyelv és irodalomtudományi közlemények* (1967): 245–55.
Füst, Milán, "A Nyugat születése," *Irodalomtörténet* (1959): 453–66.

Gellért, Oszkár, "Bartók és a Nyugat," *Élet és irodalom* (1965, No. 39).
——, "Még egyszer a Gyosz és a Nyugat," *Élet és irodalom* 8 (1964): 5.
Gulyás, Pál, "A hazai népkönyvtárügy kialakulása és mai helyzete," *Muzeumi és könyvtári értesitö* (1911): 65-84.
——, "Mit olvas a magyar nép," *Muzeumi és könyvtári értesitö* (1911): 2-3.
Hanák, Petér, "Skizzen über die Gesellschaft am Anfang des 20. Jahrhunderts," *Acta Historica* 10 (1964): 1-45.
Halmi, Bodog, "Ady Endre," *Máramaros* (1910).
Harsányi, Lajos, "O beata Ungheria," *Alkotmány* (1916, No. 68).
Heltai, Nándor, "A kecskeméti városi könyvtár," *Magyar könyvszemle* (1959) 75: 65-84.
Horváth, Pál, "Haladó ifjusági mozgalmak a budapesti egyetemen," *Felsöoktatási szemle* (1961, No. 1-2).
Horváth, Zoltán, "The Rise of Nationalism and the Nationality Problem in Hungary in the Last Decades of Dualism," *Acta Historica*, 9 (1963): 1-37.
Kamarás, István, "Olvasó portrék kétezerben," *Könyvtári Figyelö* (1974): 542-52.
Kardos, Albert, "A Nyugat Debrecenben—harminc éve," *Nyugat*, 33 (1940): 70-74.
Kardos, Pál, "A Nyugat debreceni kapcsolatai," *Acta Universitatis Debreceniensis* (1955): 85-100.
Keményfy, János, "A Nyugat irodalomtörténete," *Budapesti szemle* (1937): 86-106.
Kocsis, Vince, "Ady Endre hazafias költészete," *Kalazantium*, 16, No. -10.
Kristof, György, "Irodalmunk és közéletünk," *Uránia* (1909): 472-77.
Komlos, Aladár, "Keletiek Nyugaton," *Irodalomtörténet* (1973): 988-94.
Lackó, Miklos, "Osvát," *Uj irás* (April 1976): 92-101.
"Legfiatalabb irodalom," *Politikai hetiszemle* (1907, No. 19): 5-7.
Lukács, György, "The Importance and Influence of Ady," *New Hungarian Quarterly* 10 (1969): 56-63.
Móricz, Zsigmond, "Fenyö Miksa és a Nyugat," *Kelet népe* (1941, October 15).
——, "Huszonöt év," *Nyugat* 25 (1932): 1-4.
Nádai, Pál, "Magyar irók, külföldi irók és vásárlok," *Uj élet* (1914): 547-49.
"Nagy Lajos levelei Nagy Zoltánhoz," *Kritika* (June 1977).
Nagy, Péter, "Szabó Dezsö ideologiájának forrásai," *Irodalomtörténeti közlemények* (1963).
"Népkönyvtár és olvasó terem," *Kelet* (1910, December 1).
Nyilas, Márta, "A budapesti nyomdászkönyvtár," *Magyar könyvszemle* (1959): 163-79.
"A Nyugat temesvári matinéja," *Függetlenség* (Arad) (1909, October 20).
Pogány, Béla, "A Nyugat a történelmi fejlödes itélöszéke elött," *Gondolat* (1937): 274-80.
Pok, Lajos, "A Nyugat elözményei," *Irodalomtörténet* (1957): 285-303.
"Olvasó kedv a háboru alatt," *Könyvtári szemle* (1914): 212.
Osvát, Kálmán, "Beszélgetés Nyugat szerkesztökröl," *Erdélyi Helikon* (1930): 88-90.
Réti, László, "Az elsö orosz forradalom és a forradalmi baloldal kialakulása," *Társadalmi szemle* (1955): 50-69.
Ritóok, Emma, "A Nyugat új utja," *Társadalomtudomány* (1930): 176-85.
Ruszinyák, Márta, "A Nyugat könyvkiadó," Budapest: Egyetem 1962 (unpublished thesis).
Schöpflin, Aladár, "Az indulás," *Nyugat* (1932): 74-76.
Sos, Endre, "Ignotus és a Nyugat negyven esztendeje," *Népszava* (1948).
Staindl, Mátyás, "Mit olvas a közönség?" *Könyvtári szemle*, (1917): 79-80.
Szabó, Ervin, "Községi nyilvános könyvtár Budapesten," *Városi szemle* (1910): 446-90.
——, "Mit olvasnak és mit olvassanak?" *Népmüvelés*, (1911): 60-64.
Szabó, Miklos, "A századfordulói konzervatizmus új vonásai," *Századok* (1974): 3-65.
Szilágyi, János, "A Nyugat könyvkiadó," *A könyv*, (1964): 356-58.
Tábori, Kornél, "A ponyvairodalom társadalmi hatása," *Magyar Társadalomtudományi szemle* (1909), 122-34.
Tharaud, Jérôme et Jean, "Bolchévistes de Hongrie," *Revue des Deux Mondes* (1920): 809-30; (1921): 611-52, 757-804.
Váradi, Irma, "Egy városi fiókkönyvtár kezdetei," *Városi szemle* (1914): 829-37.
Varga, József, "A századeleji szocialista gondolat a Nyugatban," *Irodalomtörténeti közlemények*, 78, No. 1 (1974): 41-56.
Vezér, Erzsébet, "Egy századeleji irodalmár portréja," *Irodalomtörténet* (1974): 556-94.
Wessely, Anna, "A szellemi tudományok szabad iskolája és a Vasárnapi Kör," *Világosság*, 16, No. 10: 613-20.

INDEX

Áchim, András, 24, 68
Adler, Viktor, 4
Adorno, Theodor, 135
Ady, Endre, 4, 7–9, 12, 23, 30–32, 34–37, 40, 45–47, 49–52, 54, 58, 61, 62, 64, 65, 67, 68, 71, 74, 81–84, 88, 89, 91, 95, 96, 98–106, 109–114, 116–123, 125, 127–129, 131, 133, 134, 145
Altomare, Libero, 47n
Ambrus, Zoltán, 58, 71, 83, 110, 113
Anderson, Perry, 135
Andrássy, Count Gyula, 27, 54, 126, 129
Antal, Frigyes, 2, 3, 97, 98
Apollinaire, Guillaume, 33
Apponyi, Count Albert, 27, 129
Arany, János, 39, 100, 110
Arcubasev, 47n

Babits, Mihály, 7, 8, 31–35, 37, 40, 42, 45, 52, 56, 62, 63n, 71–73, 83–85, 87n, 90, 93, 99–106, 114, 115, 122, 123, 125–127, 131–133, 145
Balázs, Béla, 2, 43, 52, 64, 65, 69, 85, 88, 90, 91, 93, 97, 98, 102, 106, 115, 118, 125, 136, 146
Balzac, Honoré de, 33, 75, 101
Barta, Lajos, 106
Bartók, Béla, 2, 63–65, 74, 91
Bataille, Henri, 59
Baudelaire, Charles, 30, 33, 34, 59, 101, 118, 122
Bauer, Ervin, 64
Baumgarten (foundation), 13
Beardsley, Aubrey, 32
Bédy-Schwimmer, Rózsa, 74
Békésy, György, 3
Bélia, György, 50
Benczur, Gyula, 89
Benedek, Marcell, 98
Berény, Robert, 90n
Bethlen, Count István, 123
Biró, Lajos, 5n, 54, 61, 83, 85, 93, 95, 96, 102, 106, 110, 112
Björnson, Bjørnstjerne, 21
Blake, Robert, 11
Bodor, Aladar, 121
Bohm, Vilmos, 119
Bokányi, Dezsö, 18
Bölöni, György, 96, 144
Bone, Edith (Edith Hajos), 97
Borges, Jorge Luis, 136
Bradbury, Malcolm, 145

Braque, Georges, 90
Brecht, Berchtolt, 140n
Bresztovszky, Ernö, 49, 109, 113, 114, 118
Brod, Max, 6
Brody, Sándor, 31, 34, 82, 113, 116, 124
Bryce, Lord, 21
Buchinger, Manó, 118, 123
Burgos, Julia de, 115
Busiția, Janos, 64
Byron, Lord George, 11

Čapek brothers, 1
Caudwell, Christopher, 57, 142, 143
Cézanne, Paul, 90, 101
Cholnoky, Viktor, 39, 60
Chorin, Ferenc, 45n
Chorin, Ferenc Jr., 40, 41
Claudel, Paul, 33
Clémenceau, Georges, 21
Cocteau, Jean, 47
Coleridge, Samuel, 11
Csáth, Géza, 85, 91, 97, 112
Csécsy, Imre, 65
Csinszka (Mrs. Ady), 90
Csizmadia, Sándor, 101, 113, 118
Czigány, Dezsö, 90n
Czóbel, Béla, 90n

Daiches, David, 29
Dante, 133
Deák, Ferenc, 133
Déry, Tibor, 118
Dickens, Charles, 113
Dimitrov, Georgi, 142
Dohnányi, Ernö, 2, 91
Dorsan, Harry Russel, 70
Dostoievsky, Fyodor, 32, 33
Dózsa, György, 68
Dreyfus (affair), 128
Duhamel, Georges, 47n

Einstein, Albert, 32
Elek, Artur, 8
Engels, Friedrich, 31, 75, 136, 137, 144
Escarpit, Robert, 12, 140

Farkas, Lujza, 13
Fenyö, Miksa, 5, 35, 38–41, 43, 45, 49, 51–53, 55, 65, 69, 71–73, 76, 93, 97, 98, 105, 122n, 123, 126, 131, 144
Ferenczi, Sándor, 2, 32, 37

Fischer, Ernst, 31, 135
Fitzmaurice, Lord, 21
Flaubert, Gustave, 100, 118
Fogarasi, Béla, 97
Ford, Madox Ford, 78
Fort, Paul, 47n
Fox, Ralph, 57, 135, 140, 142
Francis, of Assisi (Saint), 118
Francis, Ferdinand (Archduke), 46
France, Anatole, 32–34, 59, 95
Freud, Sigmund, 1, 2, 4, 32, 34, 37, 75
Fülep, Lajos, 97
Füst, Milán, 8, 35, 52

Galambos, Ferenc, 59
Galilei (Circle), 94–96, 98
Gárdonyi, Géza, 39, 82
Gay, Peter, 1
Gellért, Oszkár, 8, 45, 106, 112, 115n
Gergely, Tibor, 97
Gide, André, 33
Giesswein, 26
Goethe, Johann Wolfgang, 91
Goga, Octavian, 62
Gogol, Nikolai, 113
Goldmann, Lucien, 10, 75, 135, 140, 144
Grátz, Gusztáv, 25
Gramsci, Antonio, 135
Gyömröi, Edit, 97

Hadik, Count János, 54
Hajos, Edit (Edith Bone), 97
Halász, Imre, 85
Hašek, Jaroslav, 1, 2, 4, 40
Hatvany, Lajos, 7, 8, 34, 38, 40, 41, 43, 45, 46, 50–52, 57, 58, 67, 85, 89, 93, 99, 102, 123, 133
Hauptmann, Gerhardt, 89
Hauser, Arnold, 2, 3, 93, 97, 146
Hegedüs, Loránt, 128
Heine, Heinrich, 33, 100
Heller, Ágnes, 56, 139
Heltai, Jenö, 74, 82, 116 ,124
Herceg, Ferenc, 74, 82, 116, 124
Herzl, Theodor, 4
Hevesy, György, 3
Hitler, Adolf, 33, 140
Hofmannsthal, Hugo von, 1, 2, 7
Hoggart, Richard, 112
Horthy, Miklós, 123, 133
Horváth, János, 125, 126
Horváth, Zoltán, 49, 144, 145
Hubay, Jenö, 3n
Hughes, Houghton Stuart, 92
Huysmans, Joris Karl, 30

Ibsen, Henrik, 33, 89, 100, 107, 108
Ignotus, Hugó, 5, 8, 32, 34, 40n, 43, 45, 49, 51, 53, 54, 57, 58, 62, 69, 89, 93, 110, 111, 113, 116, 118, 122, 123, 125n, 126, 131

Illyés, Gyula, 122n
Isac, Emil, 62

Jászi, Oszkár, 2, 3, 6–8, 20, 21, 37, 55, 58, 59, 65, 88, 95, 96, 98–100, 106, 123, 124, 133
Jokai, Mór, 29, 39, 57, 82, 100
Josika, Miklós, 82
Joyce, James, 31n, 75
Jozsef, Attila, 61, 145
Juhász, Gyula, 8, 19, 33–35, 44, 60, 101, 102, 112, 113n, 127

Kaffka, Margit, 8, 34, 42, 50, 64, 67n, 73, 83–85, 95, 99, 104, 106, 115, 125, 126
Kafka, Franz, 1, 2, 75
Káldor, György, 97
Kálmán, Imre, 5
Kandinsky, Vassili, 47n
Karátson, André, 30
Karinthy, Frigyes, 8, 32, 36, 55, 73, 83–85, 95, 99, 105, 118, 127, 130
Kármán, Todor, 3
Károlyi, Count Mihály, 26, 67n, 87, 99, 100, 133
Kassák, Lajos, 8, 33, 47, 48, 70, 71, 74, 106, 107, 111
Kautsky, Karl, 14n, 24
Kazantzakis, Nikos, 8, 102
Kelen, Jolán, 69, 95, 117
Kéri, Pal, 33, 109, 118
Kernstok, Károly, 90, 91, 96
Kierkegaard, Søren, 140
Kipling, Rudyard, 136
Király, István, 13
Kisfaludy (Society), 57, 67n, 123
Kodály, Zoltán, 2, 65, 91
Köhalmi, Béla, 100
Kolakowski, Leszek, 141n
Komját, Aladár, 106
Komlos, Aladár, 12, 32
Kont, Ignace, 34
Kornfeld, Baron Móricz, 45
Korvin, Otto, 118
Kossuth, Lajos, 9, 99
Kosztolányi, Dezsö, 8, 30, 33–35, 52, 70, 95, 99, 101, 110, 118, 131
Kraus, Karl, 4, 5
Kristóffy, József, 88, 108
Krudy, Gyula, 8, 83–85, 105, 106
Kubin, N., 47n
Kun, Béla, 119
Kuncz, Aladár, 8, 35, 59, 63, 96, 98, 124
Kunfi, Zsigmond, 20, 118, 123, 133

Láng, Juliska, 97
Lányi, Sarolta, 73, 85, 124
Leavis, Queenie D., 109
Lechner, Odon, 5
Lehár, Ferenc, 5
Lengyel, Géza, 8, 96, 112

INDEX

Lengyel, Menyhért, 8, 14, 34, 41, 70, 83, 84, 89, 91, 119, 123
Lenin, Nikolai, 54, 117, 135–138, 144
Lesznai, Anna, 8, 85, 90n, 97
Lopez, Robert S., 35
Löwy, Michael, 95
Lueger, Karl, 23
Lukács, György, 2, 3, 7, 22, 27, 34, 37, 53, 55, 69, 74, 75, 83, 88–90, 92–94, 100, 101, 106, 118, 119, 126, 132n, 135, 136, 139–141, 143, 145, 146
Lunacharski, A. V., 14n

Mach, Ernst, 5
Maeterlinck, Maurice, 59, 115
Magyar, Mór, 43
Mahler, Gustav, 5, 123n
Mallarmé, Stéphane, 30
Mann, Thomas, 4, 33, 71, 96
Mannheim, Károly, 2, 37, 56, 98, 146
Márffy, Ödön, 90n
Margalits (Judge), 73
Marx, Karl, 31, 75, 136, 137, 142, 144
May, Arthur J., 23
Mayakovsky, Vladimir, 137n
McCagg, William O., 94
Meinecke, Friedrich, 96
Mestrović, Iván, 47n
Mezöfi, Vilmos, 24
Michelangelo, 101
Miklós, Andor, 41
Mikszáth, Kálmán, 39, 57, 82
Moholy-Nagy, László, 2, 3
Molière, 141
Molnár, Ferenc, 34, 45, 50, 51
Monet, Charles, 101
Moore, Barrington, 11
Móricz, Zsigmond, 7, 8, 31, 34, 45, 51, 53, 58, 60, 62, 64, 66, 67, 71, 74, 76, 81–84, 90, 99, 100, 106, 110, 111, 122, 124–126, 131
Munkácsy, Mihály, 89
Münnich, Ferenc, 110, 111
Musil, Robert, 5

Nagy, Endre, 88, 89, 96, 114, 116
Nagy, Lajos, 8, 31, 47, 55, 73, 89, 106, 112, 124
Naumann, Friedrich, 96
Négyessy (Seminar), 35
Németh, László, 102n, 126
Neruda, Pablo, 9n
Neumann, János von, 3
Nietzsche, Friedrich, 32–34

Orbán, Dezsö, 90n
Ormándy, Eugene, 3n
Ostwald, Wilhelm, 5
Osvát, Ernö, 13, 35, 43, 46, 47, 49–56, 92, 93, 105, 106

Paine, Thomas, 11
Pascal, Blaise, 86
Pavel, Konstantin, 62
Petöfi, Sándor, 9, 47, 95, 99, 100, 102, 105, 110, 121, 122, 133, 134
Peyre, Henri, 32
Picasso, Pablo, 90, 142
Pikler, Gyula, 94, 106
Plekhanov, Gyorgii, 57, 137
Pogány, József, 117
Polányi, Károly, 2, 5, 7
Polányi, Mihály, 3, 7, 37, 97
Popper, David, 3n
Pór, Bertalan, 90n
Proust, Marcel, 31n, 33
Pushkin, Alexander, 57

Racine, Jean, 140
Radványi, László, 97
Rákosi, Jenö, 116, 122, 123, 132
Ranschburg, Viktor, 43
Raynal, Abbé, 141
Reinitz, Béla, 47, 89, 106
Révai, József, 95
Révai, Károly, 61
Révész, Béla, 47, 89, 106
Rilke, Rainer Maria, 2, 30, 118
Rimbaud, Arthur, 30
Rippl-Rónai, József, 89–90, 91, 128
Ritóok, Emma, 97
Róheim, Géza, 2
Rolland, Romain, 118
Rostand, Edmond, 70, 95
Rubiner, Leo, 47n

Samain, Albert, 30
Sartre, Jean-Paul, 9, 31, 66, 75, 135, 140–142
Schiller, Friedrich, 91
Schnitzler, Arthur, 2
Schönberg, Arnold, 2
Schönerer, Georg von, 23
Schöpflin, Aladár, 8, 50, 56, 64, 67n, 70, 93, 97, 98, 104, 108
Seidler, Ernö, 94
Seidler, Irma, 94
Seton-Watson, Robert W., 21
Shaw, George Bernard, 47n
Shelley, Percy B., 9n, 11
Shils, Edward, 25
Sinkó, Ervin, 97
Slamadinger, Anna, 97
Sombart, Werner, 112
Southey, Robert, 11
Stalin (Jozef Dugashvili), 93
Stephen (King), 26
Strauss, Richard, 2
Strindberg, August, 108, 113
Szabó, Dezsö, 8, 52, 59, 70, 90, 93, 98, 101, 121, 127
Szabó, Ervin, 37, 53, 98, 113, 117, 118, 130

Szabó, István Nagyatádi, 24
Szamuely, Tibor, 119
Székely, Artur, 95
Szekfü, Gyula, 6
Szentgyörgyi, Albert, 3
Szép, Ernö, 8, 42, 73, 84, 99
Szerb, Antal, 31, 33
Szigeti, József, 3n
Szilárd, Leo, 3, 6
Szilasi, Vilmos, 2, 97
Szini, Gyula, 8, 83–85, 93, 96, 106, 107, 124
Szomory, Dezsö, 8, 14, 58, 70, 83, 84, 99, 110, 118, 126
Szüllö, Géza, 124

Teller, Edward, 82
Tersánszky, Józsi-Jenö, 8, 36
Tharaud brothers, 120
Tihanyi, Lajos, 90n
Tisza, Count István, 22, 26, 27, 71, 90, 97, 127–129, 133
Tolnay, Károly, 3, 97
Tolstoy, Leo, 21, 33, 75, 113, 118, 136
Tóth, Arpad, 8, 35, 99
Tóth, Wanda, 8, 85
Trotsky, Leon, 71n, 135, 137–139, 144

Unamuno, Miguel de, 96

Vambéry, Rusztem, 96
Varga, Jenö, 2, 3, 37
Varnai, Zseni, 105
Vázsonyi, Vilmos, 26
Verhaeren, Emil, 47n, 115
Verlaine, Paul, 30, 112
Verne, Jules, 82
Vezér, Erzsébet, 39
Vincze, Sándor, 118
Vörösmarty, Mihály, 100, 110, 134

Wedekind, Franz, 89
Weltner, Jakab, 118
Wigner, Eugen, 3
Wilde, John, 97
Williams, Eric, 141
Williams, Raymond, 11
Wittgenstein, Ludwig, 1, 2, 7
Wordsworth, William, 11, 12n

Yeats, William Butler, 30
Yevtushenko, Yevgeni, 9

Zéraffa, Michel, 112
Zola, Emile, 31–34, 82, 101, 113, 118
Zsilinszky brothers, 68

PH 3042 .F46 1987x

Fenyo, Mario D.

Literature and political change